X-FORCE

Collection Editor: Alex Starbuck
Assistant Editor: Sarah Brunstad
Editors, Special Projects: Jennifer Grünwald & Mark D. Beazley
Senior Editor, Special Projects: Jeff Youngquist
SVP Print, Sales & Marketing: David Gabriel

Editor in Chief: Axel Alonso
Chief Creative Officer: Joe Quesada
Publisher: Dan Buckley
Executive Producer: Alan Fine

X-FORCE VOL. 3: ENDS/MEANS. Contains material originally published in magazine form as X-FORCE #11-15. First printing 2015. ISBN# 978-0-7851-9391-3. Published by MARVEL WORLDWIDE, INC., a subsidiary of MARVEL ENTERTAINMENT, LLC. OFFICE OF PUBLICATION: 135 West 50th Street, New York, NY 10020. Copyright © 2015 MARVEL No similarity between any of the names, characters, persons, and/or institutions in this magazine with those of any living or dead person or institution is intended, and any such similarity which may exist is purely coincidental. **Printed in Canada.** ALAN FINE, President, Marvel Entertainment; DAN BUCKLEY, President, TV, Publishing and Brand Management; JOE QUESADA, Chief Creative Officer; TOM BREVOORT, SVP of Publishing; DAVID BOGART, SVP of Operations & Procurement, Publishing; C.B. CEBULSKI, SVP of Creator & Content Development; DAVID GABRIEL, SVP Print, Sales & Marketing; JIM O'KEEFE, VP of Operations & Logistics; DAN CARR, Executive Director of Publishing Technology; SUSAN CRESPI, Editorial Operations Manager; ALEX MORALES, Publishing Operations Manager; STAN LEE, Chairman Emeritus. For information regarding advertising in Marvel Comics or on Marvel.com, please contact Niza Disla, Director of Marvel Partnerships, at ndisla@marvel.com. For Marvel subscription inquiries, please call 800-217-9158. **Manufactured between 3/6/2015 and 4/13/2015 by SOLISCO PRINTERS, SCOTT, QC, CANADA.**

10 9 8 7 6 5 4 3 2 1

X-FORCE

›› ENDS/MEANS ‹‹

WRITER
SIMON SPURRIER

ISSUES #11-12 & #14-15

ARTIST
ROCK-HE KIM

COLORISTS
ROCK-HE KIM (#11) &
JOSE VILLARRUBIA (#12, #14-15)

ISSUE #13

PENCILERS
TAN ENG HUAT
& KEVIN SHARPE

INKERS
CRAIG YEUNG **WITH**
NORMAN LEE

COLORIST
JOSE VILLARRUBIA

WITHDRAWN

LETTERER
VC'S JOE SABINO

COVER ART
ROCK-HE KIM

ASSISTANT EDITOR
XANDER JAROWEY

EDITOR
DANIEL KETCHUM

X-MEN GROUP EDITOR
MIKE MARTS

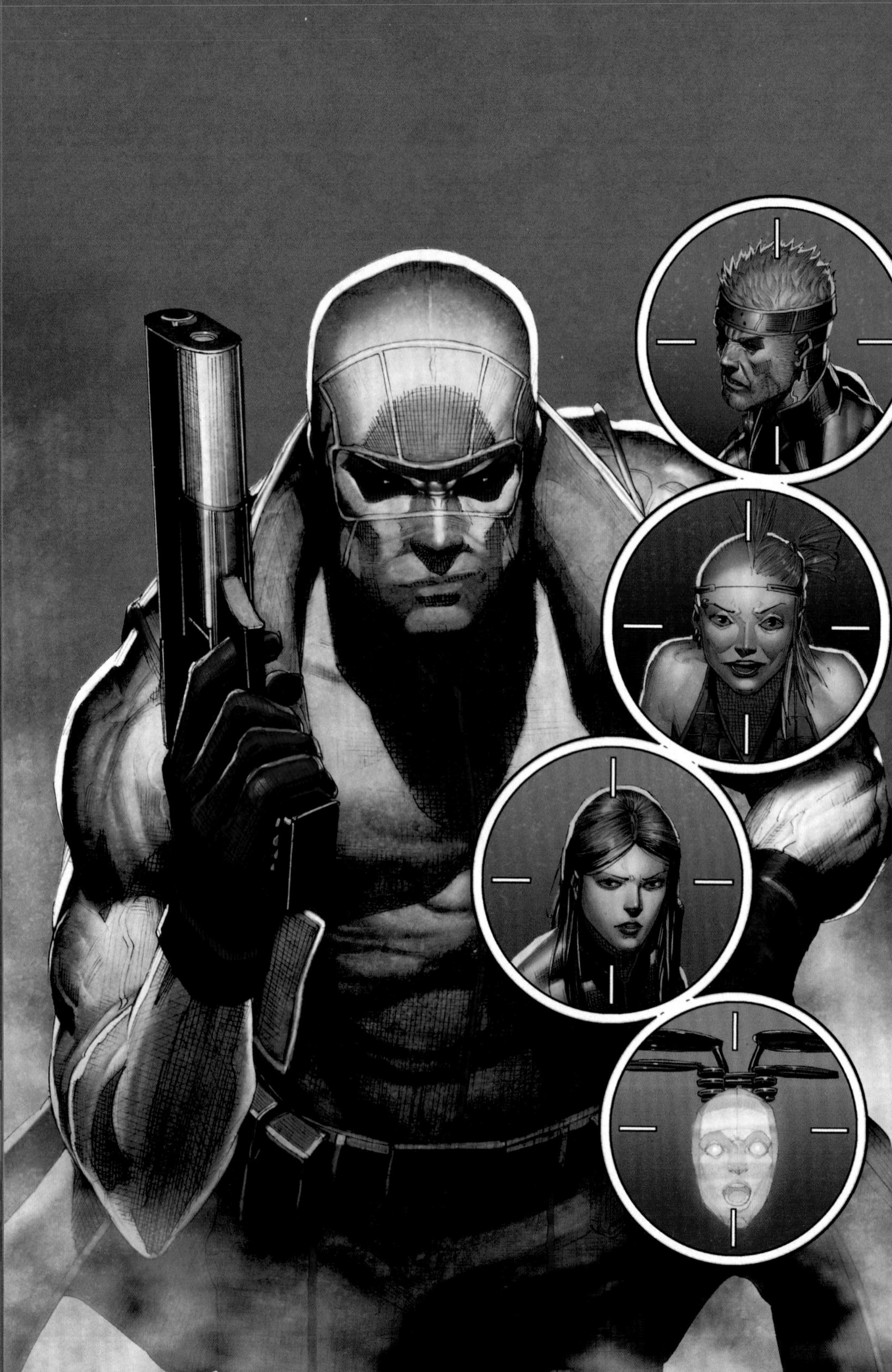

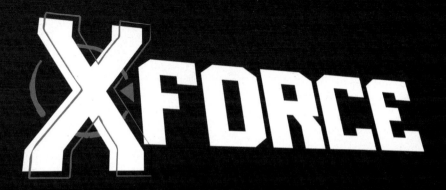

X-FORCE

>> MISSION BRIEF

A terrorist attack known as the Alexandria Incident used a weaponized mutant to claim 3,000 lives. In response, Cable re-formed the mutant black ops team X-Force to ensure that mutantkind not only has a continued place in the world, but also a stake in it.

After being informed by Pete Wisdom that an organization called the Yellow Eye has been running surveillance on every mutant in the world, X-Force set out to determine the location of this mysterious watchdog. With their only lead being a cryptic message from Wisdom regarding bugs, Doctor Nemesis was able to determine the location of the Yellow Eye by placing a tracking device on one of the mechanical flies they have been using to spy on mutants. Now, with the location of their base in hand, X-Force must infiltrate and eliminate this threat to mutantkind.

CABLE

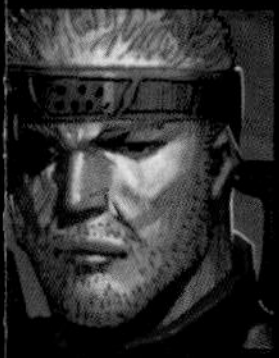

ME: Nathan
stopher Charles
mers
CIES: Mutant
LL SET: Limited
ognition and
ponized upper limb.
y trained in survival,
king, combat and
tegy.

PSYLOCKE

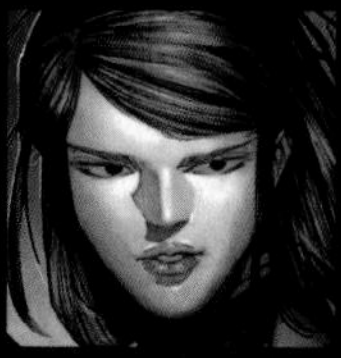

NAME: Elizabeth "Betsy" Braddock
SPECIES: Mutant
SKILL SET: Telepathy and telekinesis. Skilled martial artist.

MARROW

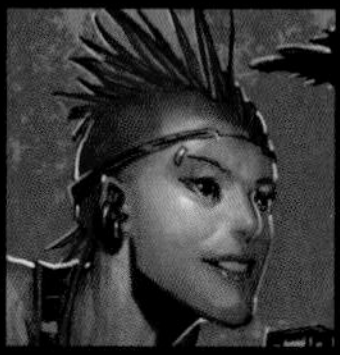

NAME: Sarah (Surname unknown)
SPECIES: De-Powered mutant
SKILL SET: Accelerated bone growth and enhanced bone durability. Healing factor. Expert in hand-to-hand combat.

FANTOMEX

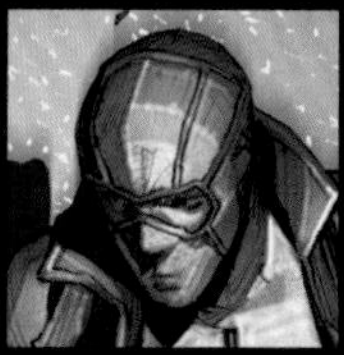

ALIAS: Jean-Phillipe
SPECIES: Mutant
SKILL SET: Externally manifested nervous system (E.V.A.). Accelerated healing and enhanced physiology and senses. Skilled marksman and hand-to-hand combatant.

MeMe

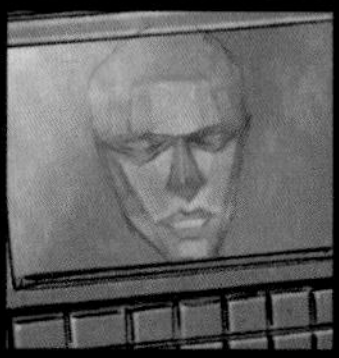

NAME: MeMe
SPECIES: Mutant
SKILL SET: Sentient data capable of infiltrating electronic networks and subverting them to her will.

DR. NEMESIS

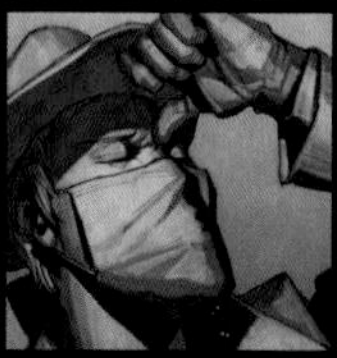

NAME: James Bradley
SPECIES: Mutant
SKILL SET: Self-evolved intellect. Cybernetic eyes. Advanced longevity and enhanced immune system.

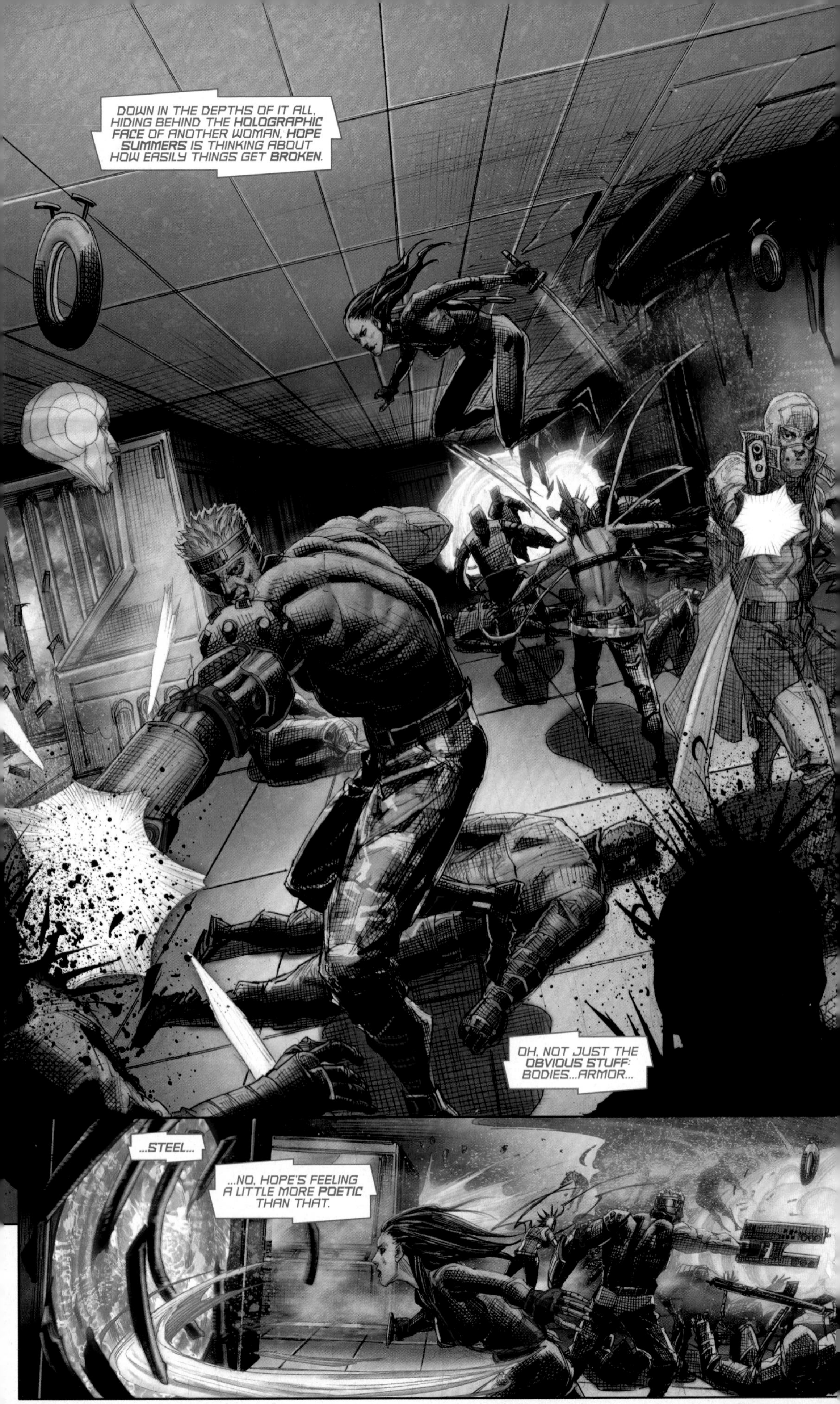
DOWN IN THE DEPTHS OF IT ALL, HIDING BEHIND THE HOLOGRAPHIC FACE OF ANOTHER WOMAN, HOPE SUMMERS IS THINKING ABOUT HOW EASILY THINGS GET BROKEN.
OH, NOT JUST THE OBVIOUS STUFF: BODIES...ARMOR...
...STEEL...
...NO, HOPE'S FEELING A LITTLE MORE POETIC THAN THAT.

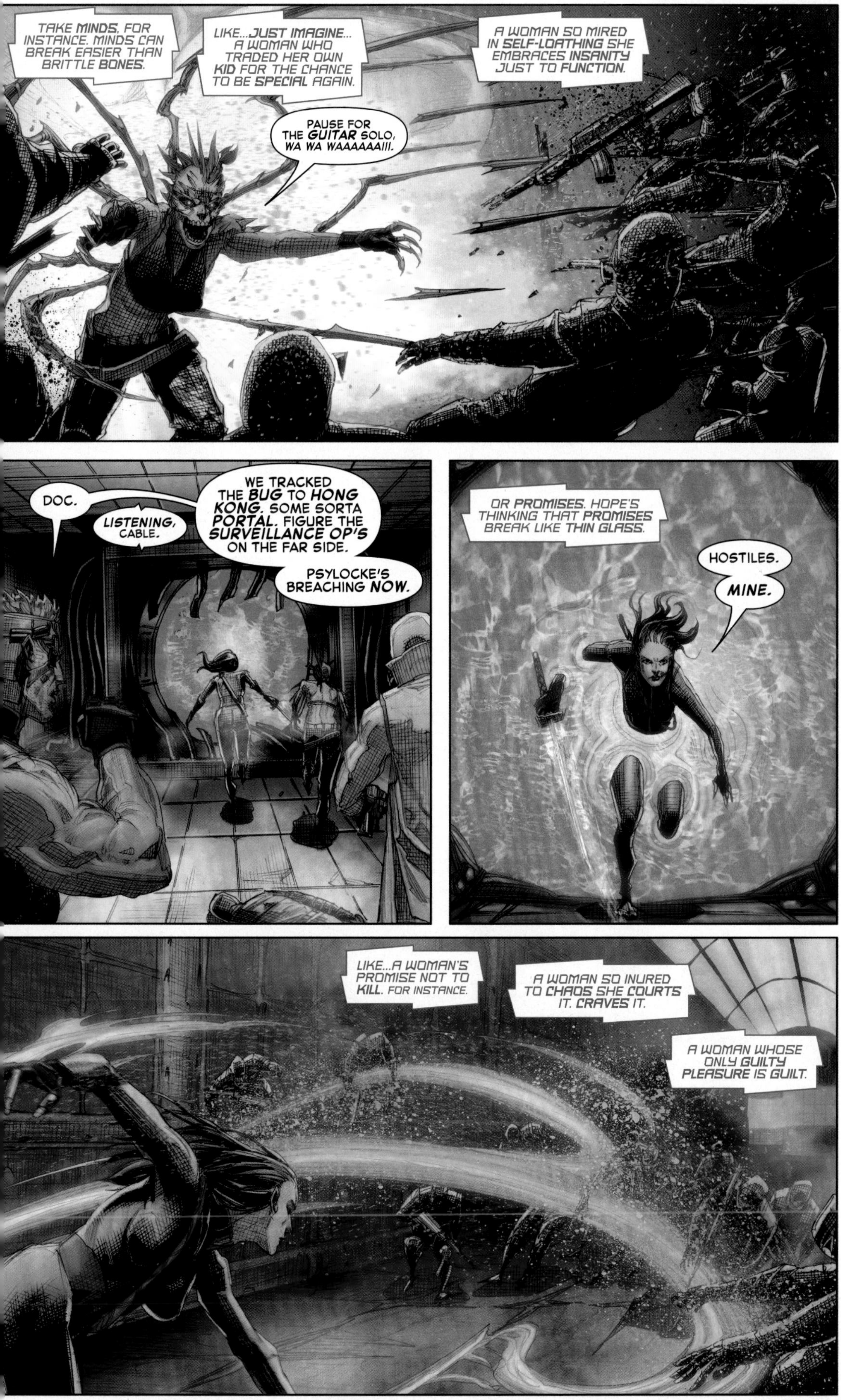
TAKE MINDS, FOR INSTANCE. MINDS CAN BREAK EASIER THAN BRITTLE BONES.
LIKE...JUST IMAGINE... A WOMAN WHO TRADED HER OWN KID FOR THE CHANCE TO BE SPECIAL AGAIN.
A WOMAN SO MIRED IN SELF-LOATHING SHE EMBRACES INSANITY JUST TO FUNCTION.
PAUSE FOR THE GUITAR SOLO, WA WA WAAAAAAIII.
DOC.
WE TRACKED THE BUG TO HONG KONG. SOME SORTA PORTAL. FIGURE THE SURVEILLANCE OP'S ON THE FAR SIDE.
LISTENING, CABLE.
PSYLOCKE'S BREACHING NOW.
OR PROMISES. HOPE'S THINKING THAT PROMISES BREAK LIKE THIN GLASS.
HOSTILES.
MINE.
LIKE...A WOMAN'S PROMISE NOT TO KILL. FOR INSTANCE.
A WOMAN SO INURED TO CHAOS SHE COURTS IT. CRAVES IT.
A WOMAN WHOSE ONLY GUILTY PLEASURE IS GUILT.

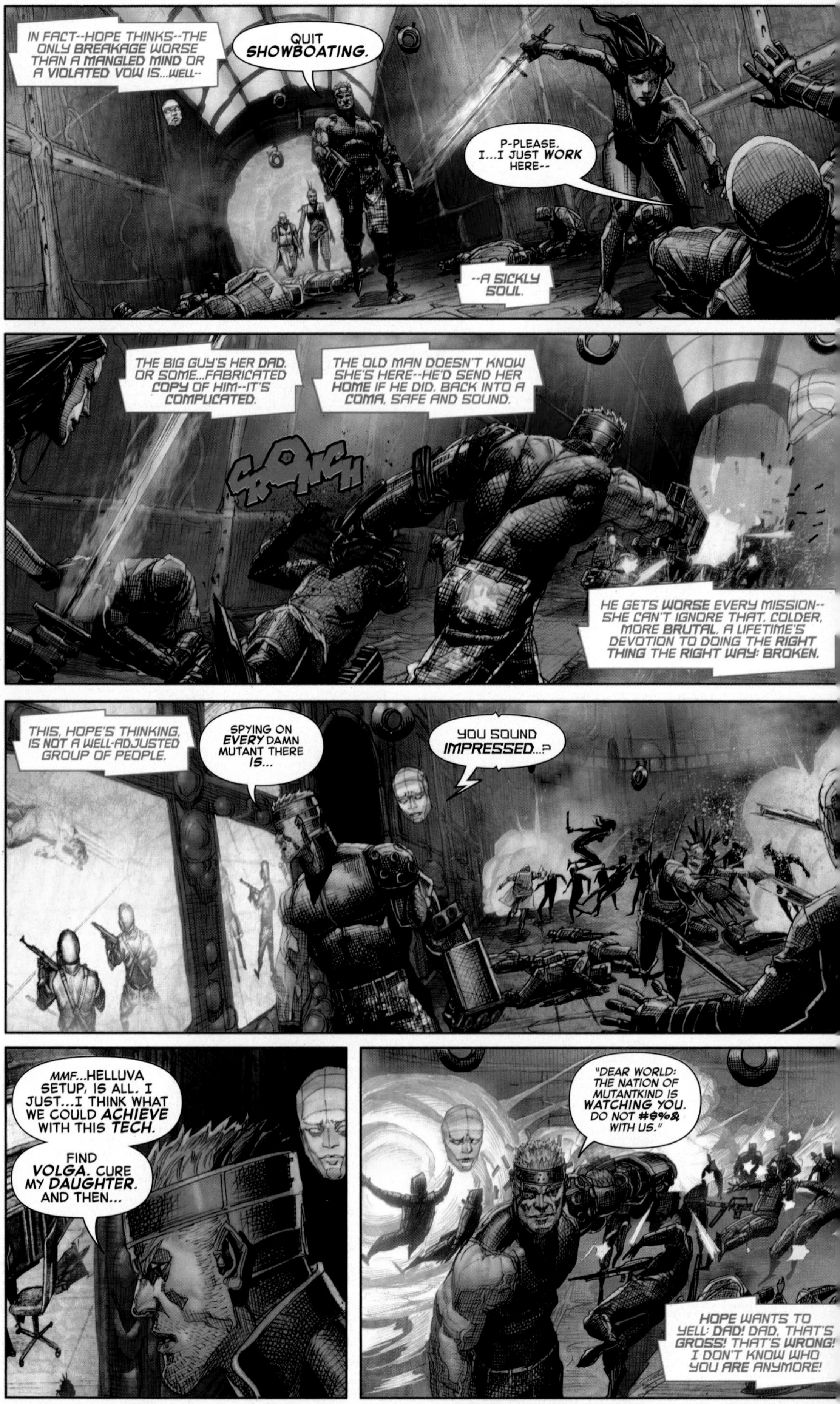
IN FACT--HOPE THINKS--THE ONLY BREAKAGE WORSE THAN A MANGLED MIND OR A VIOLATED VOW IS...WELL--
QUIT SHOWBOATING.
P-PLEASE. I...I JUST WORK HERE--
--A SICKLY SOUL.
THE BIG GUY'S HER DAD. OR SOME...FABRICATED COPY OF HIM--IT'S COMPLICATED.
THE OLD MAN DOESN'T KNOW SHE'S HERE--HE'D SEND HER HOME IF HE DID. BACK INTO A COMA, SAFE AND SOUND.
CRONCH
HE GETS WORSE EVERY MISSION--SHE CAN'T IGNORE THAT. COLDER, MORE BRUTAL. A LIFETIME'S DEVOTION TO DOING THE RIGHT THING THE RIGHT WAY: BROKEN.
THIS, HOPE'S THINKING, IS NOT A WELL-ADJUSTED GROUP OF PEOPLE.
SPYING ON EVERY DAMN MUTANT THERE IS...
YOU SOUND IMPRESSED...?
MMF...HELLUVA SETUP, IS ALL. I JUST...I THINK WHAT WE COULD ACHIEVE WITH THIS TECH.
FIND VOLGA. CURE MY DAUGHTER. AND THEN...
"DEAR WORLD: THE NATION OF MUTANTKIND IS WATCHING YOU. DO NOT #$%& WITH US."
HOPE WANTS TO YELL: DAD! DAD, THAT'S GROSS! THAT'S WRONG! I DON'T KNOW WHO YOU ARE ANYMORE!

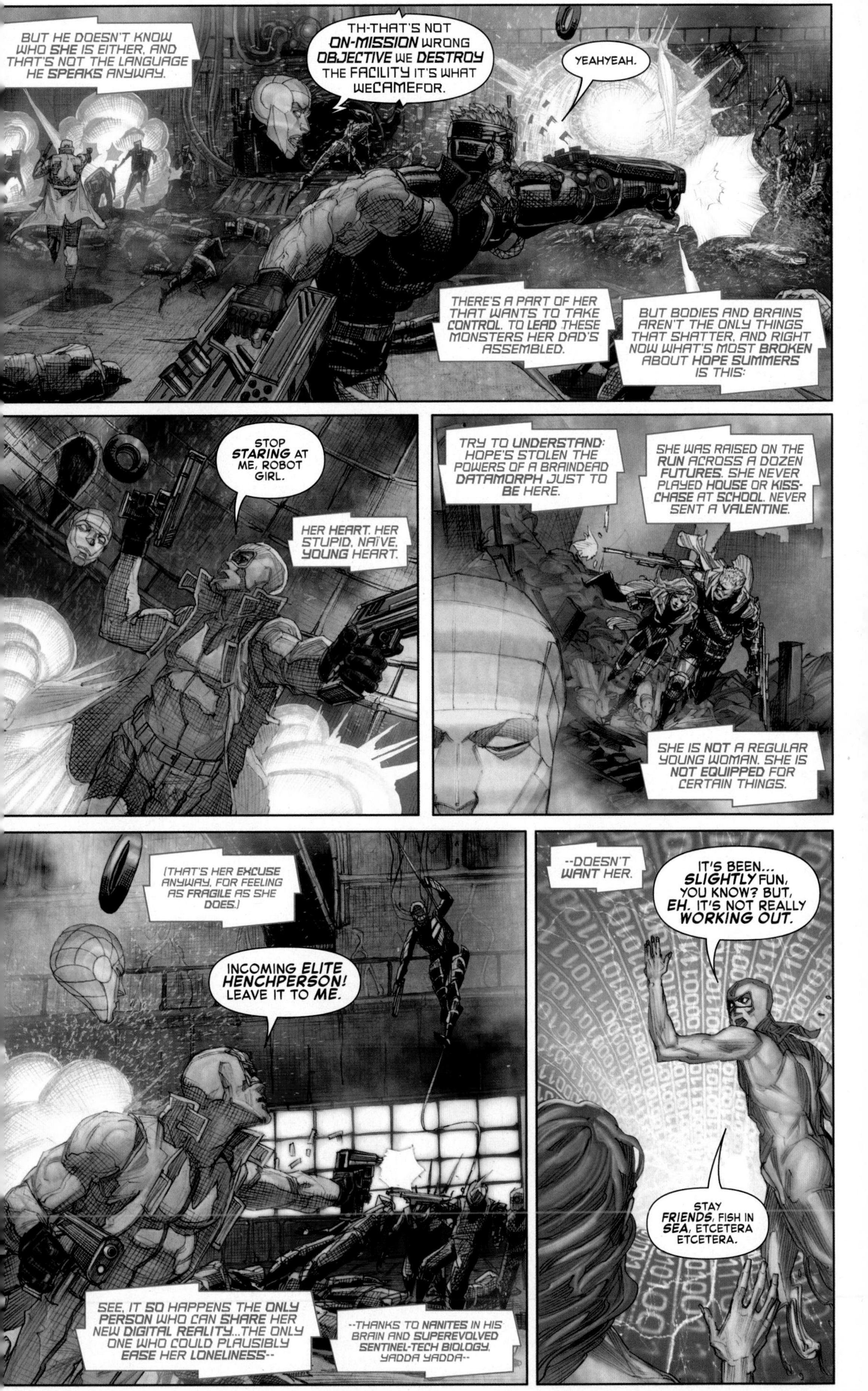
BUT HE DOESN'T KNOW WHO SHE IS EITHER, AND THAT'S NOT THE LANGUAGE HE SPEAKS ANYWAY.
TH-THAT'S NOT ON-MISSION WRONG OBJECTIVE WE DESTROY THE FACILITY IT'S WHAT WECAMEFOR.
YEAHYEAH.
THERE'S A PART OF HER THAT WANTS TO TAKE CONTROL. TO LEAD THESE MONSTERS HER DAD'S ASSEMBLED.
BUT BODIES AND BRAINS AREN'T THE ONLY THINGS THAT SHATTER, AND RIGHT NOW WHAT'S MOST BROKEN ABOUT HOPE SUMMERS IS THIS:
STOP STARING AT ME, ROBOT GIRL.
HER HEART. HER STUPID, NAÏVE, YOUNG HEART.
TRY TO UNDERSTAND: HOPE'S STOLEN THE POWERS OF A BRAINDEAD DATAMORPH JUST TO BE HERE.
SHE WAS RAISED ON THE RUN ACROSS A DOZEN FUTURES. SHE NEVER PLAYED HOUSE OR KISS-CHASE AT SCHOOL. NEVER SENT A VALENTINE.
SHE IS NOT A REGULAR YOUNG WOMAN. SHE IS NOT EQUIPPED FOR CERTAIN THINGS.
(THAT'S HER EXCUSE ANYWAY, FOR FEELING AS FRAGILE AS SHE DOES.)
INCOMING ELITE HENCHPERSON! LEAVE IT TO ME.
SEE, IT SO HAPPENS THE ONLY PERSON WHO CAN SHARE HER NEW DIGITAL REALITY...THE ONLY ONE WHO COULD PLAUSIBLY EASE HER LONELINESS--
--THANKS TO NANITES IN HIS BRAIN AND SUPEREVOLVED SENTINEL-TECH BIOLOGY, YADDA YADDA--
--DOESN'T WANT HER.
IT'S BEEN... SLIGHTLY FUN, YOU KNOW? BUT, EH. IT'S NOT REALLY WORKING OUT.
STAY FRIENDS, FISH IN SEA, ETCETERA ETCETERA.

HENCE THE HEARTACHE.
AND HENCE THE BROKEN
CONCENTRATION.

OUTTA THE
WAY, HOLO-
DUMMY!

IMBÉCILES!
I TOLD YOU TO
LEAVE THIS ONE
TO ME!

SHE TELLS HERSELF SHE'S
BEING STUPID. HE'S A LOWLIFE
ANYWAY, RIGHT? AN ARROGANT
FAKE-FRENCHMAN NEVER MORE
THAN AN INCH FROM A TANTRUM.

IT'S NOT LIKE IT WENT REAL
FAR ANYWAY--AS IF INTANGIBLE
NON-JUNK-RELATED DATA-
COMMUNING EVER COULD.

AND...SHE'S KISSED OTHER
GUYS...BEEN ON DATES. THIS
SHOULDN'T MATTER. BUT...

...THAT FIRST TIME
YOU'RE DITCHED? THAT
STAYS WITH YOU.

MINE!
MY KILL!
ME!

THIS POOR LITTLE WOULD-BE
WARRIOR SIMPLY DOESN'T
KNOW WHAT TO DO WITH
THE REJECT-BIN FEELING.

ONLY THAT
SHE WANTS TO
UNDERSTAND
THE "WHY."

AND THAT, TO BRING YOU
UP TO SPEED, IS WHY HOPE
SUMMERS IS SECRETLY HACKING
THE BRAIN OF AN UNSTABLE
MACHINE-MAN IN THE MIDDLE OF
A CRAZY SUPER HERO FIGHT.

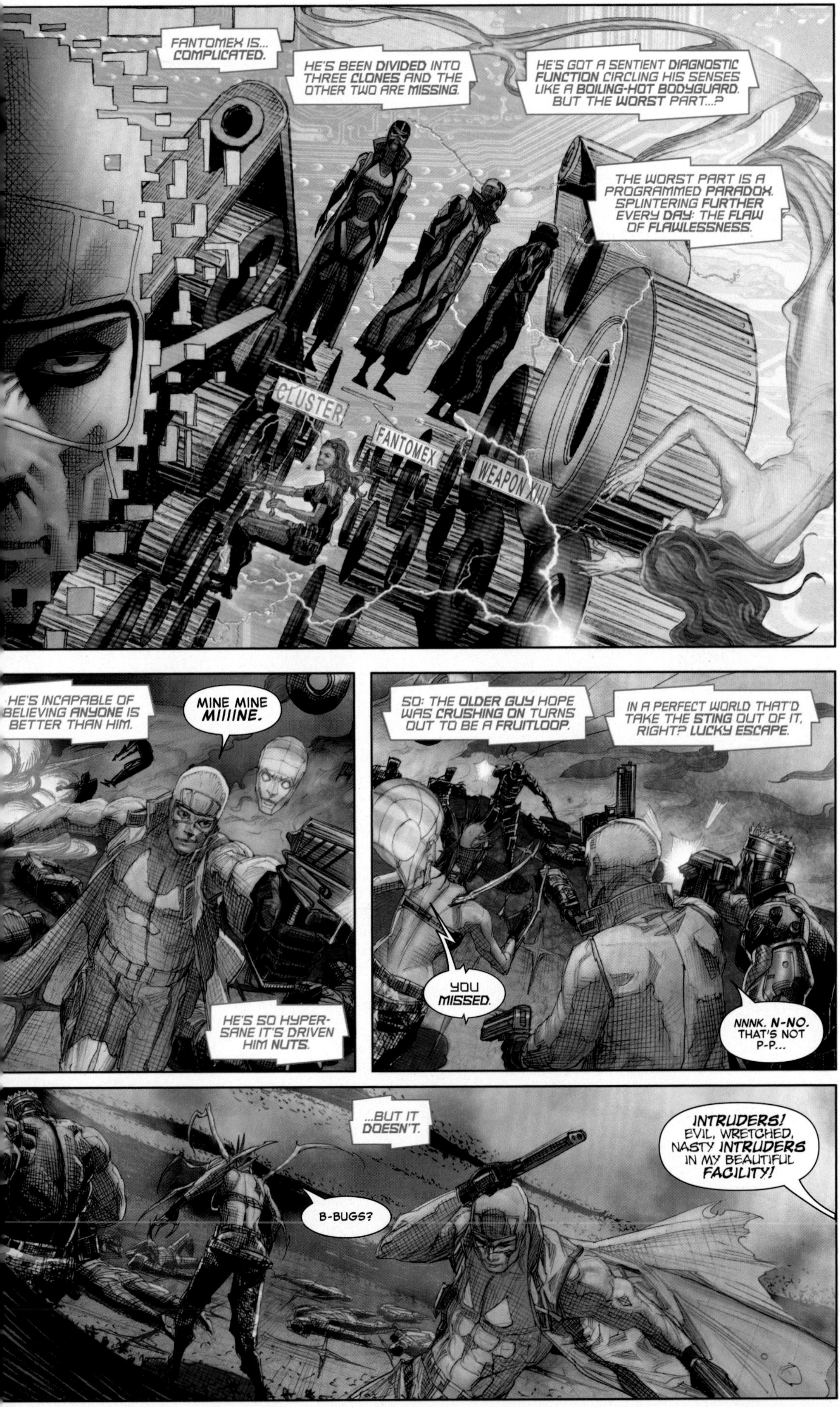
FANTOMEX IS... COMPLICATED.
HE'S BEEN DIVIDED INTO THREE CLONES AND THE OTHER TWO ARE MISSING.
HE'S GOT A SENTIENT DIAGNOSTIC FUNCTION CIRCLING HIS SENSES LIKE A BOILING-HOT BODYGUARD. BUT THE WORST PART...?
THE WORST PART IS A PROGRAMMED PARADOX, SPLINTERING FURTHER EVERY DAY: THE FLAW OF FLAWLESSNESS.
CLUSTER
FANTOMEX
WEAPON XIII
HE'S INCAPABLE OF BELIEVING ANYONE IS BETTER THAN HIM.
MINE MINE MIIIINE.
HE'S SO HYPER-SANE IT'S DRIVEN HIM NUTS.
SO: THE OLDER GUY HOPE WAS CRUSHING ON TURNS OUT TO BE A FRUITLOOP.
IN A PERFECT WORLD THAT'D TAKE THE STING OUT OF IT, RIGHT? LUCKY ESCAPE.
YOU MISSED.
NNNK. N-NO. THAT'S NOT P-P...
...BUT IT DOESN'T.
B-BUGS?
INTRUDERS! EVIL, WRETCHED, NASTY INTRUDERS IN MY BEAUTIFUL FACILITY!

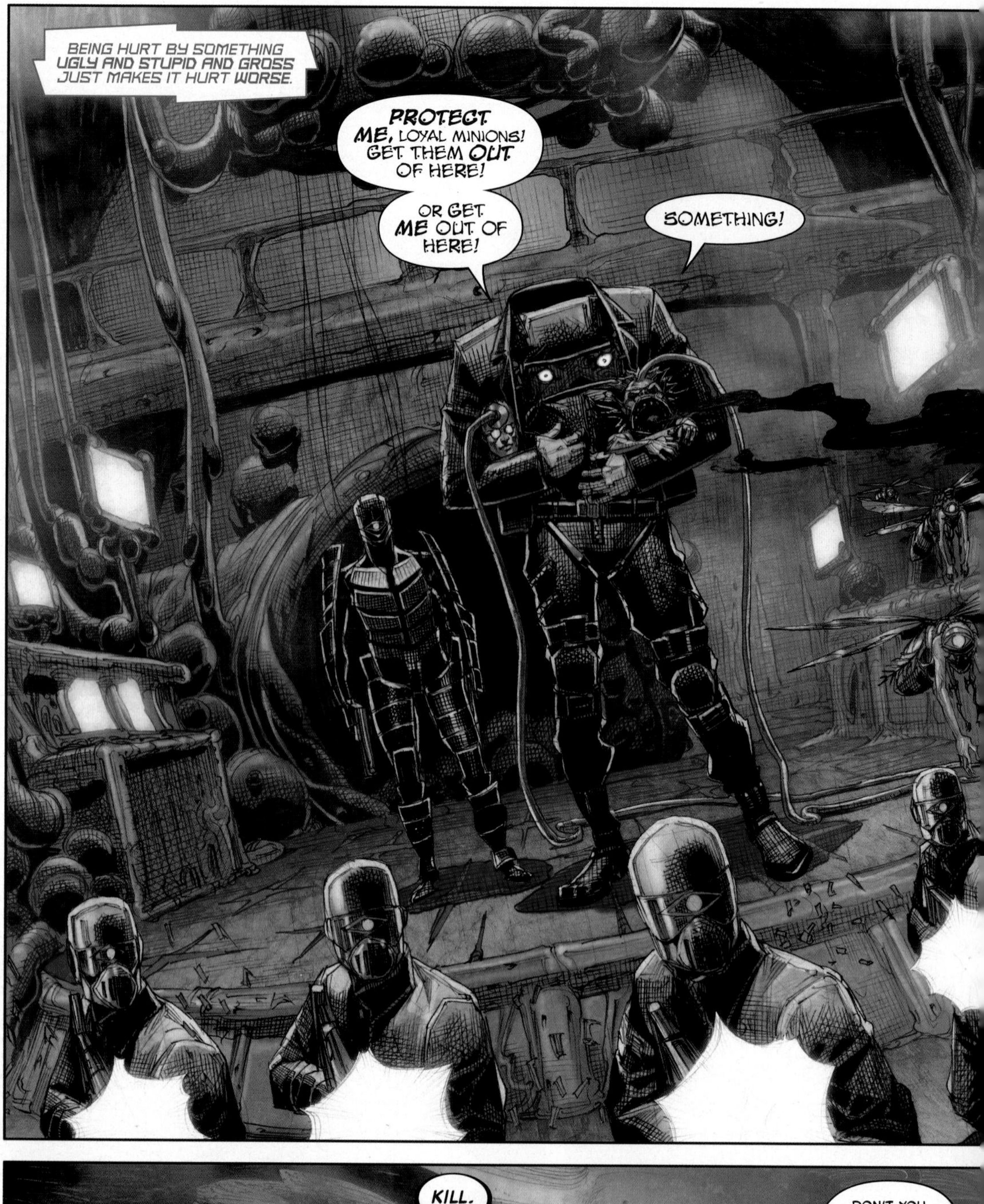
BEING HURT BY SOMETHING UGLY AND STUPID AND GROSS JUST MAKES IT HURT WORSE.
PROTECT ME, LOYAL MINIONS! GET THEM OUT OF HERE!
OR GET ME OUT OF HERE!
SOMETHING!

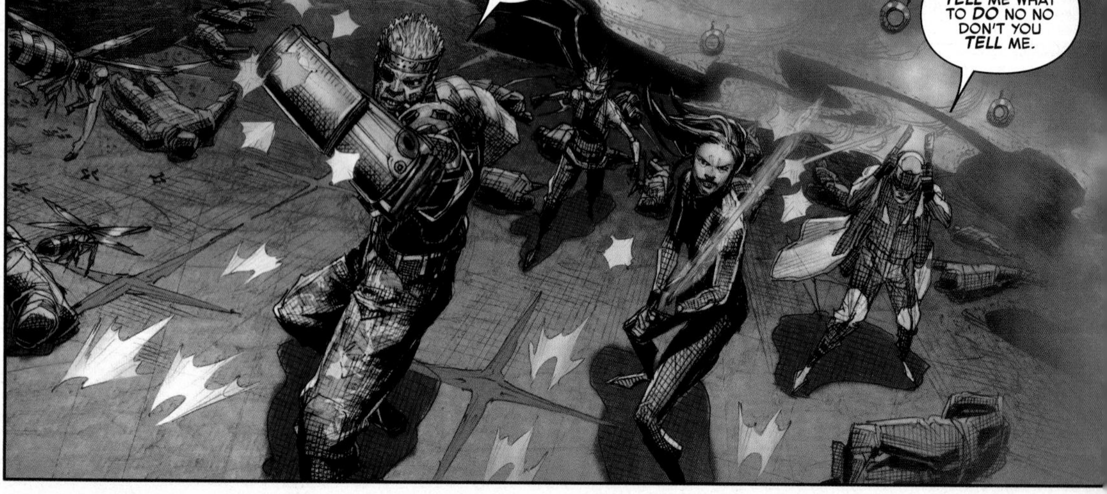
KILL.
DON'T YOU TELL ME WHAT TO DO NO NO DON'T YOU TELL ME.

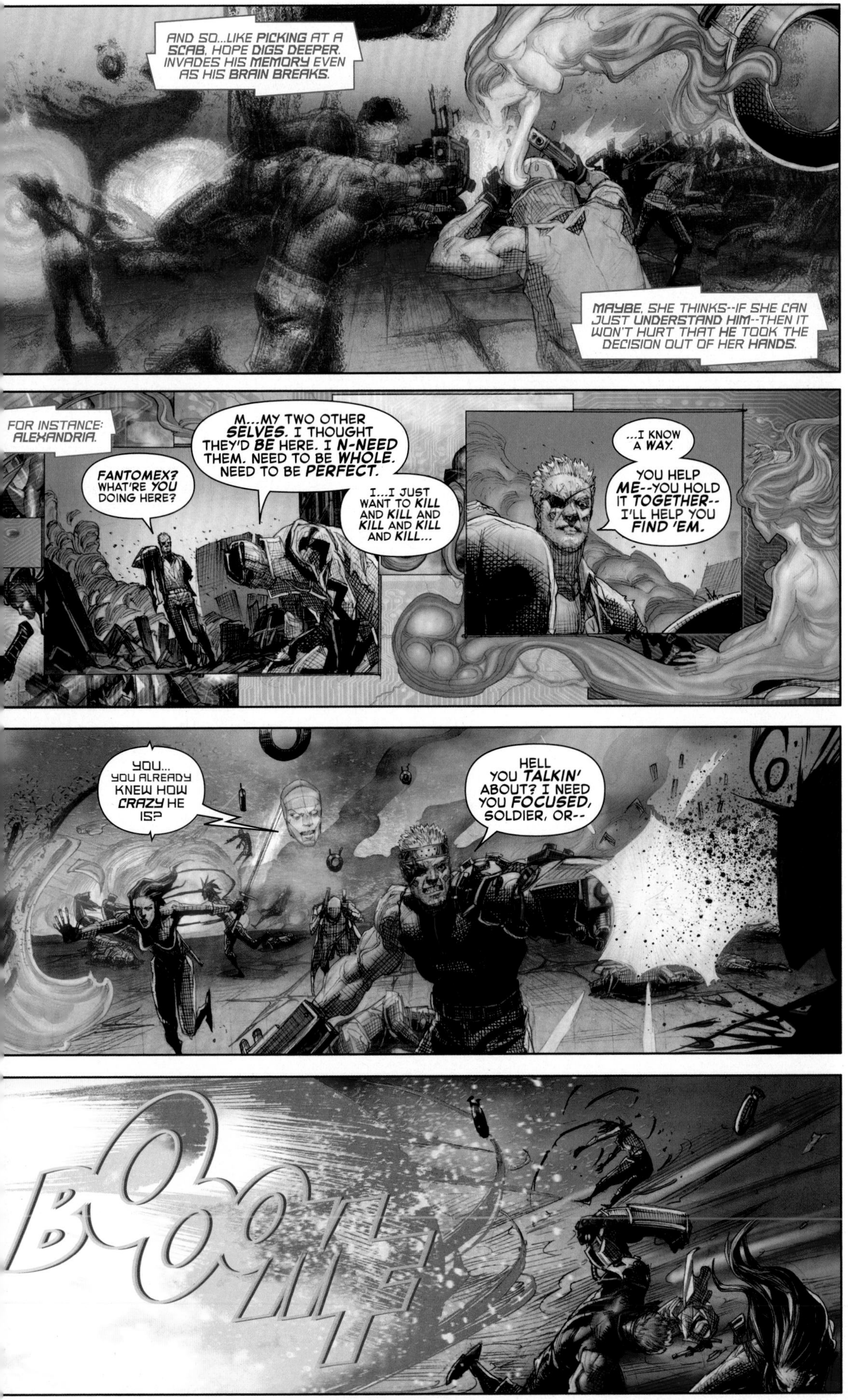

AND SO...LIKE PICKING AT A SCAB, HOPE DIGS DEEPER. INVADES HIS MEMORY EVEN AS HIS BRAIN BREAKS.
MAYBE, SHE THINKS--IF SHE CAN JUST UNDERSTAND HIM--THEN IT WON'T HURT THAT HE TOOK THE DECISION OUT OF HER HANDS.
FOR INSTANCE: ALEXANDRIA.
FANTOMEX? WHAT'RE YOU DOING HERE?
M...MY TWO OTHER SELVES. I THOUGHT THEY'D BE HERE. I N-NEED THEM. NEED TO BE WHOLE. NEED TO BE PERFECT.
I...I JUST WANT TO KILL AND KILL AND KILL AND KILL AND KILL...
...I KNOW A WAY.
YOU HELP ME--YOU HOLD IT TOGETHER--I'LL HELP YOU FIND 'EM.
YOU... YOU ALREADY KNEW HOW CRAZY HE IS?
HELL YOU TALKIN' ABOUT? I NEED YOU FOCUSED, SOLDIER, OR--

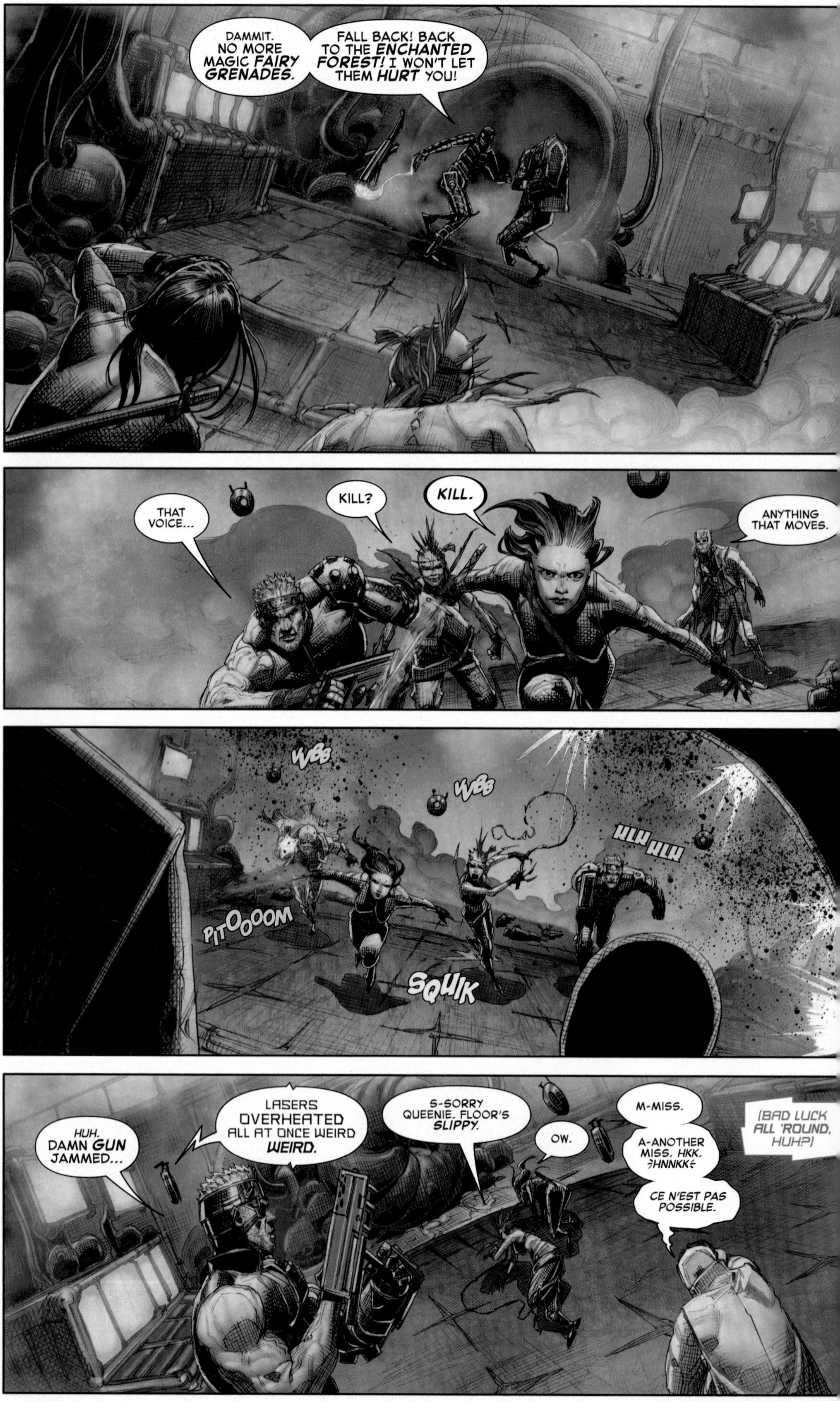
DAMMIT. NO MORE MAGIC FAIRY GRENADES.
FALL BACK! BACK TO THE ENCHANTED FOREST! I WON'T LET THEM HURT YOU!
THAT VOICE...
KILL?
KILL.
ANYTHING THAT MOVES.
VVBB
VVBB
KLK KLK
PITOOOOM
SQUIK
HUH. DAMN GUN JAMMED...
LASERS OVERHEATED ALL AT ONCE WEIRD WEIRD.
S-SORRY QUEENIE. FLOOR'S SLIPPY.
OW.
M-MISS.
A-ANOTHER MISS. HKK. HNNKK
CE N'EST PAS POSSIBLE.
(BAD LUCK ALL 'ROUND, HUH?)

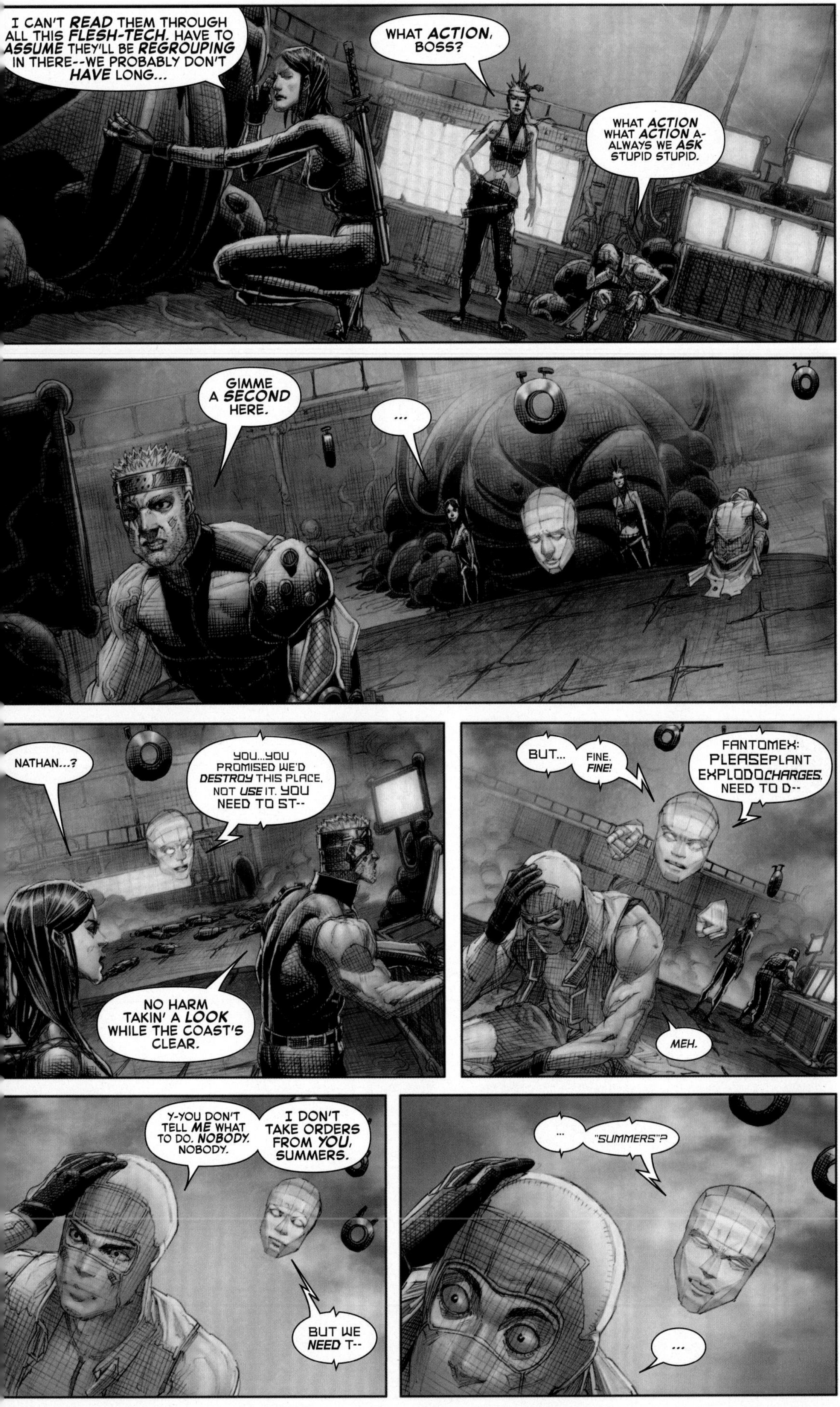
I CAN'T READ THEM THROUGH ALL THIS FLESH-TECH. HAVE TO ASSUME THEY'LL BE REGROUPING IN THERE--WE PROBABLY DON'T HAVE LONG...
WHAT ACTION, BOSS?
WHAT ACTION WHAT ACTION A-ALWAYS WE ASK STUPID STUPID.
GIMME A SECOND HERE.
...
NATHAN...?
YOU...YOU PROMISED WE'D DESTROY THIS PLACE, NOT USE IT. YOU NEED TO ST--
NO HARM TAKIN' A LOOK WHILE THE COAST'S CLEAR.
BUT...
FINE. FINE!
FANTOMEX: PLEASEPLANT EXPLODOCHARGES. NEED TO D--
MEH.
Y-YOU DON'T TELL ME WHAT TO DO. NOBODY. NOBODY.
I DON'T TAKE ORDERS FROM YOU, SUMMERS.
BUT WE NEED T--
...
"SUMMERS"?
...

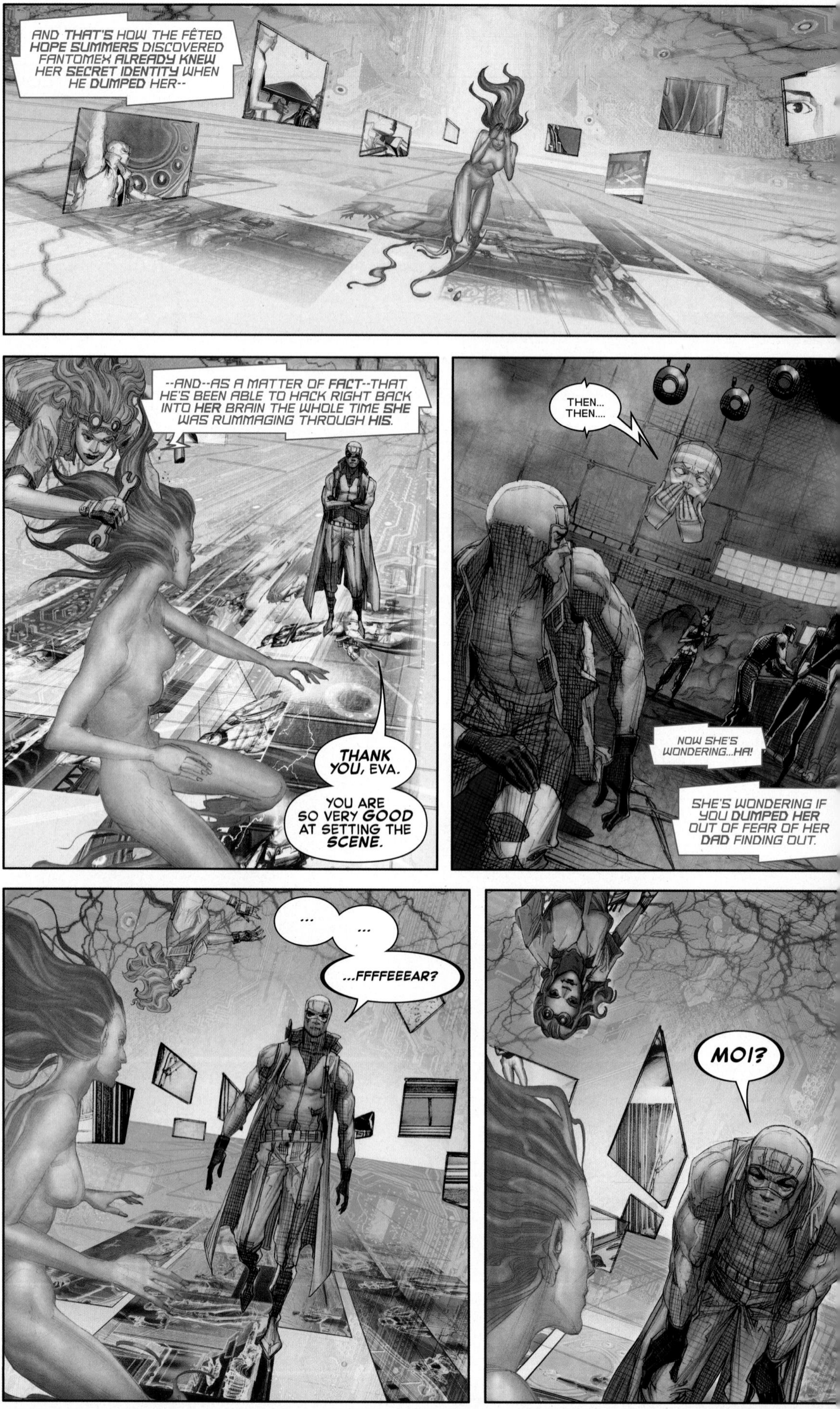
AND THAT'S HOW THE FÊTED HOPE SUMMERS DISCOVERED FANTOMEX ALREADY KNEW HER SECRET IDENTITY WHEN HE DUMPED HER--
--AND--AS A MATTER OF FACT--THAT HE'S BEEN ABLE TO HACK RIGHT BACK INTO HER BRAIN THE WHOLE TIME SHE WAS RUMMAGING THROUGH HIS.
THANK YOU, EVA.
YOU ARE SO VERY GOOD AT SETTING THE SCENE.
THEN... THEN....
NOW SHE'S WONDERING...HA!
SHE'S WONDERING IF YOU DUMPED HER OUT OF FEAR OF HER DAD FINDING OUT.
...
...
...FFFFEEEAR?
MOI?

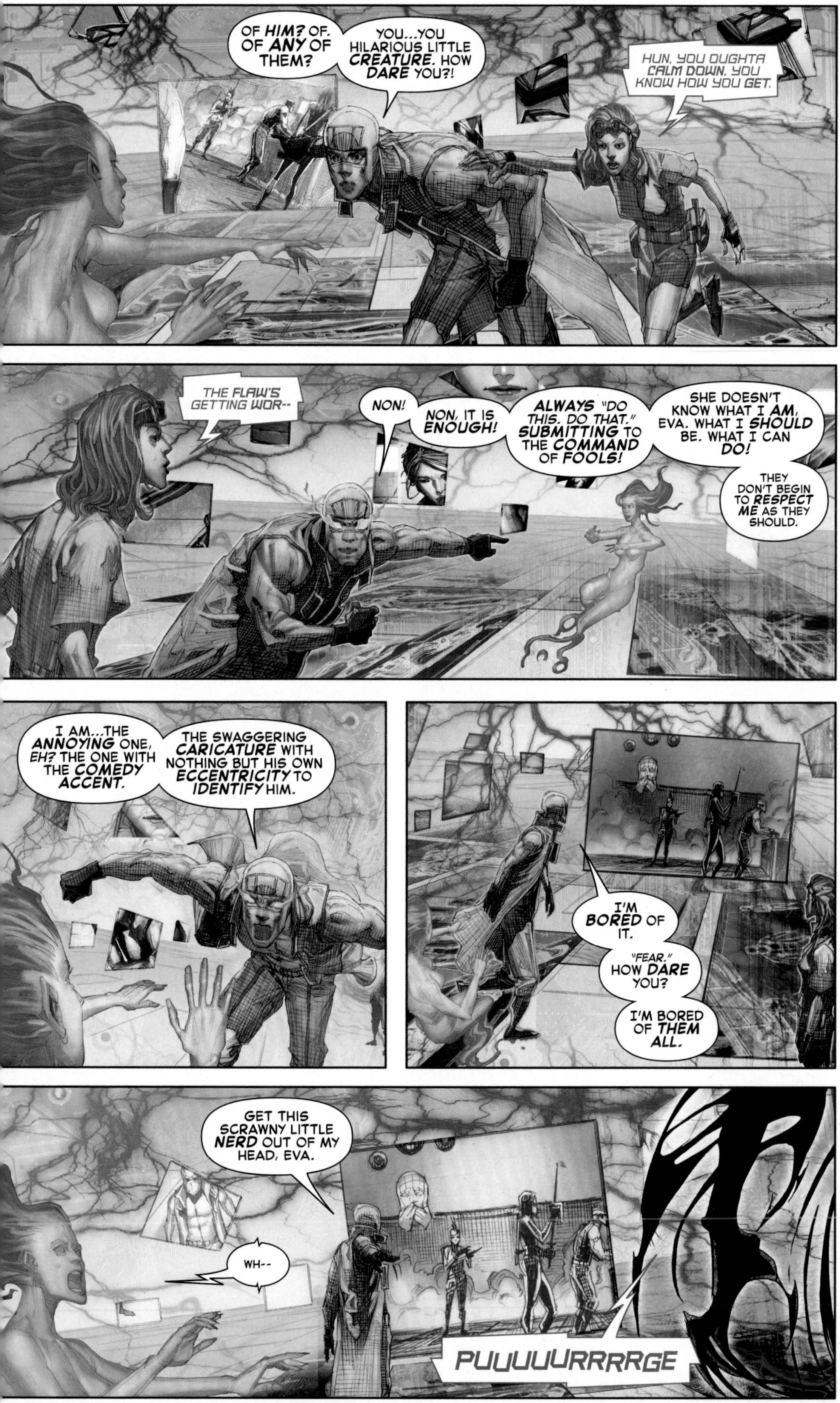
OF HIM? OF. OF ANY OF THEM?
YOU...YOU HILARIOUS LITTLE CREATURE. HOW DARE YOU?!
HUN, YOU OUGHTA CALM DOWN. YOU KNOW HOW YOU GET.
THE FLAW'S GETTING WOR--
NON!
NON, IT IS ENOUGH!
ALWAYS "DO THIS. DO THAT." SUBMITTING TO THE COMMAND OF FOOLS!
SHE DOESN'T KNOW WHAT I AM, EVA. WHAT I SHOULD BE. WHAT I CAN DO!
THEY DON'T BEGIN TO RESPECT ME AS THEY SHOULD.
I AM...THE ANNOYING ONE, EH? THE ONE WITH THE COMEDY ACCENT.
THE SWAGGERING CARICATURE WITH NOTHING BUT HIS OWN ECCENTRICITY TO IDENTIFY HIM.
I'M BORED OF IT.
"FEAR." HOW DARE YOU?
I'M BORED OF THEM ALL.
GET THIS SCRAWNY LITTLE NERD OUT OF MY HEAD, EVA.
WH--
PUUUUURRRRGE

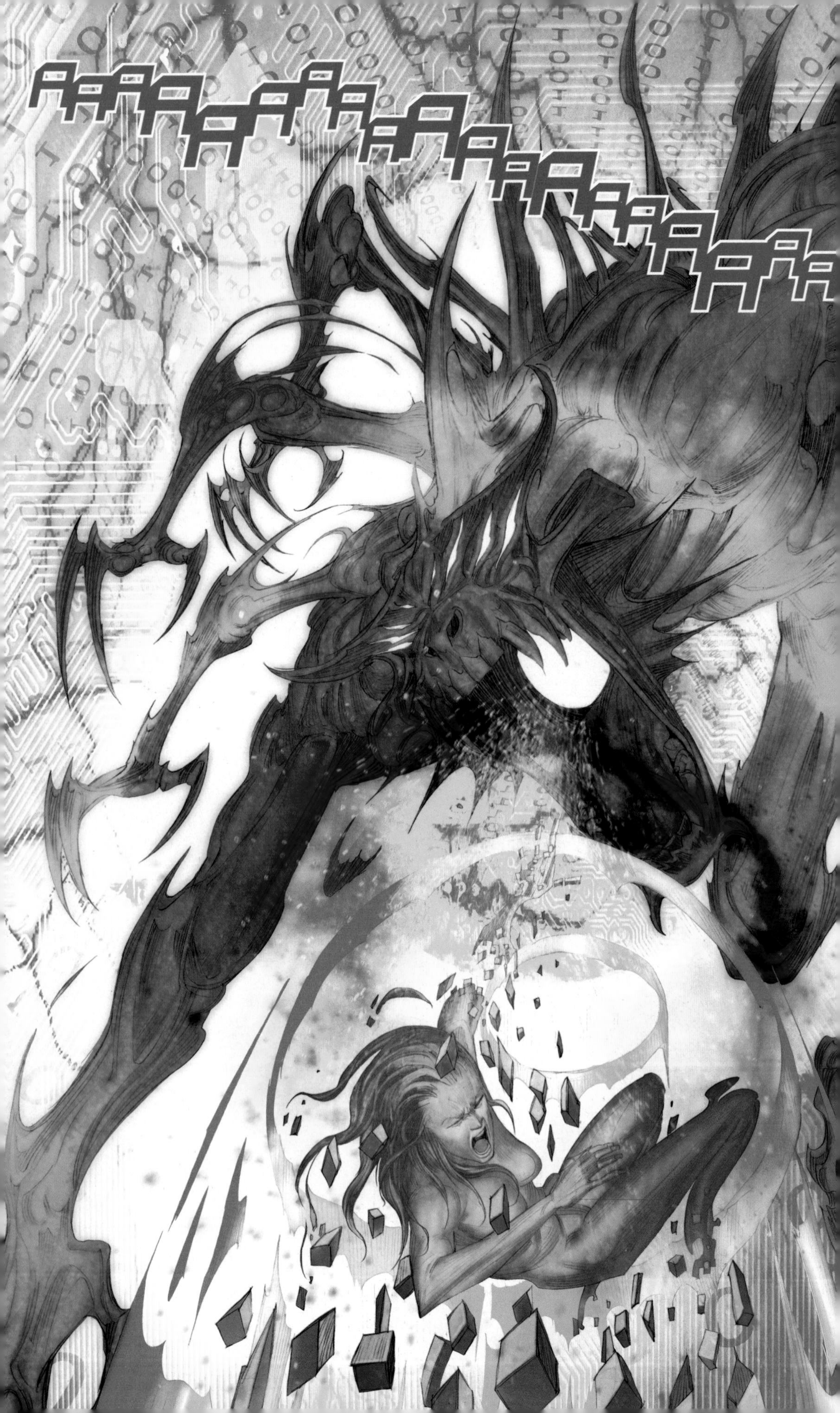
AAAAAAAAAAAAAAAAAAA

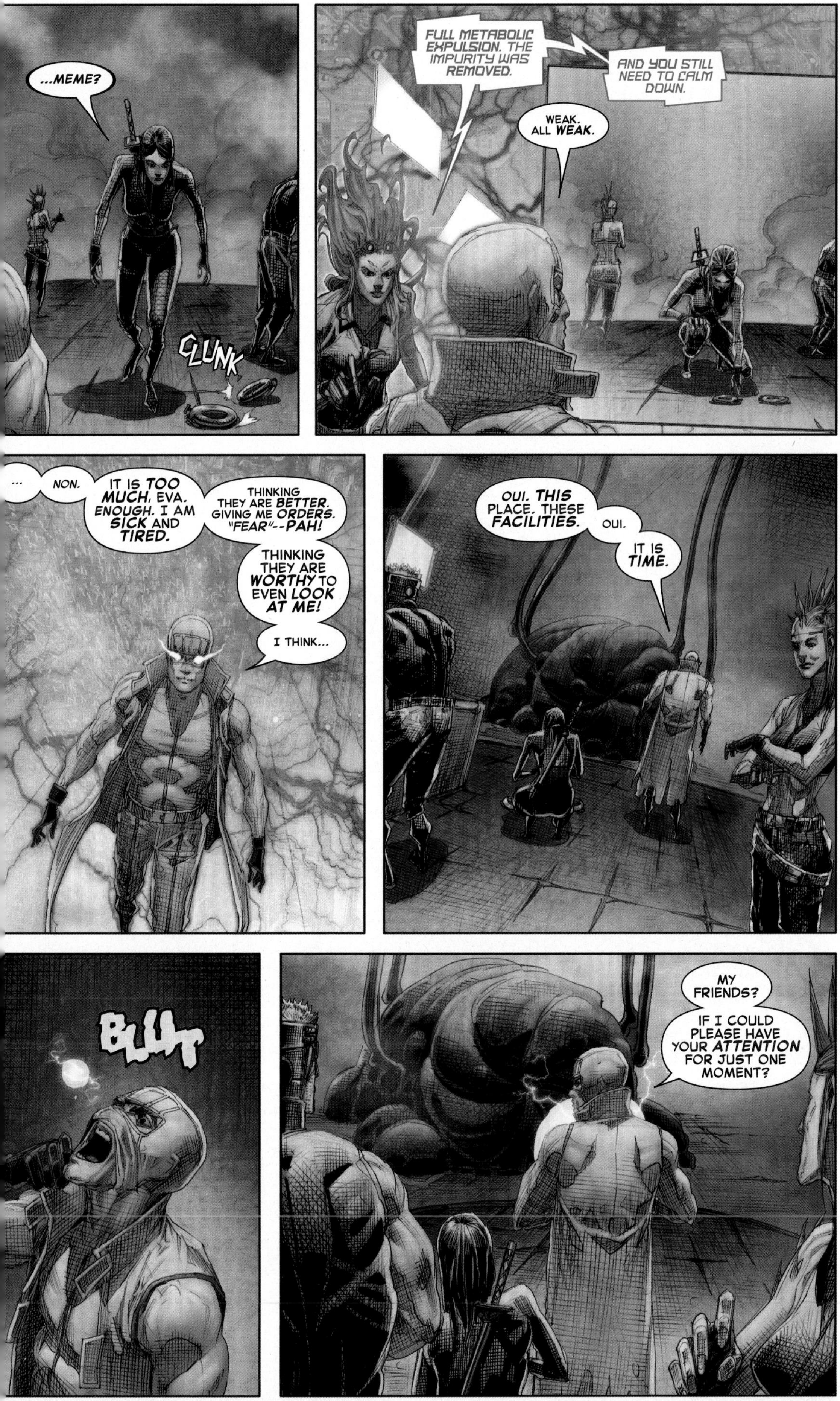
...MEME?
CLUNK
FULL METABOLIC EXPULSION. THE IMPURITY WAS REMOVED.
AND YOU STILL NEED TO CALM DOWN.
WEAK. ALL WEAK.
...
NON.
IT IS TOO MUCH, EVA. ENOUGH. I AM SICK AND TIRED.
THINKING THEY ARE BETTER. GIVING ME ORDERS. "FEAR"--PAH!
THINKING THEY ARE WORTHY TO EVEN LOOK AT ME!
I THINK...
OUI. THIS PLACE. THESE FACILITIES.
OUI.
IT IS TIME.
BLUT
MY FRIENDS?
IF I COULD PLEASE HAVE YOUR ATTENTION FOR JUST ONE MOMENT?

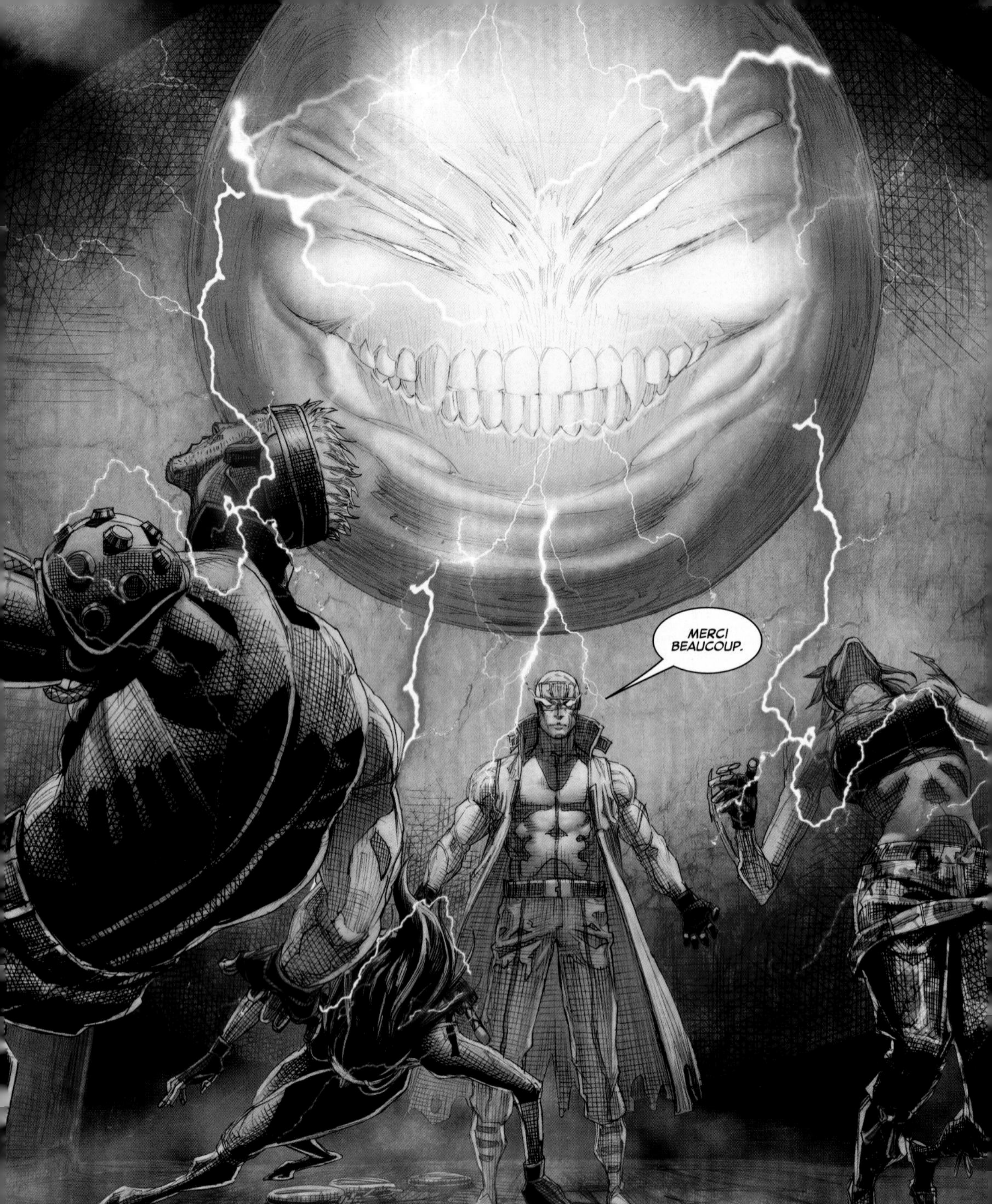
MERCI BEAUCOUP.

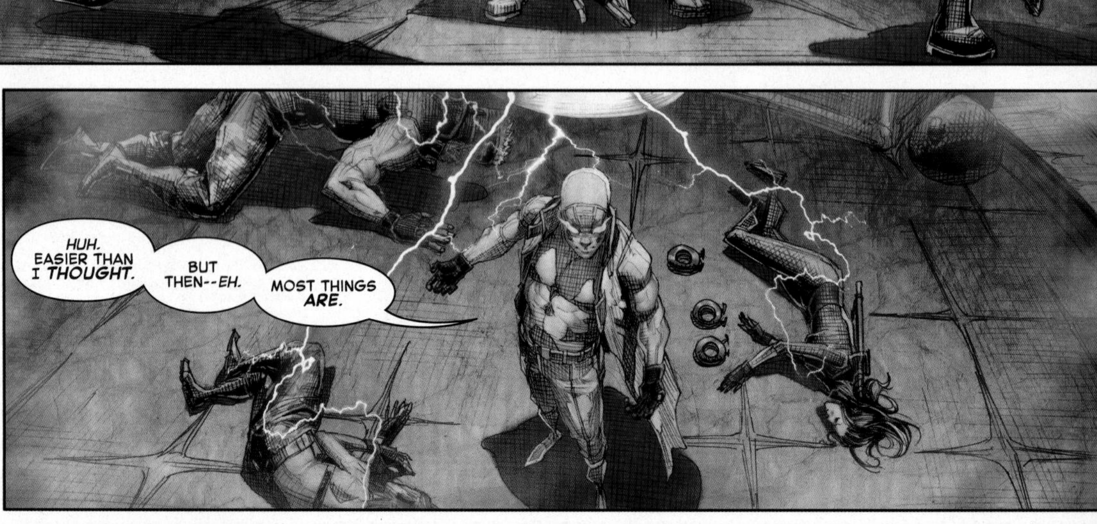
HUH. EASIER THAN I THOUGHT.
BUT THEN--EH.
MOST THINGS ARE.

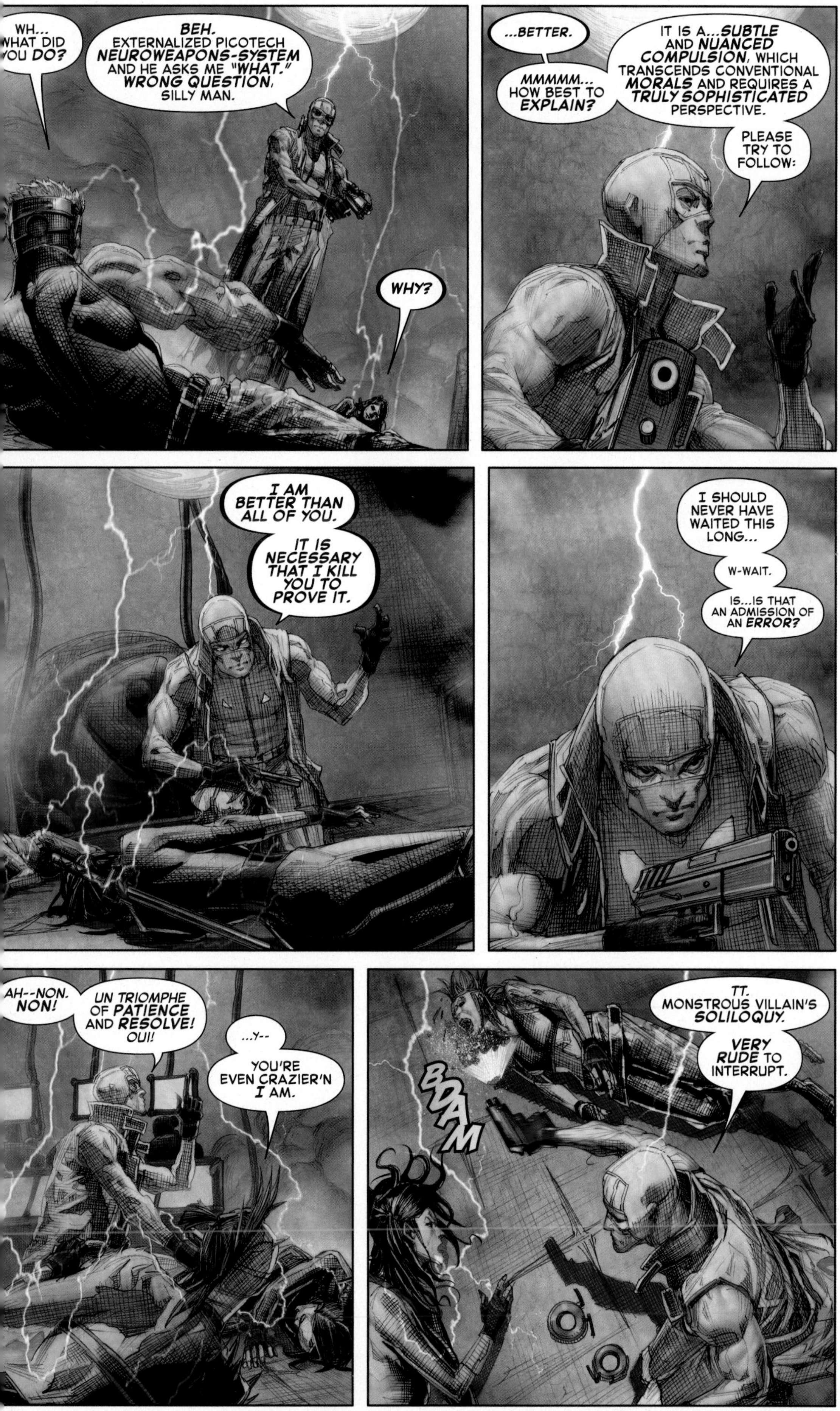
WH... WHAT DID YOU DO?
BEH. EXTERNALIZED PICOTECH NEUROWEAPONS-SYSTEM AND HE ASKS ME "WHAT." WRONG QUESTION, SILLY MAN.
WHY?
...BETTER.
MMMMM... HOW BEST TO EXPLAIN?
IT IS A...SUBTLE AND NUANCED COMPULSION, WHICH TRANSCENDS CONVENTIONAL MORALS AND REQUIRES A TRULY SOPHISTICATED PERSPECTIVE.
PLEASE TRY TO FOLLOW:
I AM BETTER THAN ALL OF YOU.
IT IS NECESSARY THAT I KILL YOU TO PROVE IT.
I SHOULD NEVER HAVE WAITED THIS LONG...
W-WAIT.
IS...IS THAT AN ADMISSION OF AN ERROR?
AH--NON. NON!
UN TRIOMPHE OF PATIENCE AND RESOLVE! OUI!
...Y--
YOU'RE EVEN CRAZIER'N I AM.
BDAM
TT. MONSTROUS VILLAIN'S SOLILOQUY.
VERY RUDE TO INTERRUPT.

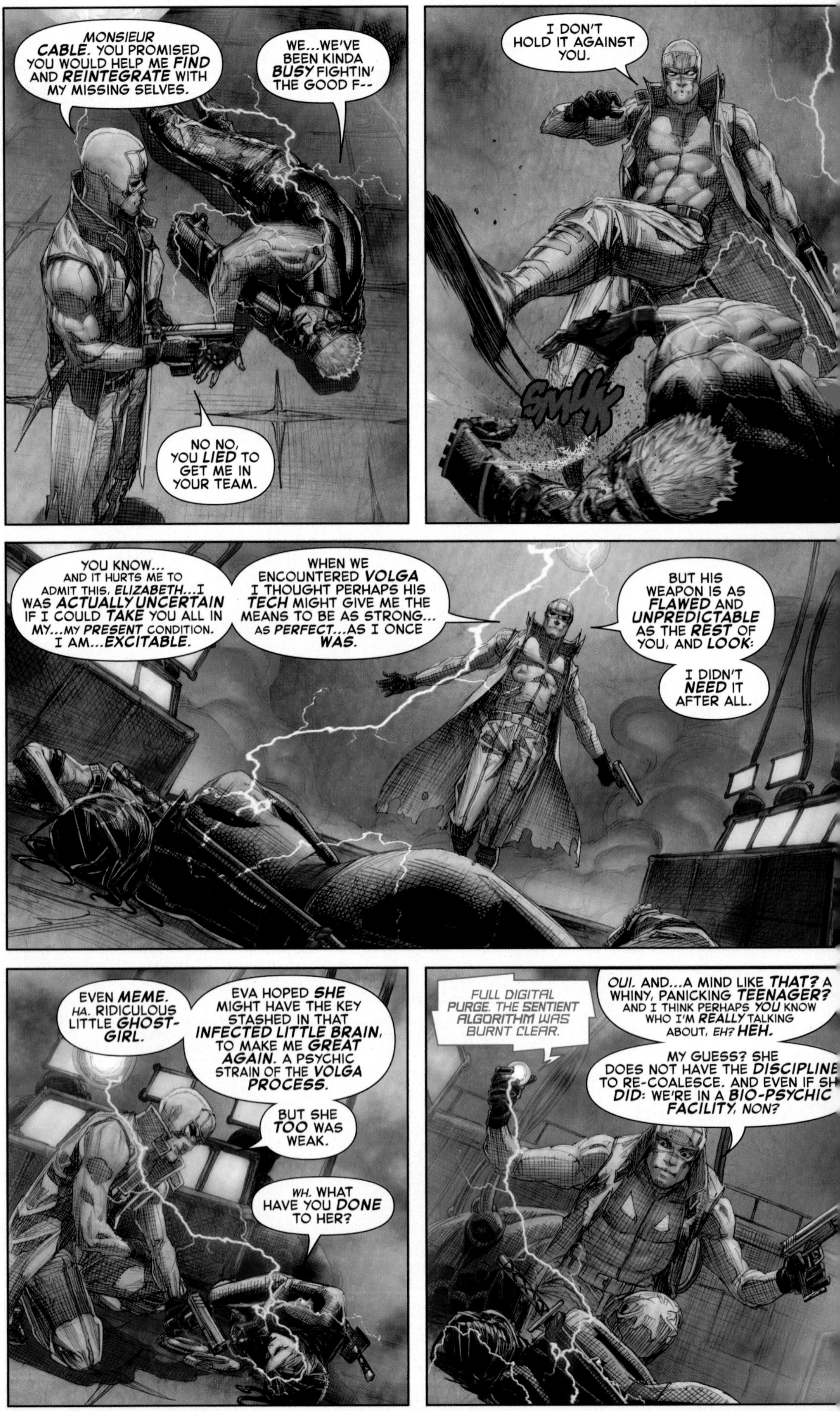
MONSIEUR CABLE. YOU PROMISED YOU WOULD HELP ME FIND AND REINTEGRATE WITH MY MISSING SELVES.
WE...WE'VE BEEN KINDA BUSY FIGHTIN' THE GOOD F--
NO NO, YOU LIED TO GET ME IN YOUR TEAM.
I DON'T HOLD IT AGAINST YOU.
SMAKK
YOU KNOW... AND IT HURTS ME TO ADMIT THIS, ELIZABETH...I WAS ACTUALLY UNCERTAIN IF I COULD TAKE YOU ALL IN MY...MY PRESENT CONDITION. I AM...EXCITABLE.
WHEN WE ENCOUNTERED VOLGA I THOUGHT PERHAPS HIS TECH MIGHT GIVE ME THE MEANS TO BE AS STRONG... AS PERFECT...AS I ONCE WAS.
BUT HIS WEAPON IS AS FLAWED AND UNPREDICTABLE AS THE REST OF YOU, AND LOOK:
I DIDN'T NEED IT AFTER ALL.
EVEN MEME. HA. RIDICULOUS LITTLE GHOST-GIRL.
EVA HOPED SHE MIGHT HAVE THE KEY STASHED IN THAT INFECTED LITTLE BRAIN, TO MAKE ME GREAT AGAIN. A PSYCHIC STRAIN OF THE VOLGA PROCESS.
BUT SHE TOO WAS WEAK.
WH. WHAT HAVE YOU DONE TO HER?
FULL DIGITAL PURGE. THE SENTIENT ALGORITHM WAS BURNT CLEAR.
OUI. AND...A MIND LIKE THAT? A WHINY, PANICKING TEENAGER? AND I THINK PERHAPS YOU KNOW WHO I'M REALLY TALKING ABOUT, EH? HEH.
MY GUESS? SHE DOES NOT HAVE THE DISCIPLINE TO RE-COALESCE. AND EVEN IF SH DID: WE'RE IN A BIO-PSYCHIC FACILITY, NON?

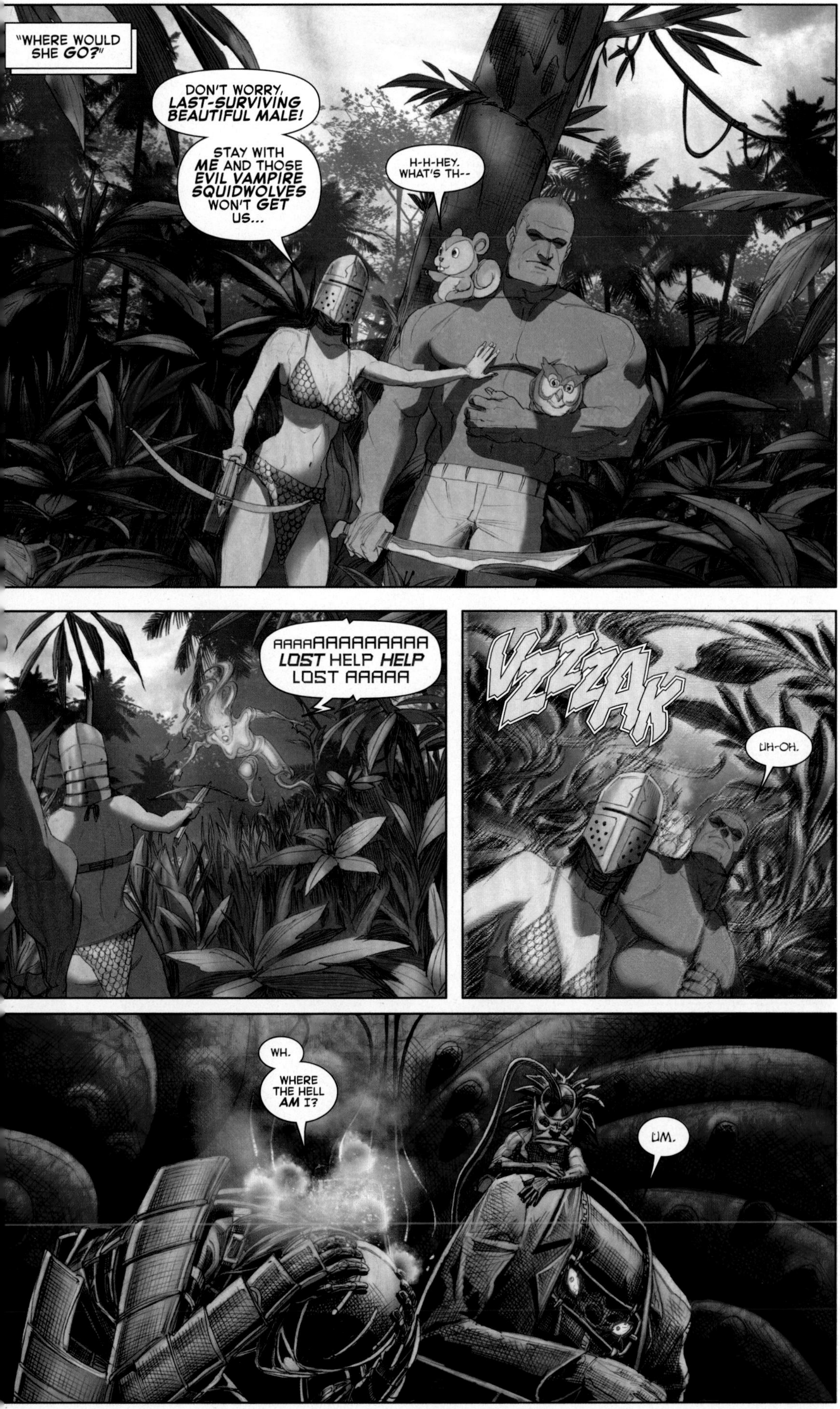
"WHERE WOULD SHE GO?"
DON'T WORRY, LAST-SURVIVING BEAUTIFUL MALE!
STAY WITH ME AND THOSE EVIL VAMPIRE SQUIDWOLVES WON'T GET US...
H-H-HEY. WHAT'S TH--
AAAAAAAAAAAAAA LOST HELP HELP LOST AAAAA
VZZZAK
UH-OH.
WH.
WHERE THE HELL AM I?
UM.

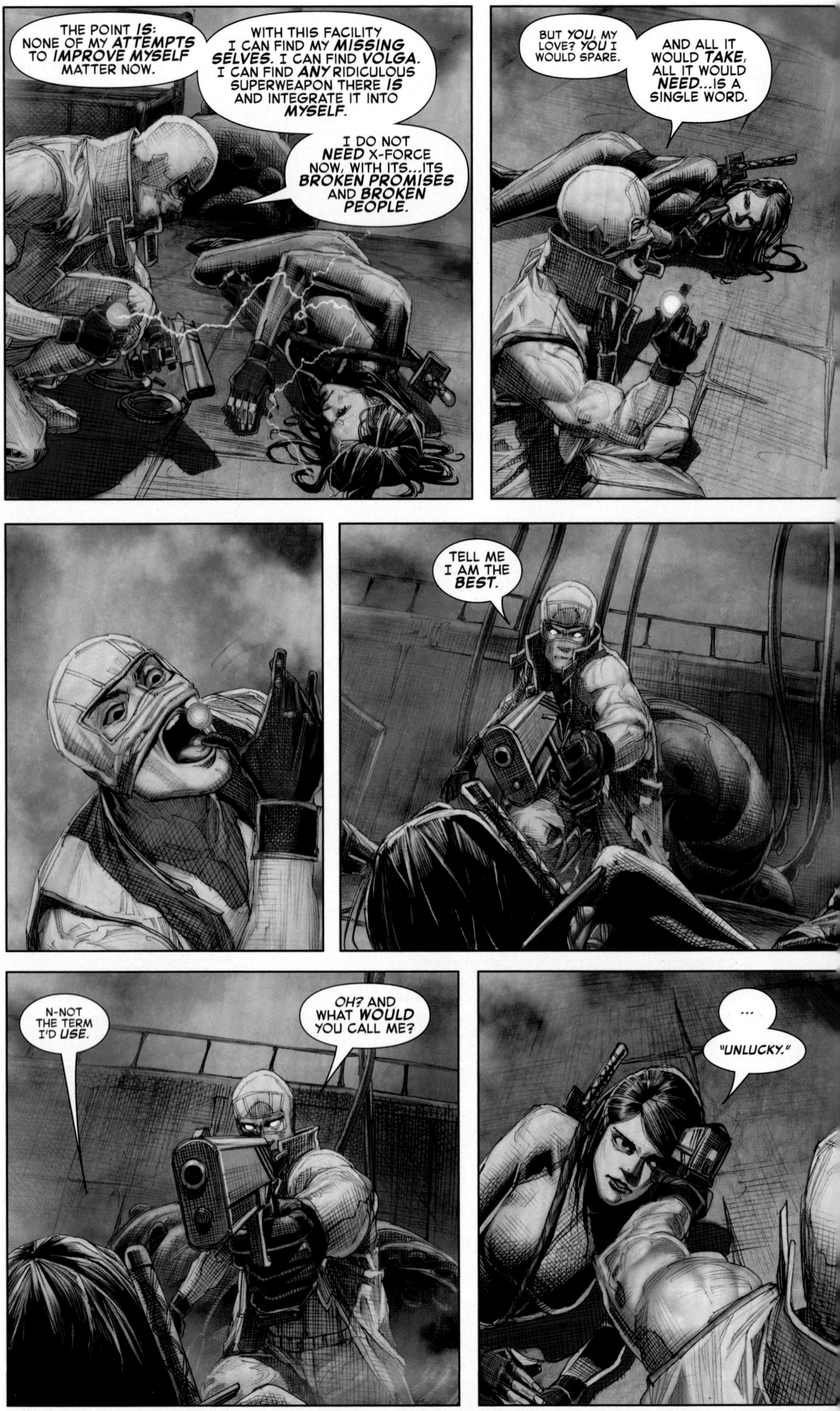
THE POINT IS: NONE OF MY ATTEMPTS TO IMPROVE MYSELF MATTER NOW.
WITH THIS FACILITY I CAN FIND MY MISSING SELVES. I CAN FIND VOLGA. I CAN FIND ANY RIDICULOUS SUPERWEAPON THERE IS AND INTEGRATE IT INTO MYSELF.
I DO NOT NEED X-FORCE NOW, WITH ITS...ITS BROKEN PROMISES AND BROKEN PEOPLE.
BUT YOU, MY LOVE? YOU I WOULD SPARE.
AND ALL IT WOULD TAKE, ALL IT WOULD NEED...IS A SINGLE WORD.
TELL ME I AM THE BEST.
N-NOT THE TERM I'D USE.
OH? AND WHAT WOULD YOU CALL ME?
...
"UNLUCKY."

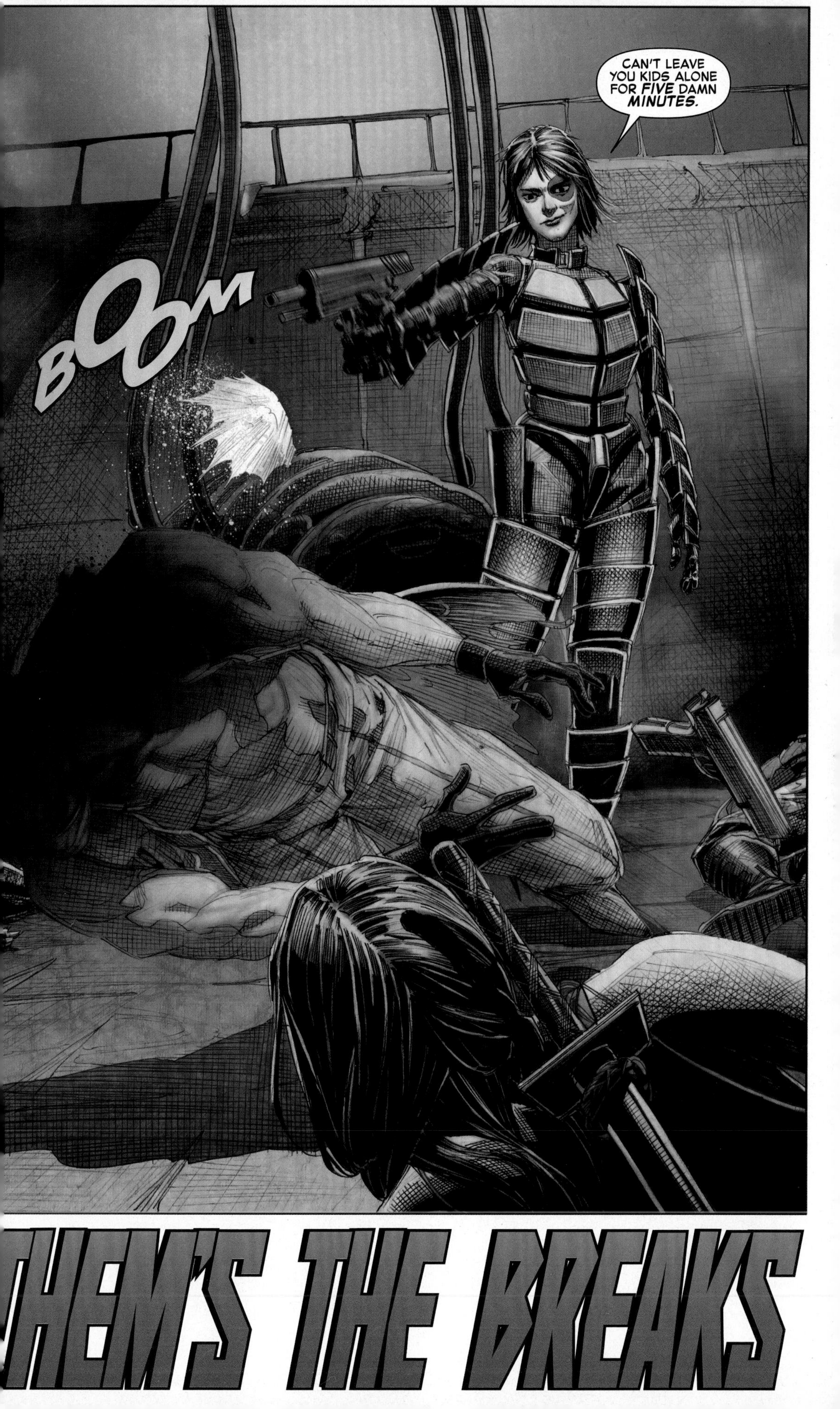
CAN'T LEAVE YOU KIDS ALONE FOR *FIVE* DAMN *MINUTES.*
BOOM
THEM'S THE BREAKS

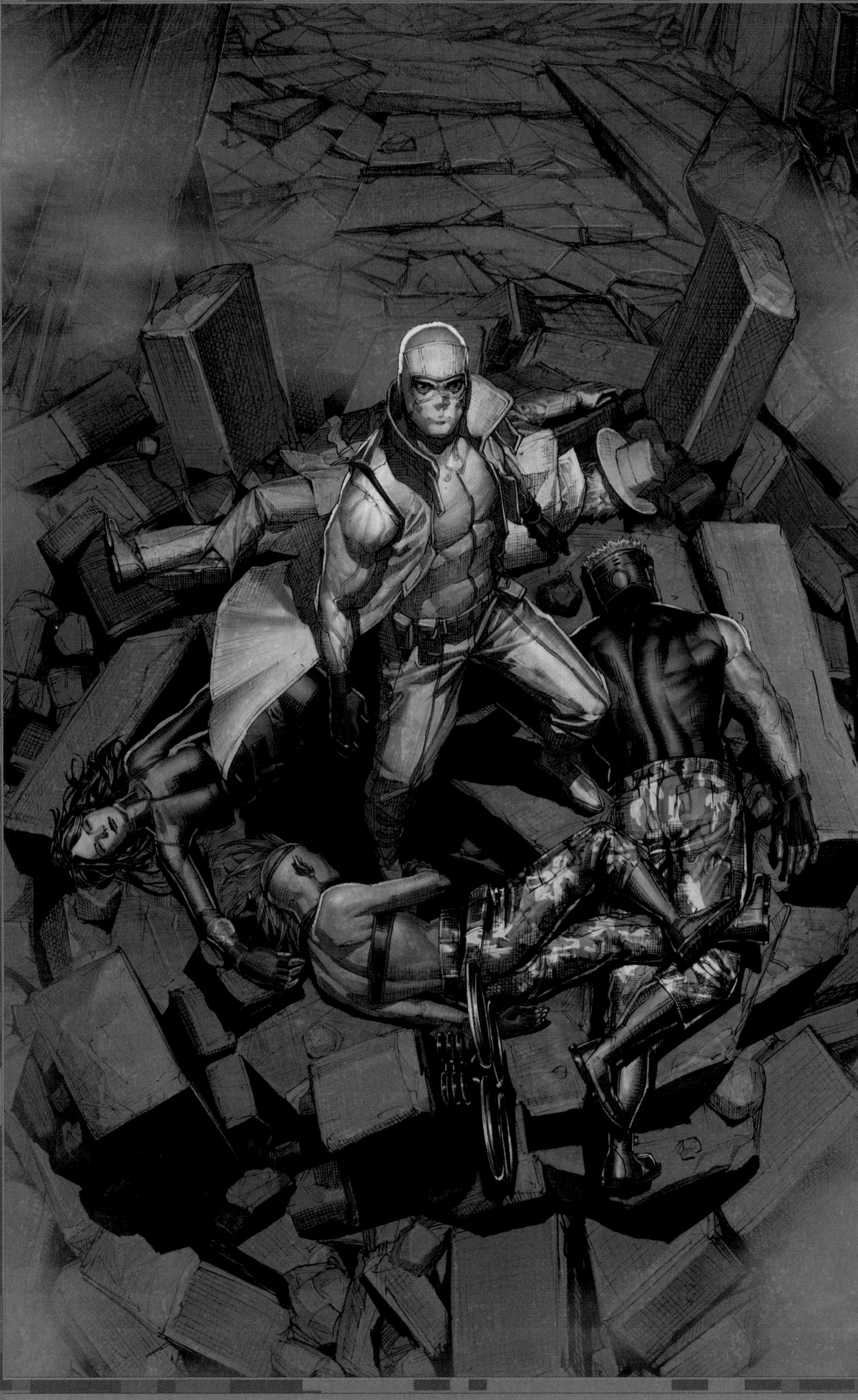

>> 12 <<

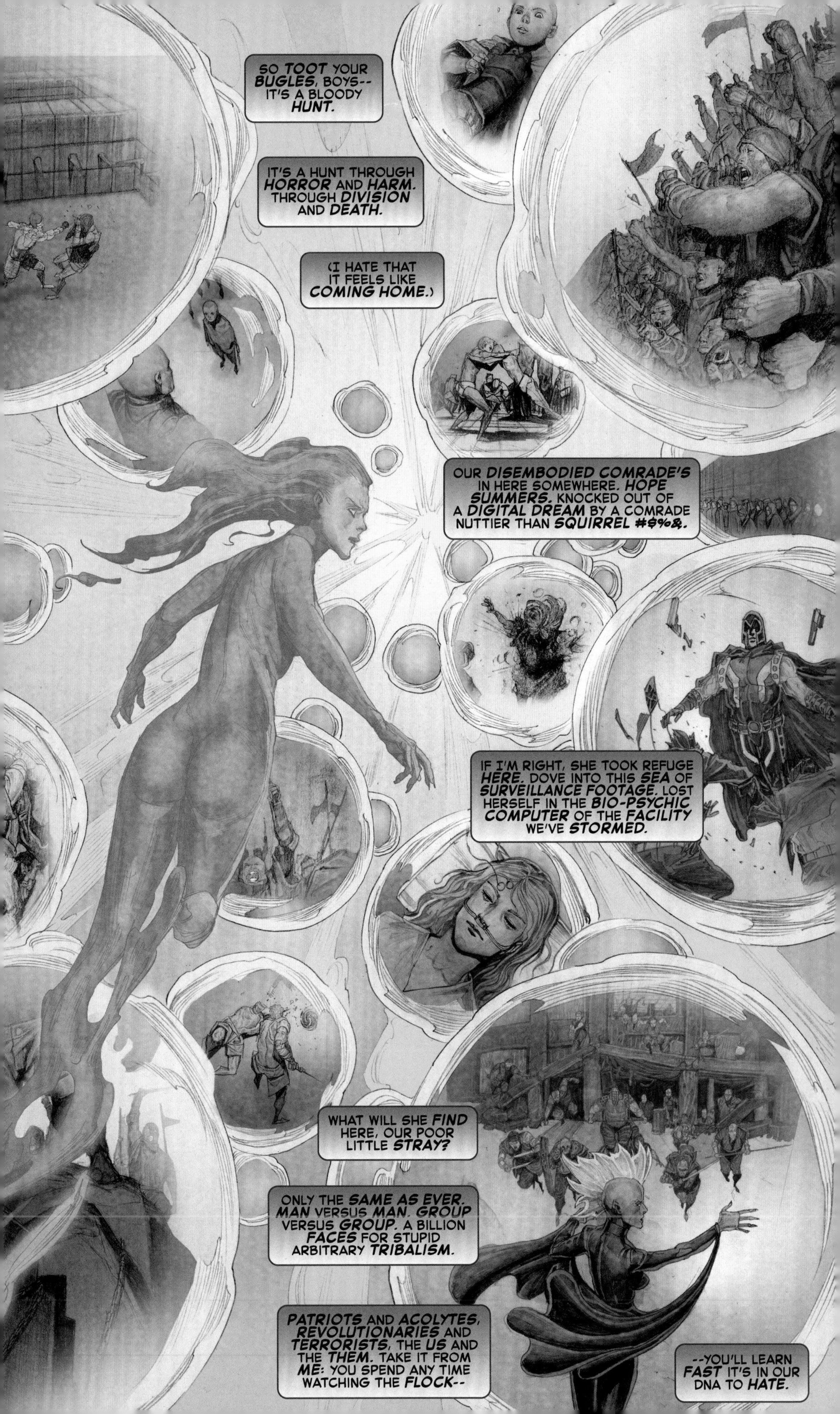

SO TOOT YOUR BUGLES, BOYS-- IT'S A BLOODY HUNT.
IT'S A HUNT THROUGH HORROR AND HARM. THROUGH DIVISION AND DEATH.
(I HATE THAT IT FEELS LIKE COMING HOME.)
OUR DISEMBODIED COMRADE'S IN HERE SOMEWHERE. HOPE SUMMERS. KNOCKED OUT OF A DIGITAL DREAM BY A COMRADE NUTTIER THAN SQUIRREL #$%&.
IF I'M RIGHT, SHE TOOK REFUGE HERE. DOVE INTO THIS SEA OF SURVEILLANCE FOOTAGE. LOST HERSELF IN THE BIO-PSYCHIC COMPUTER OF THE FACILITY WE'VE STORMED.
WHAT WILL SHE FIND HERE, OUR POOR LITTLE STRAY?
ONLY THE SAME AS EVER. MAN VERSUS MAN. GROUP VERSUS GROUP. A BILLION FACES FOR STUPID ARBITRARY TRIBALISM.
PATRIOTS AND ACOLYTES, REVOLUTIONARIES AND TERRORISTS, THE US AND THE THEM. TAKE IT FROM ME: YOU SPEND ANY TIME WATCHING THE FLOCK--
--YOU'LL LEARN FAST IT'S IN OUR DNA TO HATE.

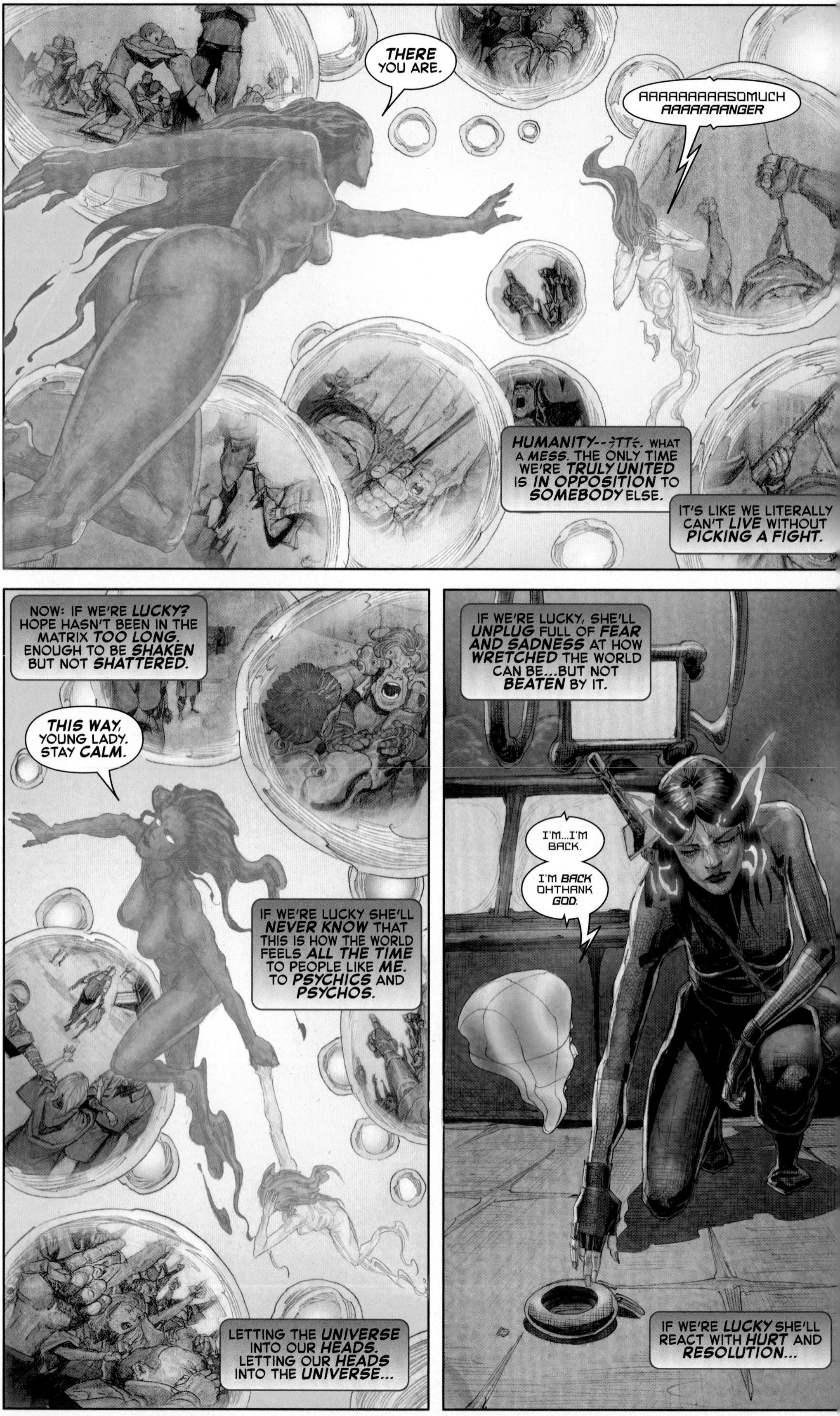
THERE YOU ARE.
AAAAAAAAASOMUCH AAAAAAAANGER
HUMANITY--TT. WHAT A MESS. THE ONLY TIME WE'RE TRULY UNITED IS IN OPPOSITION TO SOMEBODY ELSE.
IT'S LIKE WE LITERALLY CAN'T LIVE WITHOUT PICKING A FIGHT.
NOW: IF WE'RE LUCKY? HOPE HASN'T BEEN IN THE MATRIX TOO LONG. ENOUGH TO BE SHAKEN BUT NOT SHATTERED.
THIS WAY, YOUNG LADY. STAY CALM.
IF WE'RE LUCKY SHE'LL NEVER KNOW THAT THIS IS HOW THE WORLD FEELS ALL THE TIME TO PEOPLE LIKE ME. TO PSYCHICS AND PSYCHOS.
LETTING THE UNIVERSE INTO OUR HEADS. LETTING OUR HEADS INTO THE UNIVERSE...
IF WE'RE LUCKY, SHE'LL UNPLUG FULL OF FEAR AND SADNESS AT HOW WRETCHED THE WORLD CAN BE...BUT NOT BEATEN BY IT.
I'M...I'M BACK.
I'M BACK OHTHANK GOD.
IF WE'RE LUCKY SHE'LL REACT WITH HURT AND RESOLUTION...

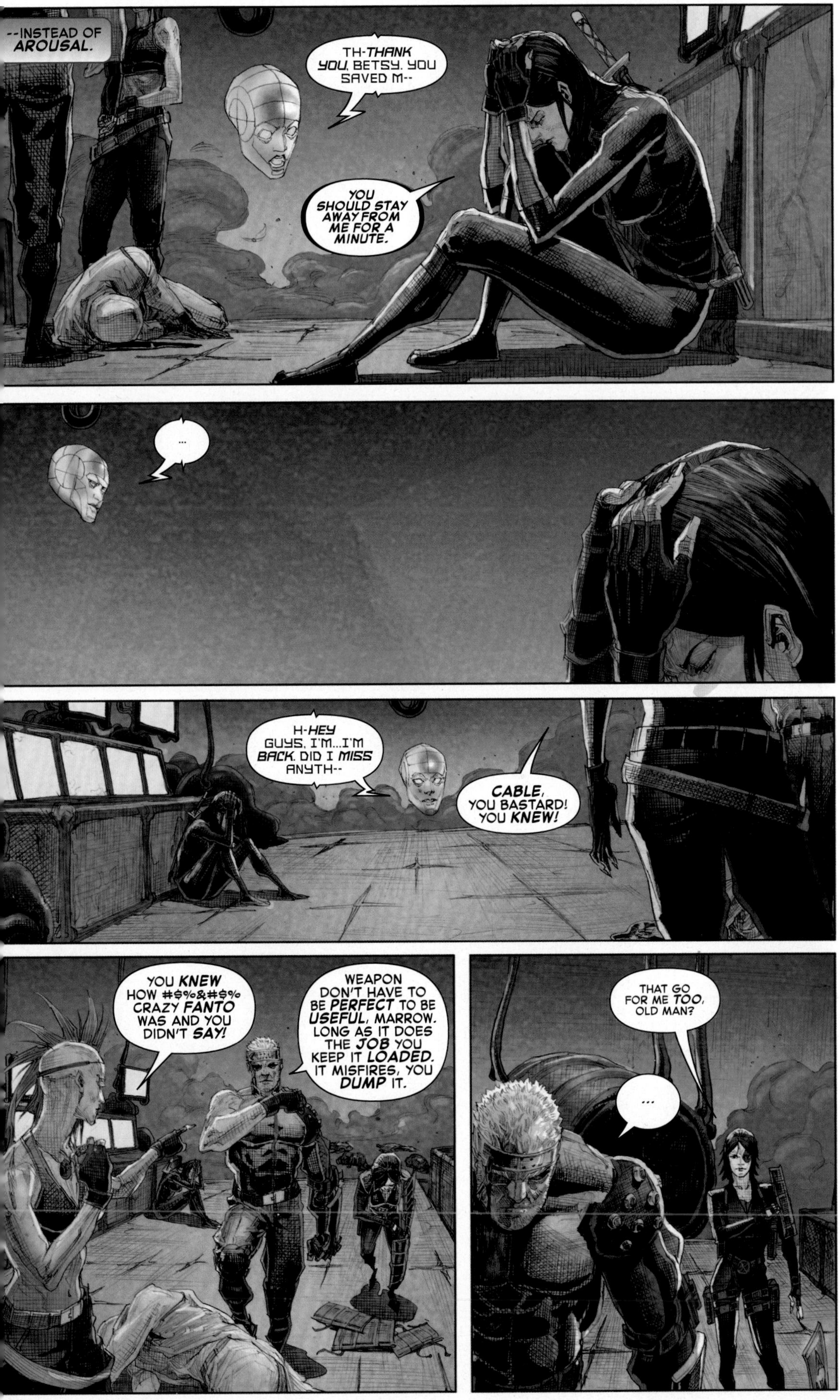
--INSTEAD OF AROUSAL.
TH-THANK YOU, BETSY. YOU SAVED M--
YOU SHOULD STAY AWAY FROM ME FOR A MINUTE.
...
H-HEY GUYS, I'M...I'M BACK. DID I MISS ANYTH--
CABLE, YOU BASTARD! YOU KNEW!
YOU KNEW HOW #$%&#$% CRAZY FANTO WAS AND YOU DIDN'T SAY!
WEAPON DON'T HAVE TO BE PERFECT TO BE USEFUL, MARROW. LONG AS IT DOES THE JOB YOU KEEP IT LOADED. IT MISFIRES, YOU DUMP IT.
THAT GO FOR ME TOO, OLD MAN?
...

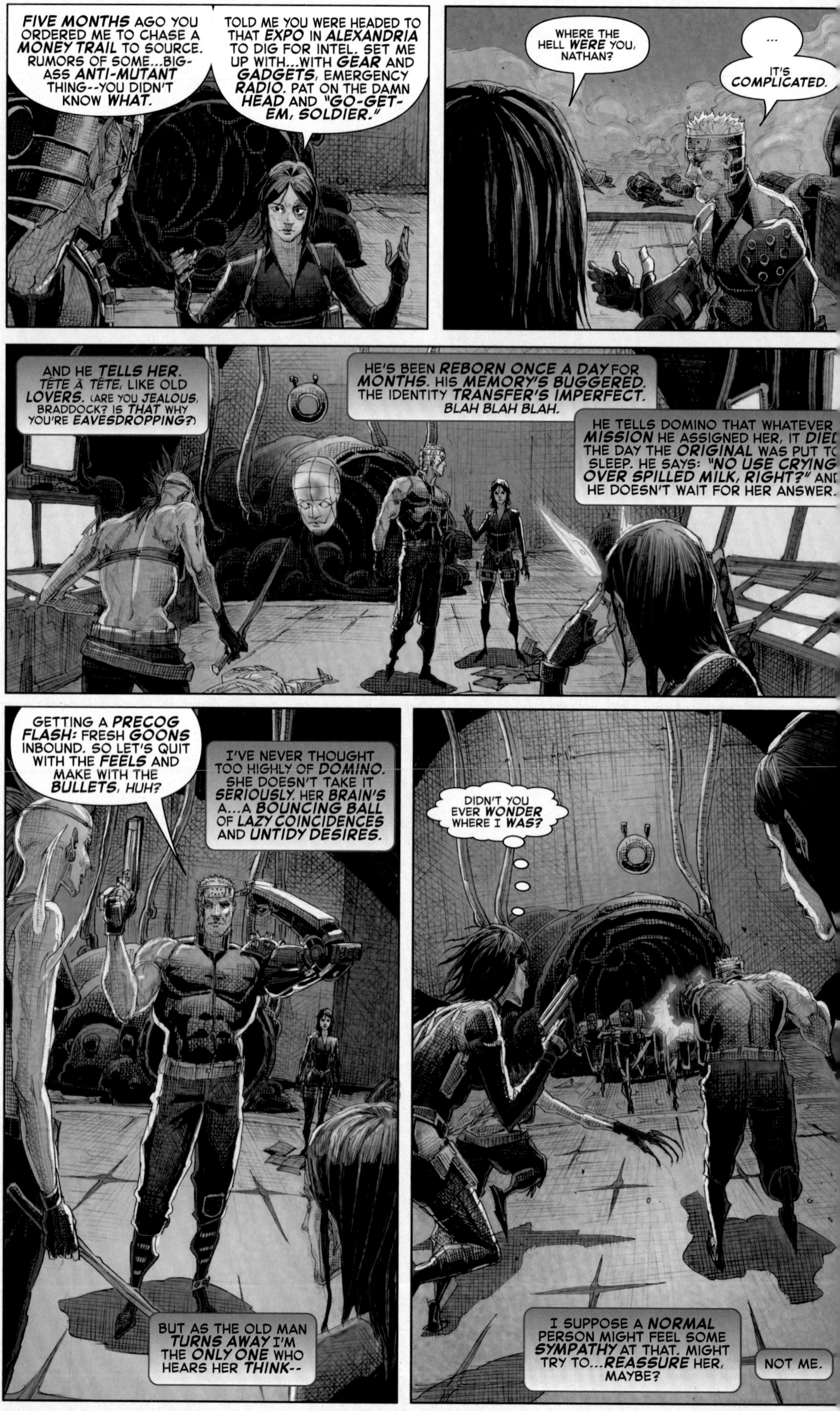
FIVE MONTHS AGO YOU ORDERED ME TO CHASE A MONEY TRAIL TO SOURCE. RUMORS OF SOME...BIG-ASS ANTI-MUTANT THING--YOU DIDN'T KNOW WHAT.
TOLD ME YOU WERE HEADED TO THAT EXPO IN ALEXANDRIA TO DIG FOR INTEL. SET ME UP WITH...WITH GEAR AND GADGETS, EMERGENCY RADIO. PAT ON THE DAMN HEAD AND "GO-GET-EM, SOLDIER."
WHERE THE HELL WERE YOU, NATHAN?
...
IT'S COMPLICATED.
AND HE TELLS HER. TÊTE À TÊTE, LIKE OLD LOVERS. (ARE YOU JEALOUS, BRADDOCK? IS THAT WHY YOU'RE EAVESDROPPING?)
HE'S BEEN REBORN ONCE A DAY FOR MONTHS. HIS MEMORY'S BUGGERED. THE IDENTITY TRANSFER'S IMPERFECT. BLAH BLAH BLAH.
HE TELLS DOMINO THAT WHATEVER MISSION HE ASSIGNED HER, IT DIED THE DAY THE ORIGINAL WAS PUT TO SLEEP. HE SAYS: "NO USE CRYING OVER SPILLED MILK, RIGHT?" AND HE DOESN'T WAIT FOR HER ANSWER.
GETTING A PRECOG FLASH: FRESH GOONS INBOUND. SO LET'S QUIT WITH THE FEELS AND MAKE WITH THE BULLETS, HUH?
I'VE NEVER THOUGHT TOO HIGHLY OF DOMINO. SHE DOESN'T TAKE IT SERIOUSLY. HER BRAIN'S A...A BOUNCING BALL OF LAZY COINCIDENCES AND UNTIDY DESIRES.
BUT AS THE OLD MAN TURNS AWAY I'M THE ONLY ONE WHO HEARS HER THINK--
DIDN'T YOU EVER WONDER WHERE I WAS?
I SUPPOSE A NORMAL PERSON MIGHT FEEL SOME SYMPATHY AT THAT. MIGHT TRY TO...REASSURE HER, MAYBE?
NOT ME.

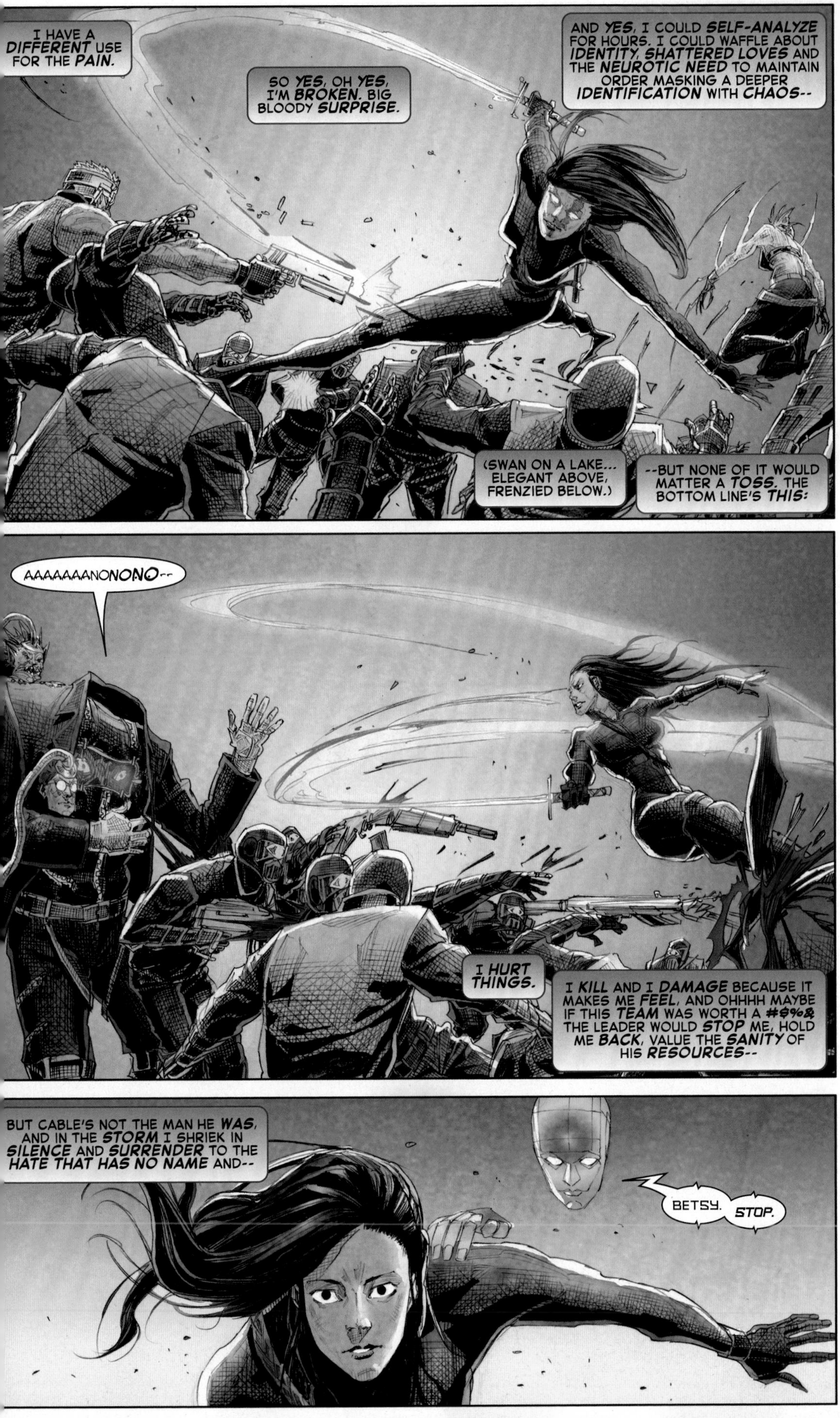

I HAVE A DIFFERENT USE FOR THE PAIN.
SO YES, OH YES, I'M BROKEN. BIG BLOODY SURPRISE.
AND YES, I COULD SELF-ANALYZE FOR HOURS. I COULD WAFFLE ABOUT IDENTITY, SHATTERED LOVES AND THE NEUROTIC NEED TO MAINTAIN ORDER MASKING A DEEPER IDENTIFICATION WITH CHAOS--
(SWAN ON A LAKE... ELEGANT ABOVE, FRENZIED BELOW.)
--BUT NONE OF IT WOULD MATTER A TOSS. THE BOTTOM LINE'S THIS:
AAAAAAANONONO--
I HURT THINGS.
I KILL AND I DAMAGE BECAUSE IT MAKES ME FEEL, AND OHHHH MAYBE IF THIS TEAM WAS WORTH A #$%& THE LEADER WOULD STOP ME, HOLD ME BACK, VALUE THE SANITY OF HIS RESOURCES--
BUT CABLE'S NOT THE MAN HE WAS, AND IN THE STORM I SHRIEK IN SILENCE AND SURRENDER TO THE HATE THAT HAS NO NAME AND--
BETSY. STOP.

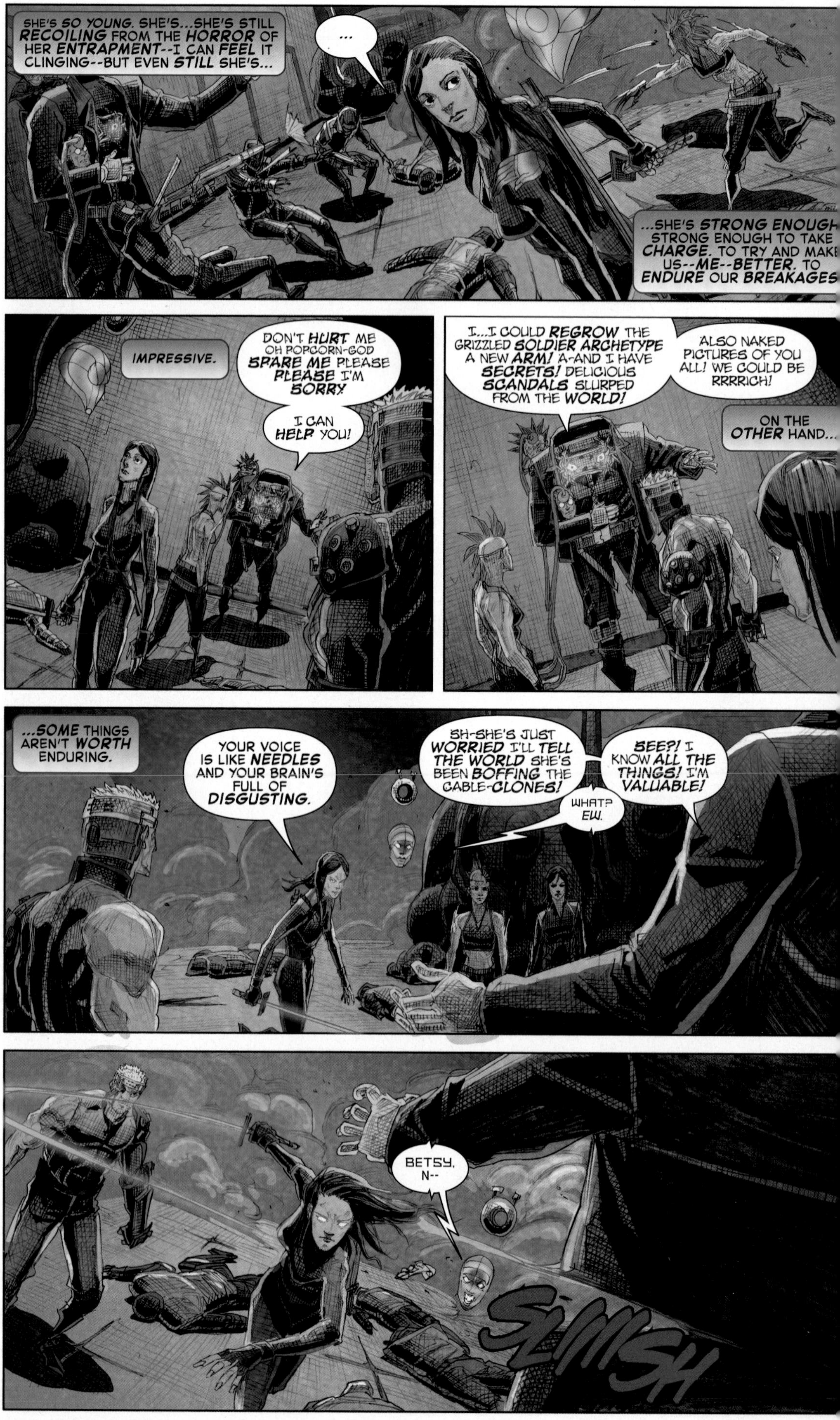
SHE'S SO YOUNG. SHE'S...SHE'S STILL RECOILING FROM THE HORROR OF HER ENTRAPMENT--I CAN FEEL IT CLINGING--BUT EVEN STILL SHE'S...
...
...SHE'S STRONG ENOUGH STRONG ENOUGH TO TAKE CHARGE. TO TRY AND MAKE US--ME--BETTER. TO ENDURE OUR BREAKAGES
IMPRESSIVE.
DON'T HURT ME OH POPCORN-GOD SPARE ME PLEASE PLEASE I'M SORRY
I CAN HELP YOU!
I...I COULD REGROW THE GRIZZLED SOLDIER ARCHETYPE A NEW ARM! A-AND I HAVE SECRETS! DELICIOUS SCANDALS SLURPED FROM THE WORLD!
ALSO NAKED PICTURES OF YOU ALL! WE COULD BE RRRRICH!
ON THE OTHER HAND...
...SOME THINGS AREN'T WORTH ENDURING.
YOUR VOICE IS LIKE NEEDLES AND YOUR BRAIN'S FULL OF DISGUSTING.
SH-SHE'S JUST WORRIED I'LL TELL THE WORLD SHE'S BEEN BOFFING THE CABLE-CLONES!
SEE?! I KNOW ALL THE THINGS! I'M VALUABLE!
WHAT? EW.
BETSY, N--
SLIIISH

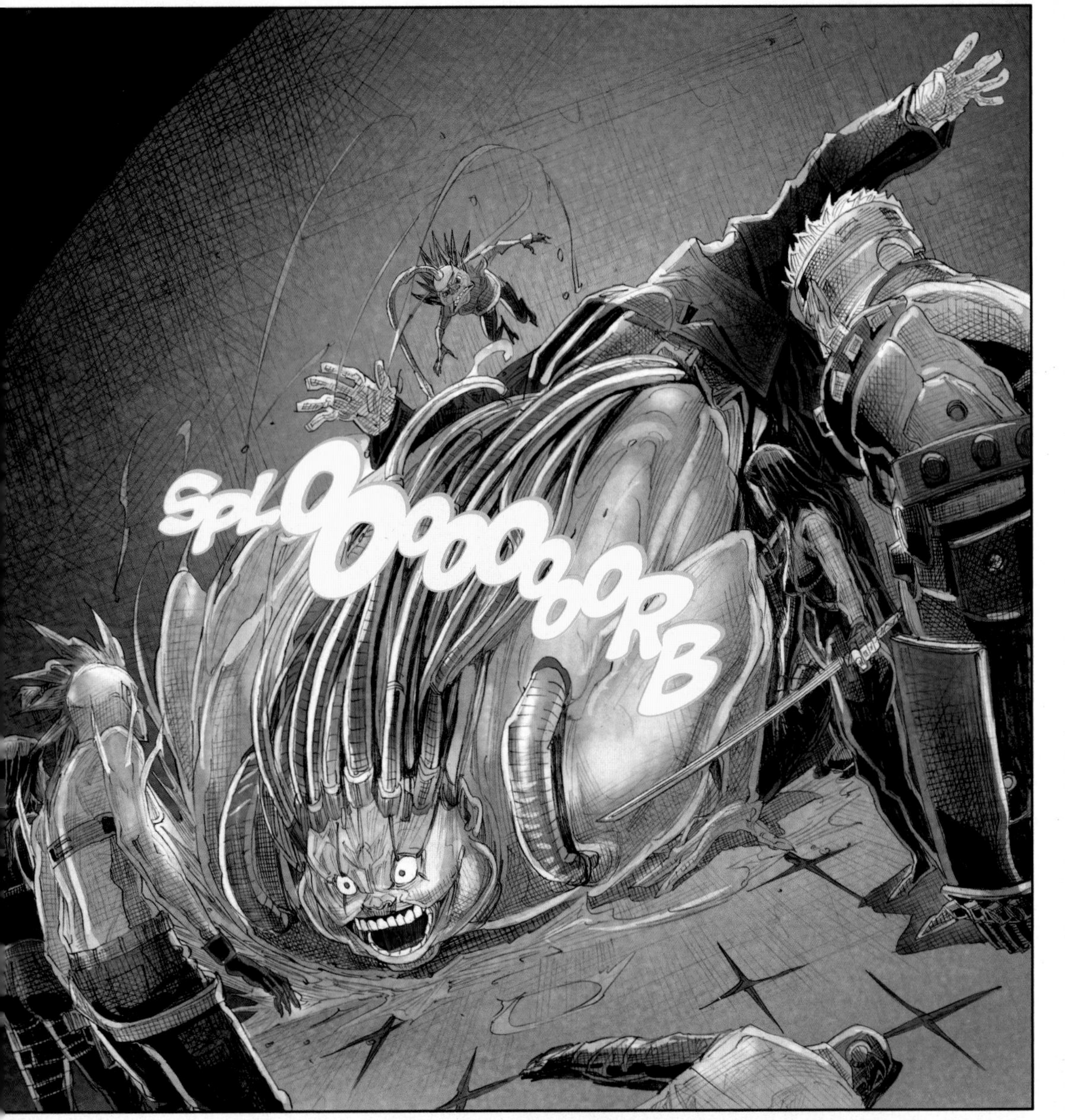
SPLOOOOOOOOORB

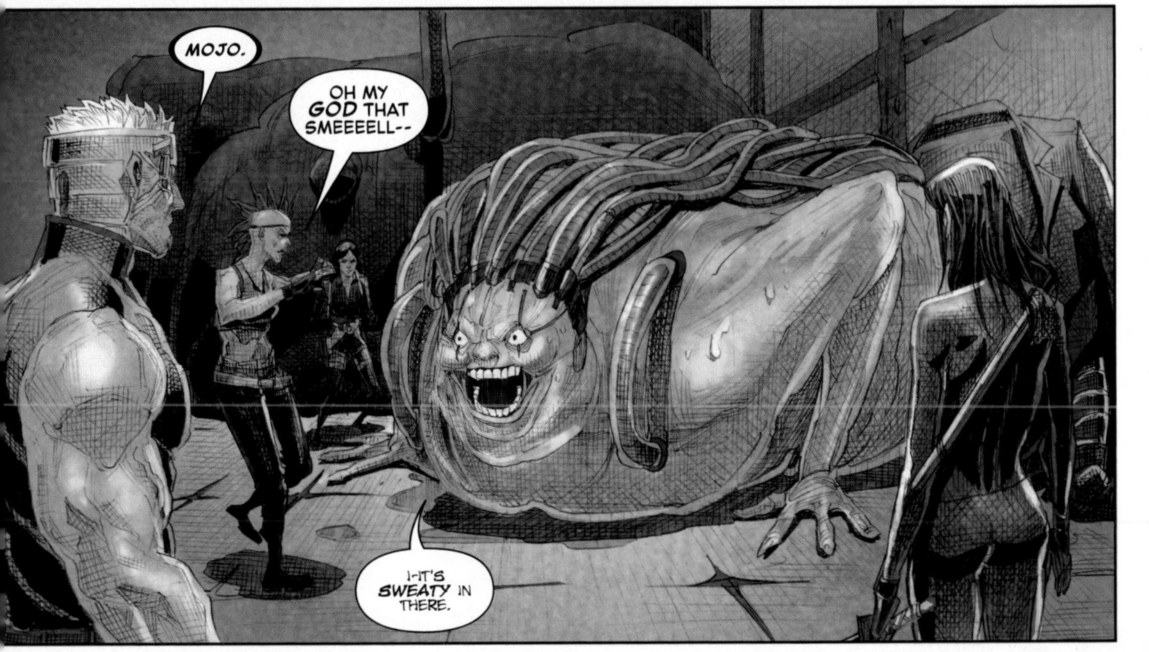
MOJO.
OH MY GOD THAT SMEEEELL--
I-IT'S SWEATY IN THERE.

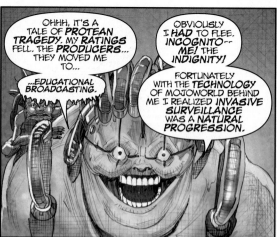

OHHH, IT'S A TALE OF *PROTEAN TRAGEDY.* MY *RATINGS* FELL. THE *PRODUCERS...* THEY MOVED ME TO...

...EDUCATIONAL BROADCASTING.

OBVIOUSLY I *HAD* TO FLEE, INCOGNITO-- *ME!* THE INDIGNITY!

FORTUNATELY WITH THE *TECHNOLOGY* OF *MOJOWORLD* BEHIND ME I REALIZED *INVASIVE SURVEILLANCE* WAS A *NATURAL PROGRESSION.*

I COLLECTED *ASSETS*--SWARM-DEMON *BE'EL* HERE, *SYDNEY* THE *SOVIET PSYKER*--TO PERFECT MY *PERVY VOYEURISM,* AND I OFFERED THEM THE *INCENTIVE* OF SPENDING THEIR LIVES IN A HALLUCINOGENIC *PARADISE FANTASY* OF THEIR OWN *CHOOSING!*

LASTLY, WITH *ANTI-MUTANT RHETORIC* AT AN ALL TIME HIGH, IT MADE SENSE TO CONCENTRAT MY ATTENTION ON TH--

HEY.

NOBODY ASKED FOR AN *EXPOSITION CATCH-UP,* FATSO.

WHO ARE YOU EVEN *TALKING* TO?

I...I JUST THOUGHT PEOPLE MIGHT APPRECIATE THE *INSIGHT.* I'M THE DISGUSTING INVERTEBRATE SUPER VILLAIN FOLKS *HATE* TO L--

NUDGE

YOU WILL TURN OVER CONTROL OF THIS *FACILITY* TO ME OR I WILL *HATE TO LOVE* YOUR *BRAINS* ALL OVER THE *WALL.*

HEY, *NO,* WAITWAIT. THAT' NOT WHAT WE'RE HERE F--

B-BUT I CAN'T!

TH...THE *CORE* SHUT DOWN THE SECOND YOU HIT THE *CONTROL-HUB.* THE FILES ARE BEING *PURGED* FROM THE *SERVER ROOM* AS WE SPEAK.

YOUR *FUNERAL.*

NO NO NO *WAIT* I HAVE MORE DELICIOUS *SCURRILOUS SSSSSECRETS!*

B-B-BONY *LADY* LIKES TO WATCH *SCIENCE GUY* WHILE HE SLEEPS!

WHY YOU SLUG-ASSED SONUVAB--

INSANE FAKE-FRENCH *EVILGUY* WAS HAVING A *SURREAL NONPHYSICAL DALLIANCE* WITH *ROBOT GIRL!*

NOT *GOOD* ENOUGH.

A-AND AS FOR *HER*-- *SHOCKING! DRAMATIC!* TWIST!

OH, *HELL*--

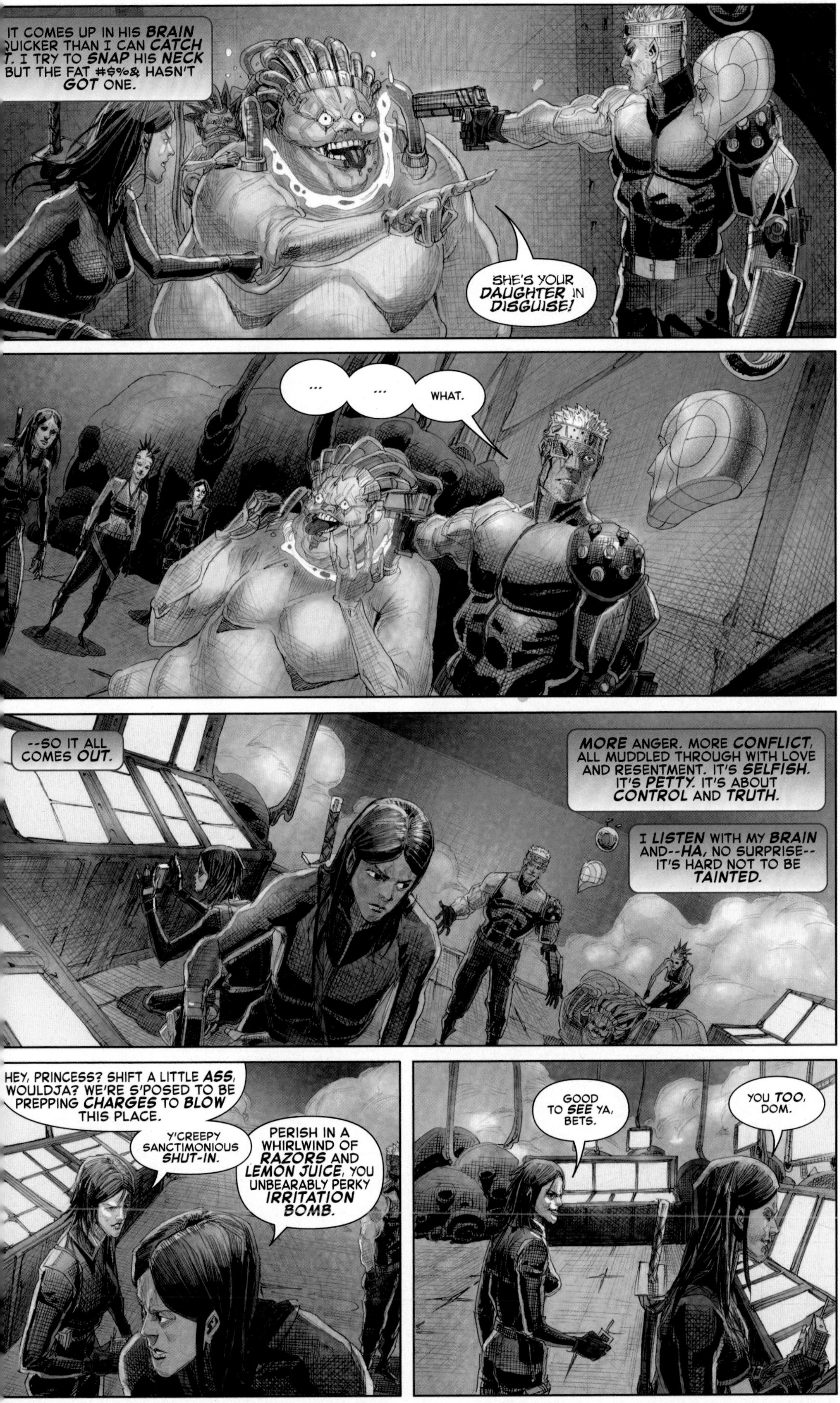

IT COMES UP IN HIS BRAIN QUICKER THAN I CAN CATCH IT. I TRY TO SNAP HIS NECK BUT THE FAT #$%& HASN'T GOT ONE.
SHE'S YOUR DAUGHTER IN DISGUISE!
...
...
WHAT.
--SO IT ALL COMES OUT.
MORE ANGER. MORE CONFLICT, ALL MUDDLED THROUGH WITH LOVE AND RESENTMENT. IT'S SELFISH. IT'S PETTY. IT'S ABOUT CONTROL AND TRUTH.
I LISTEN WITH MY BRAIN AND--HA, NO SURPRISE-- IT'S HARD NOT TO BE TAINTED.
HEY, PRINCESS? SHIFT A LITTLE ASS, WOULDJA? WE'RE S'POSED TO BE PREPPING CHARGES TO BLOW THIS PLACE.
Y'CREEPY SANCTIMONIOUS SHUT-IN.
PERISH IN A WHIRLWIND OF RAZORS AND LEMON JUICE, YOU UNBEARABLY PERKY IRRITATION BOMB.
GOOD TO SEE YA, BETS.
YOU TOO, DOM.

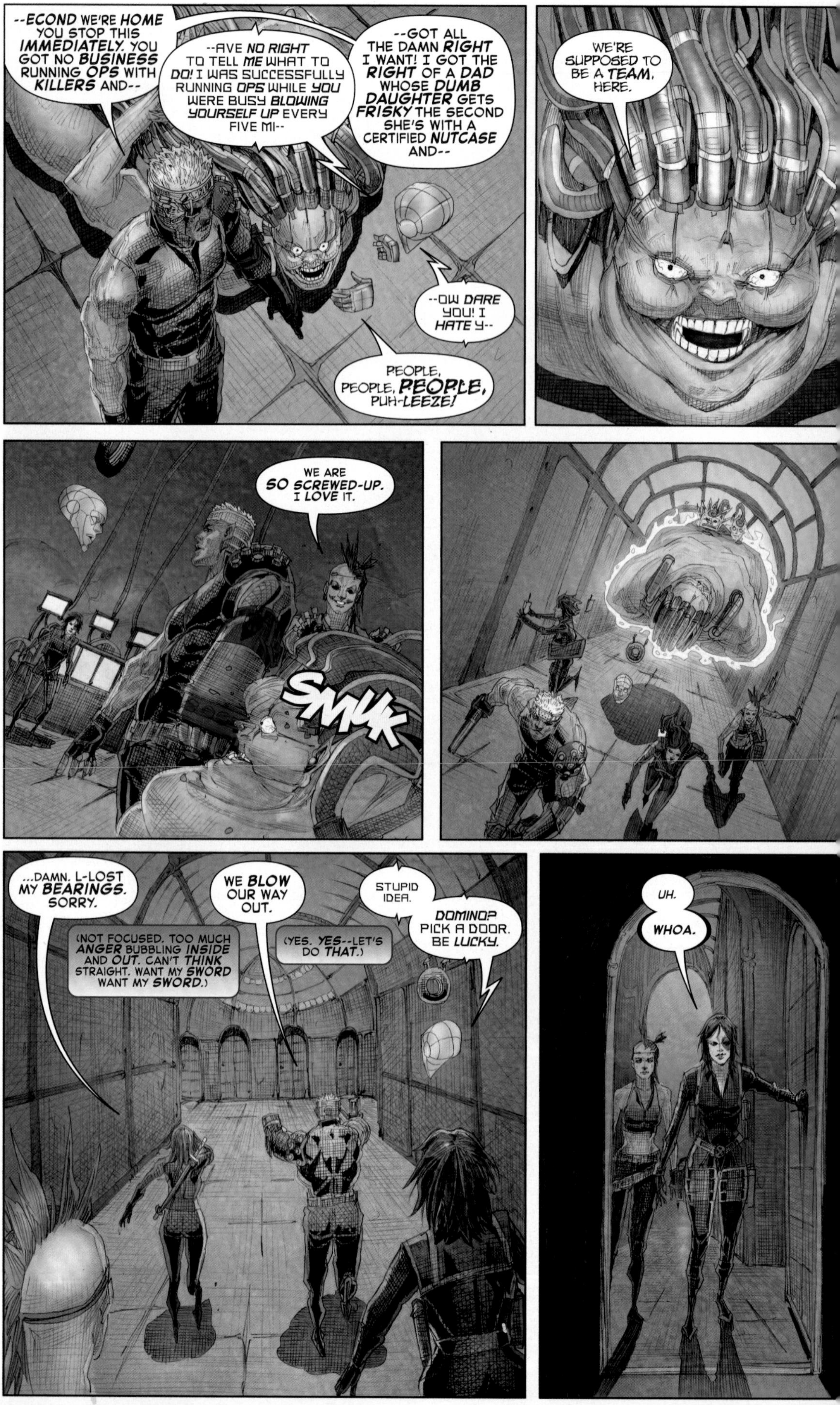
--ECOND WE'RE HOME YOU STOP THIS IMMEDIATELY. YOU GOT NO BUSINESS RUNNING OPS WITH KILLERS AND--
--AVE NO RIGHT TO TELL ME WHAT TO DO! I WAS SUCCESSFULLY RUNNING OPS WHILE YOU WERE BUSY BLOWING YOURSELF UP EVERY FIVE MI--
--GOT ALL THE DAMN RIGHT I WANT! I GOT THE RIGHT OF A DAD WHOSE DUMB DAUGHTER GETS FRISKY THE SECOND SHE'S WITH A CERTIFIED NUTCASE AND--
--OW DARE YOU! I HATE Y--
PEOPLE, PEOPLE, PEOPLE, PUH-LEEZE!
WE'RE SUPPOSED TO BE A TEAM, HERE.
WE ARE SO SCREWED-UP. I LOVE IT.
SMUK
...DAMN. L-LOST MY BEARINGS. SORRY.
(NOT FOCUSED. TOO MUCH ANGER BUBBLING INSIDE AND OUT. CAN'T THINK STRAIGHT. WANT MY SWORD WANT MY SWORD.)
WE BLOW OUR WAY OUT.
(YES. YES--LET'S DO THAT.)
STUPID IDEA.
DOMINO? PICK A DOOR. BE LUCKY.
UH.
WHOA.

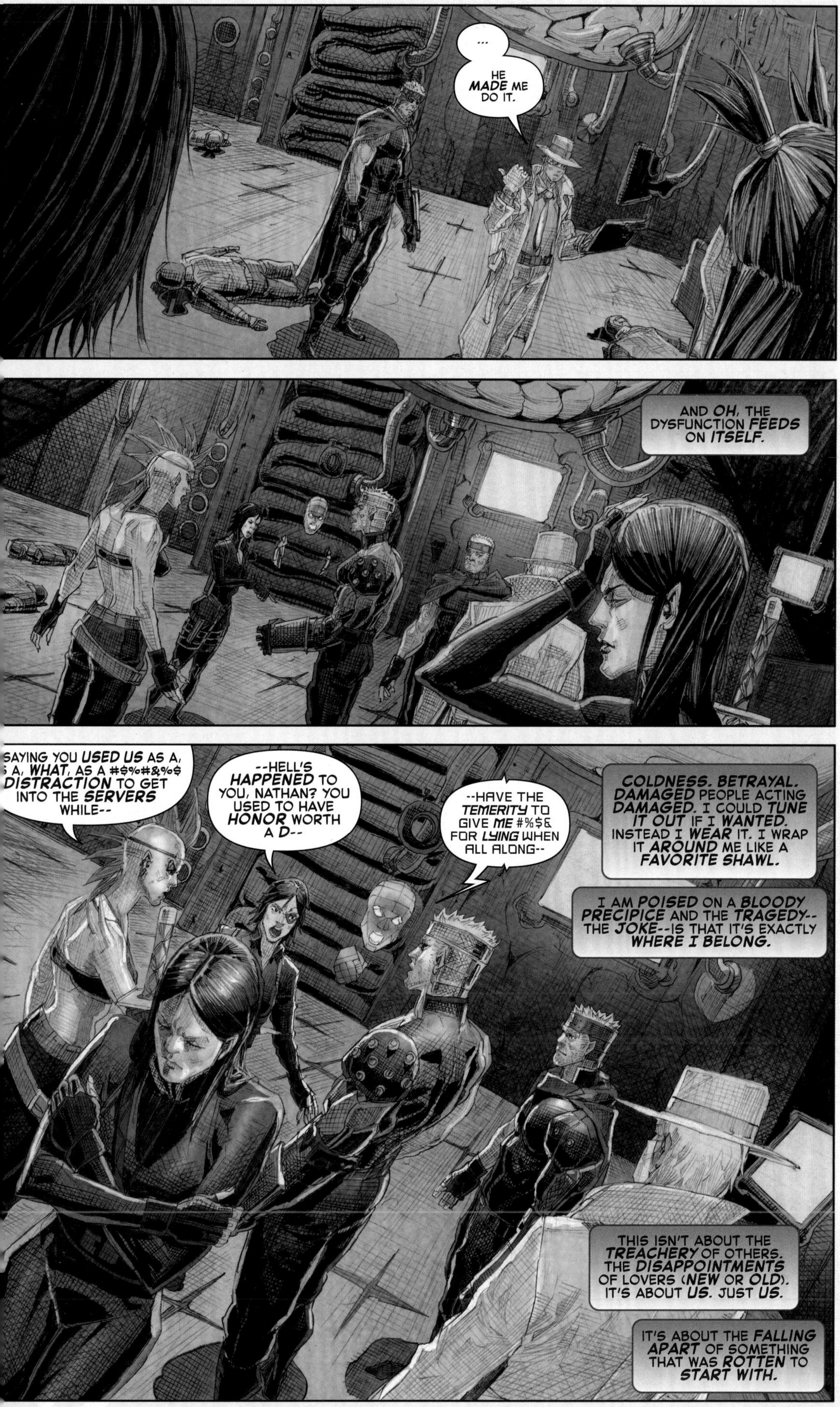
...
HE MADE ME DO IT.
AND OH, THE DYSFUNCTION FEEDS ON ITSELF.
SAYING YOU USED US AS A, A, WHAT, AS A #$%#&%$ DISTRACTION TO GET INTO THE SERVERS WHILE--
--HELL'S HAPPENED TO YOU, NATHAN? YOU USED TO HAVE HONOR WORTH A D--
--HAVE THE TEMERITY TO GIVE ME #%$& FOR LYING WHEN ALL ALONG--
COLDNESS. BETRAYAL. DAMAGED PEOPLE ACTING DAMAGED. I COULD TUNE IT OUT IF I WANTED. INSTEAD I WEAR IT. I WRAP IT AROUND ME LIKE A FAVORITE SHAWL.
I AM POISED ON A BLOODY PRECIPICE AND THE TRAGEDY--THE JOKE--IS THAT IT'S EXACTLY WHERE I BELONG.
THIS ISN'T ABOUT THE TREACHERY OF OTHERS. THE DISAPPOINTMENTS OF LOVERS (NEW OR OLD). IT'S ABOUT US. JUST US.
IT'S ABOUT THE FALLING APART OF SOMETHING THAT WAS ROTTEN TO START WITH.

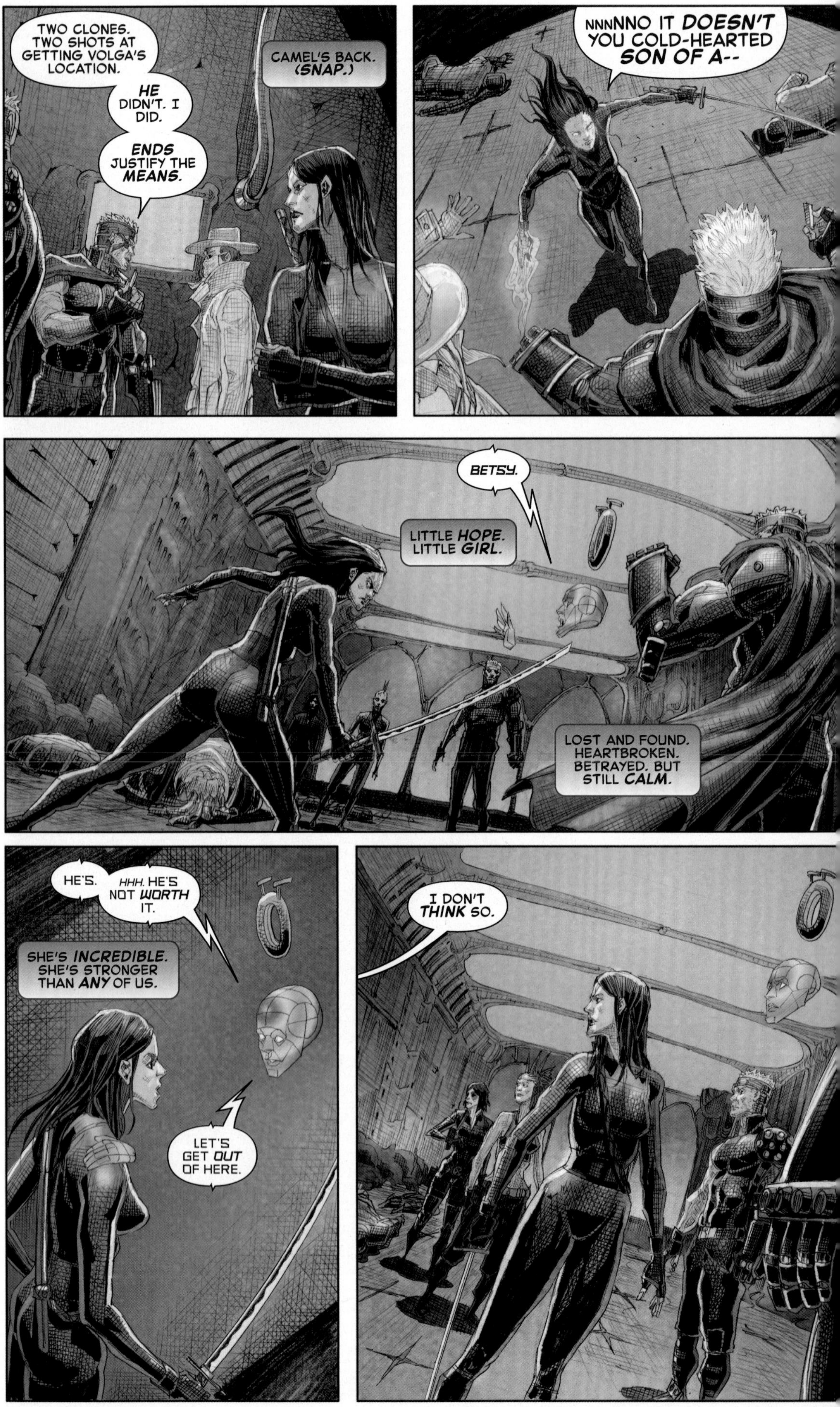
TWO CLONES. TWO SHOTS AT GETTING VOLGA'S LOCATION.
CAMEL'S BACK. (SNAP.)
HE DIDN'T. I DID.
ENDS JUSTIFY THE MEANS.
NNNNNO IT DOESN'T YOU COLD-HEARTED SON OF A--
BETSY.
LITTLE HOPE. LITTLE GIRL.
LOST AND FOUND. HEARTBROKEN. BETRAYED. BUT STILL CALM.
HE'S.
HHH. HE'S NOT WORTH IT.
SHE'S INCREDIBLE. SHE'S STRONGER THAN ANY OF US.
LET'S GET OUT OF HERE.
I DON'T THINK SO.

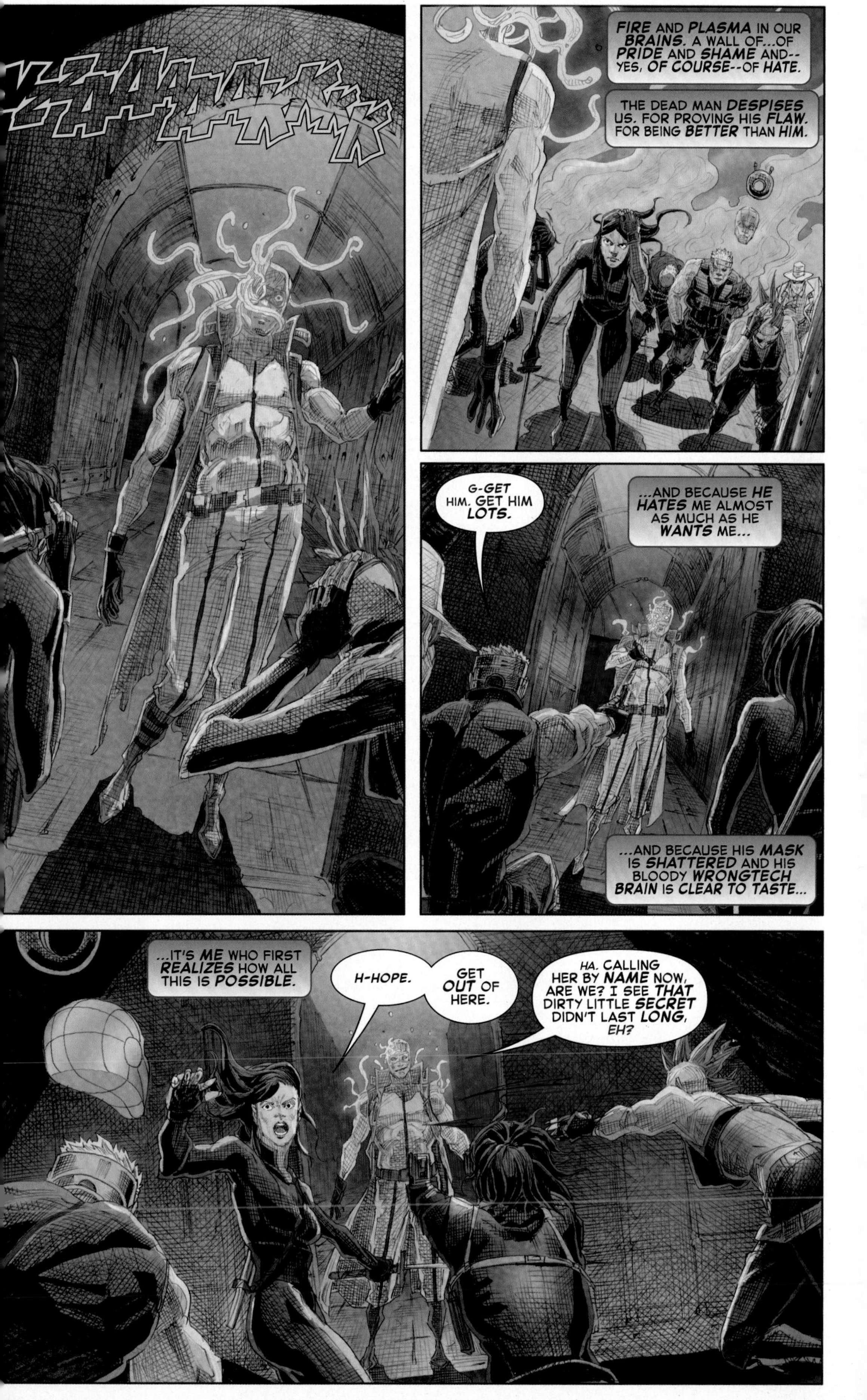

KZAAAAKK
FIRE AND PLASMA IN OUR BRAINS. A WALL OF...OF PRIDE AND SHAME AND--YES, OF COURSE--OF HATE.
THE DEAD MAN DESPISES US. FOR PROVING HIS FLAW. FOR BEING BETTER THAN HIM.
G-GET HIM. GET HIM LOTS.
...AND BECAUSE HE HATES ME ALMOST AS MUCH AS HE WANTS ME...
...AND BECAUSE HIS MASK IS SHATTERED AND HIS BLOODY WRONGTECH BRAIN IS CLEAR TO TASTE...
...IT'S ME WHO FIRST REALIZES HOW ALL THIS IS POSSIBLE.
H-HOPE.
GET OUT OF HERE.
HA. CALLING HER BY NAME NOW, ARE WE? I SEE THAT DIRTY LITTLE SECRET DIDN'T LAST LONG, EH?

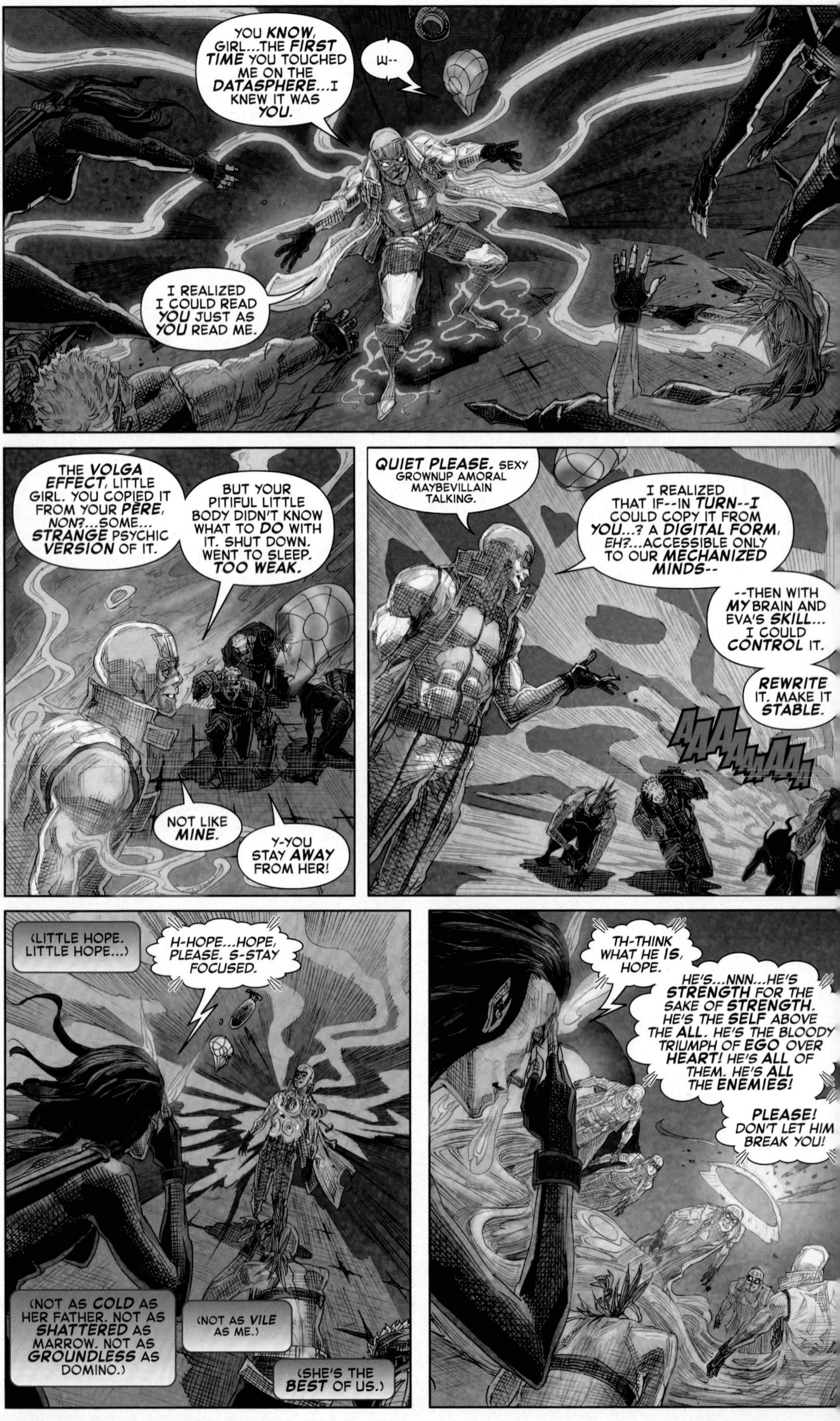
YOU KNOW, GIRL...THE FIRST TIME YOU TOUCHED ME ON THE DATASPHERE...I KNEW IT WAS YOU.
W--
I REALIZED I COULD READ YOU JUST AS YOU READ ME.
THE VOLGA EFFECT, LITTLE GIRL. YOU COPIED IT FROM YOUR PÈRE, NON?...SOME... STRANGE PSYCHIC VERSION OF IT.
BUT YOUR PITIFUL LITTLE BODY DIDN'T KNOW WHAT TO DO WITH IT. SHUT DOWN. WENT TO SLEEP. TOO WEAK.
NOT LIKE MINE.
Y-YOU STAY AWAY FROM HER!
QUIET PLEASE. SEXY GROWNUP AMORAL MAYBEVILLAIN TALKING.
I REALIZED THAT IF--IN TURN--I COULD COPY IT FROM YOU...? A DIGITAL FORM, EH?...ACCESSIBLE ONLY TO OUR MECHANIZED MINDS--
--THEN WITH MY BRAIN AND EVA'S SKILL... I COULD CONTROL IT.
REWRITE IT. MAKE IT STABLE.
AAAAAAAAAA
(LITTLE HOPE. LITTLE HOPE...)
H-HOPE...HOPE, PLEASE. S-STAY FOCUSED.
(NOT AS COLD AS HER FATHER. NOT AS SHATTERED AS MARROW. NOT AS GROUNDLESS AS DOMINO.)
(NOT AS VILE AS ME.)
(SHE'S THE BEST OF US.)
TH-THINK WHAT HE IS, HOPE.
HE'S...NNN...HE'S STRENGTH FOR THE SAKE OF STRENGTH. HE'S THE SELF ABOVE THE ALL. HE'S THE BLOODY TRIUMPH OF EGO OVER HEART! HE'S ALL OF THEM. HE'S ALL THE ENEMIES!
PLEASE! DON'T LET HIM BREAK YOU!

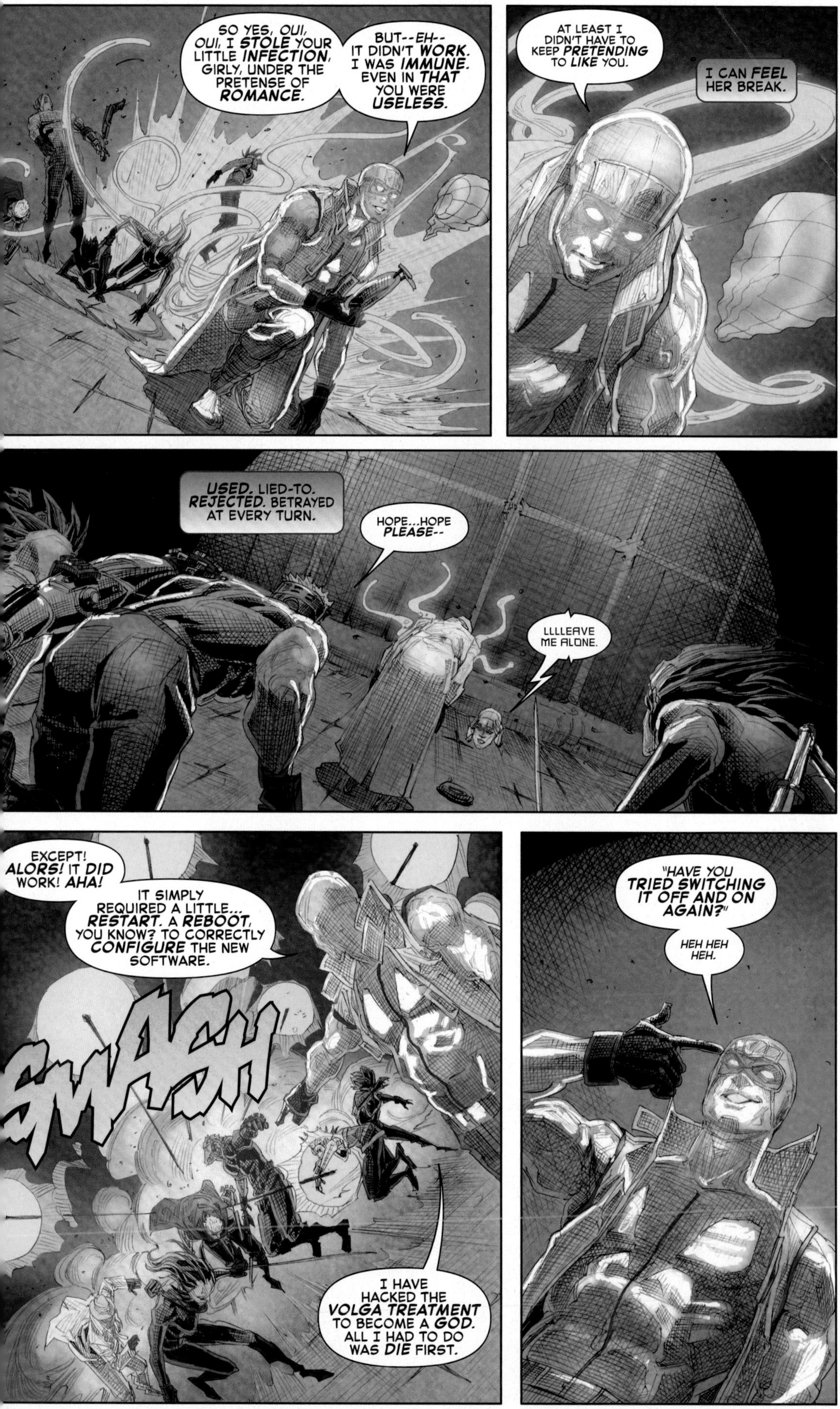

SO YES, OUI, OUI, I STOLE YOUR LITTLE INFECTION, GIRLY, UNDER THE PRETENSE OF ROMANCE.
BUT--EH-- IT DIDN'T WORK. I WAS IMMUNE. EVEN IN THAT YOU WERE USELESS.
AT LEAST I DIDN'T HAVE TO KEEP PRETENDING TO LIKE YOU.
I CAN FEEL HER BREAK.
USED. LIED-TO. REJECTED. BETRAYED AT EVERY TURN.
HOPE...HOPE PLEASE--
LLLLEAVE ME ALONE.
EXCEPT! ALORS! IT DID WORK! AHA!
IT SIMPLY REQUIRED A LITTLE... RESTART. A REBOOT, YOU KNOW? TO CORRECTLY CONFIGURE THE NEW SOFTWARE.
SMASH
I HAVE HACKED THE VOLGA TREATMENT TO BECOME A GOD. ALL I HAD TO DO WAS DIE FIRST.
"HAVE YOU TRIED SWITCHING IT OFF AND ON AGAIN?"
HEH HEH HEH.

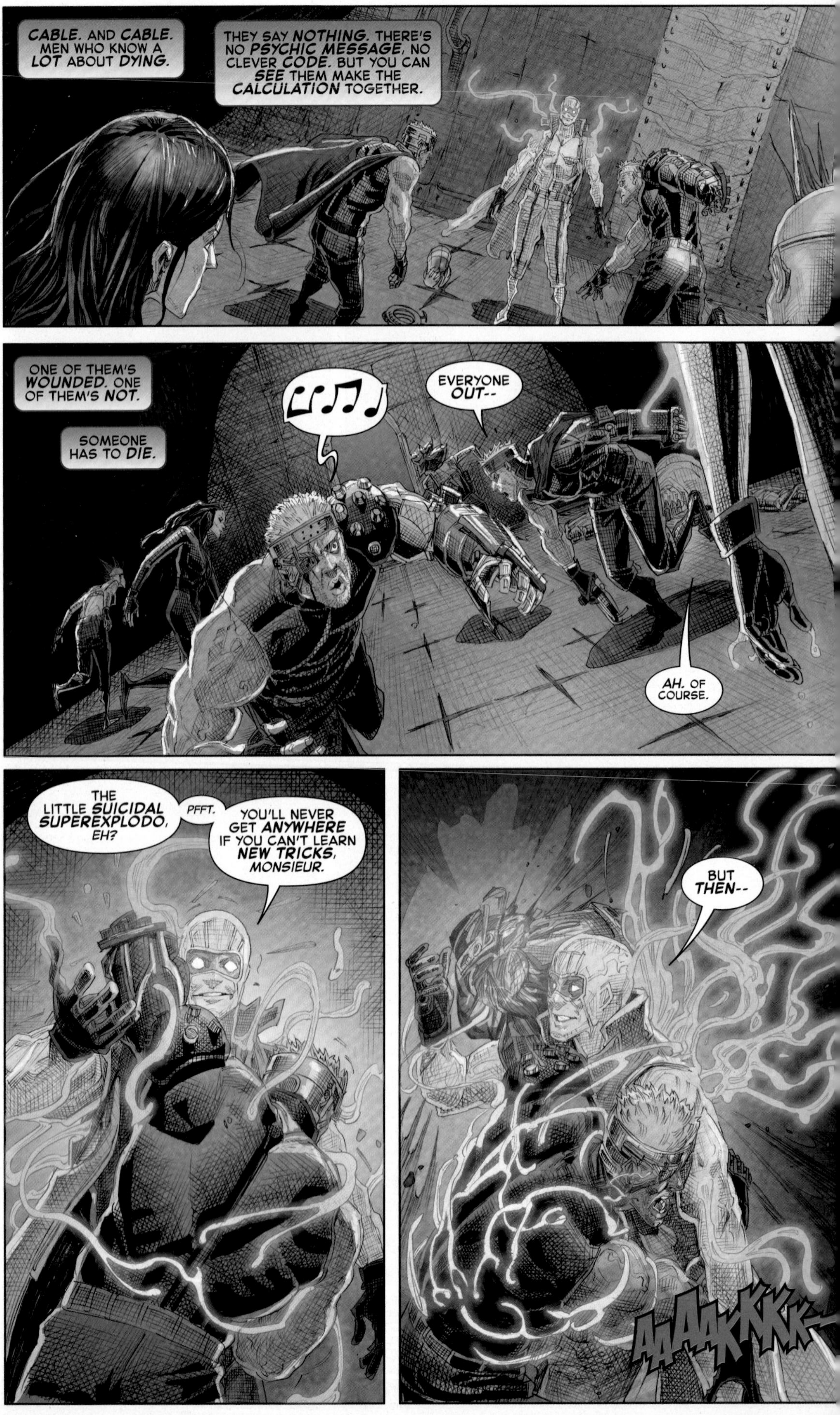
CABLE. AND CABLE. MEN WHO KNOW A LOT ABOUT DYING.
THEY SAY NOTHING. THERE'S NO PSYCHIC MESSAGE, NO CLEVER CODE. BUT YOU CAN SEE THEM MAKE THE CALCULATION TOGETHER.
ONE OF THEM'S WOUNDED. ONE OF THEM'S NOT.
SOMEONE HAS TO DIE.
♫♫♪
EVERYONE OUT--
AH. OF COURSE.
THE LITTLE SUICIDAL SUPEREXPLODO, EH?
PFFT.
YOU'LL NEVER GET ANYWHERE IF YOU CAN'T LEARN NEW TRICKS, MONSIEUR.
BUT THEN--
AAAAKKKK

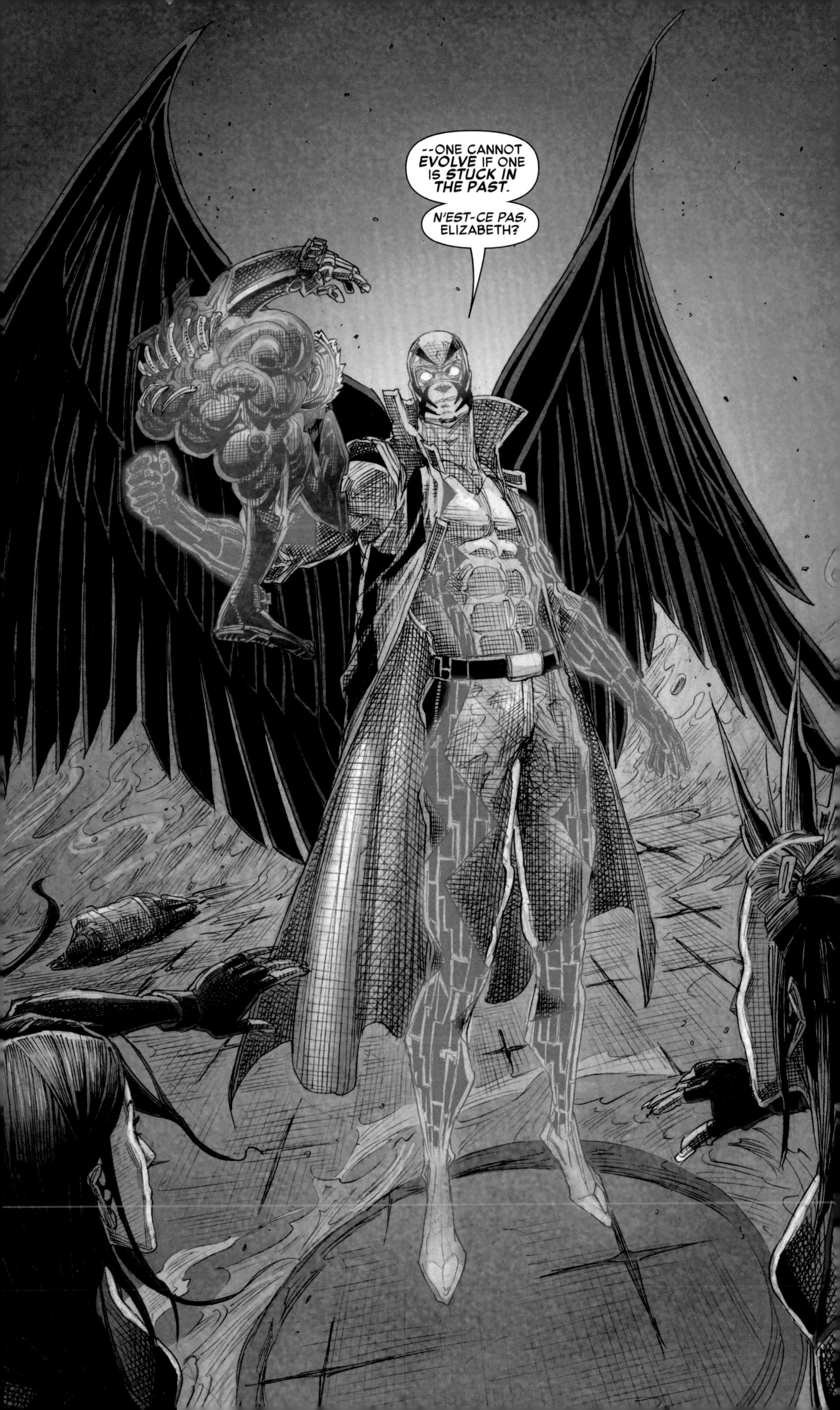
--ONE CANNOT EVOLVE IF ONE IS STUCK IN THE PAST.
N'EST-CE PAS, ELIZABETH?

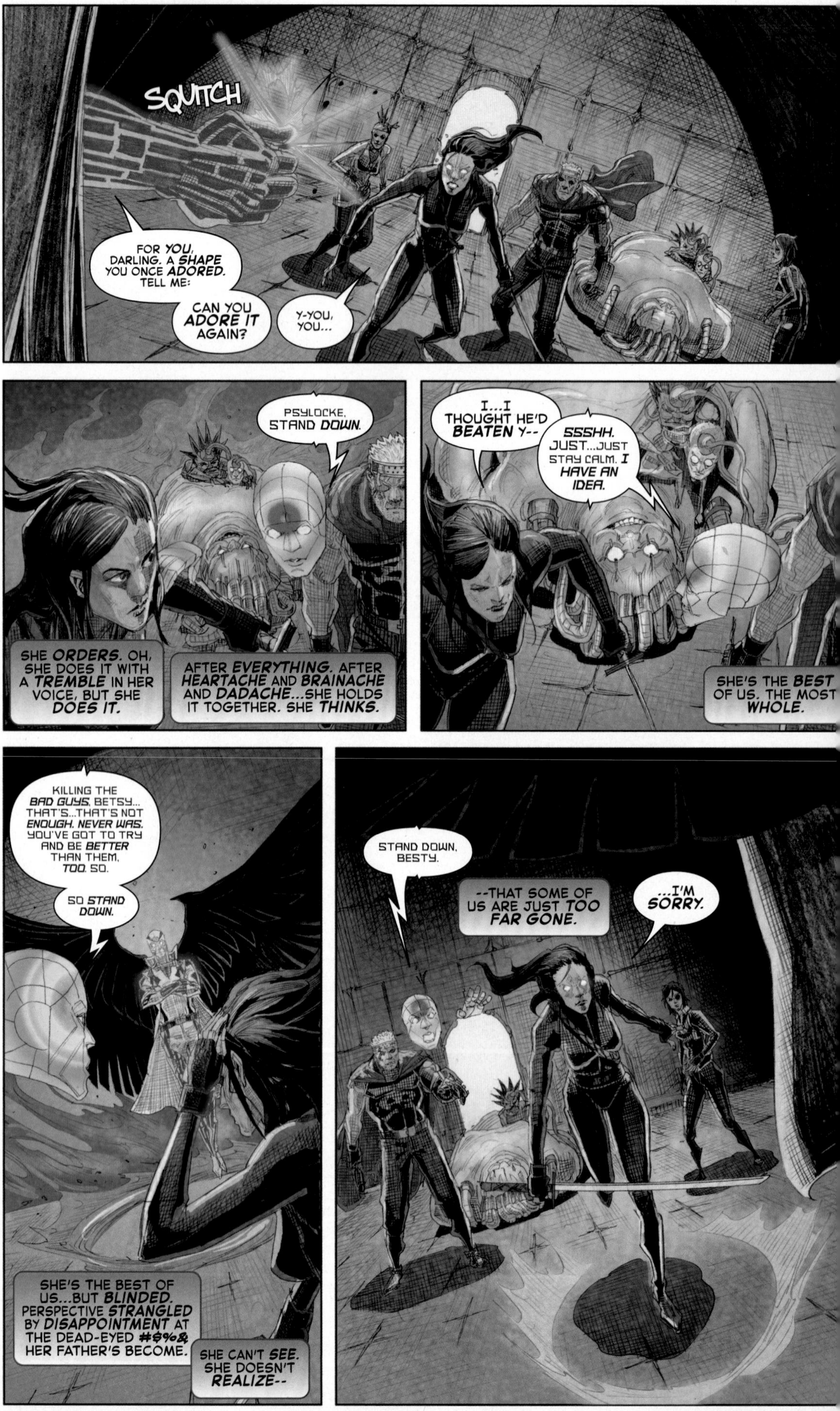
SQUITCH
FOR YOU, DARLING. A SHAPE YOU ONCE ADORED. TELL ME:
CAN YOU ADORE IT AGAIN?
Y-YOU, YOU...
PSYLOCKE, STAND DOWN.
SHE ORDERS. OH, SHE DOES IT WITH A TREMBLE IN HER VOICE, BUT SHE DOES IT.
AFTER EVERYTHING. AFTER HEARTACHE AND BRAINACHE AND DADACHE...SHE HOLDS IT TOGETHER. SHE THINKS.
I...I THOUGHT HE'D BEATEN Y--
SSSHH. JUST...JUST STAY CALM. I HAVE AN IDEA.
SHE'S THE BEST OF US. THE MOST WHOLE.
KILLING THE BAD GUYS, BETSY... THAT'S...THAT'S NOT ENOUGH. NEVER WAS. YOU'VE GOT TO TRY AND BE BETTER THAN THEM, TOO. SO.
SO STAND DOWN.
SHE'S THE BEST OF US...BUT BLINDED. PERSPECTIVE STRANGLED BY DISAPPOINTMENT AT THE DEAD-EYED #$%& HER FATHER'S BECOME.
SHE CAN'T SEE. SHE DOESN'T REALIZE--
STAND DOWN, BESTY.
--THAT SOME OF US ARE JUST TOO FAR GONE.
...I'M SORRY.

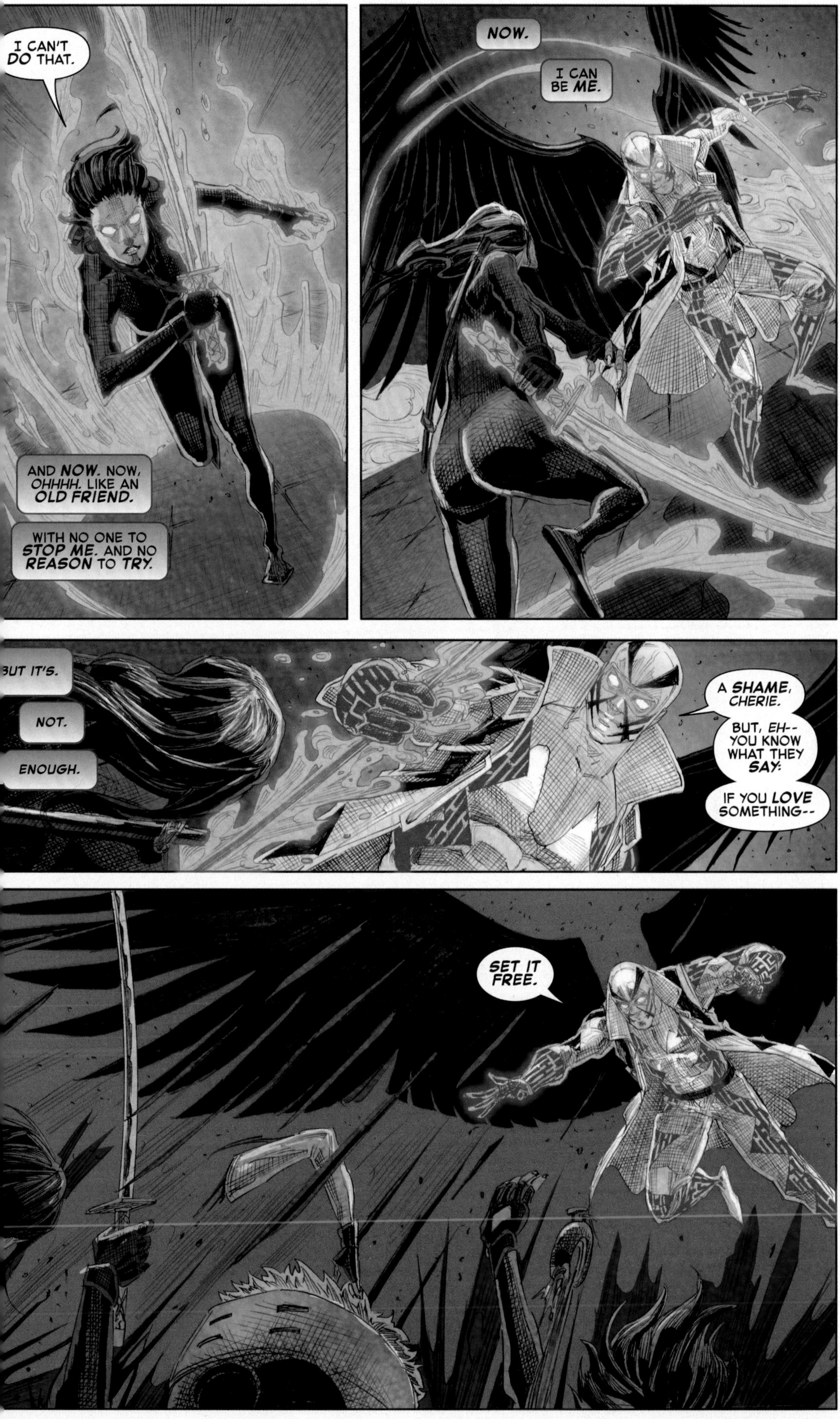
I CAN'T DO THAT.
NOW.
I CAN BE ME.
AND NOW. NOW, OHHHH. LIKE AN OLD FRIEND.
WITH NO ONE TO STOP ME. AND NO REASON TO TRY.
BUT IT'S.
NOT.
ENOUGH.
A SHAME, CHERIE.
BUT, EH-- YOU KNOW WHAT THEY SAY:
IF YOU LOVE SOMETHING--
SET IT FREE.

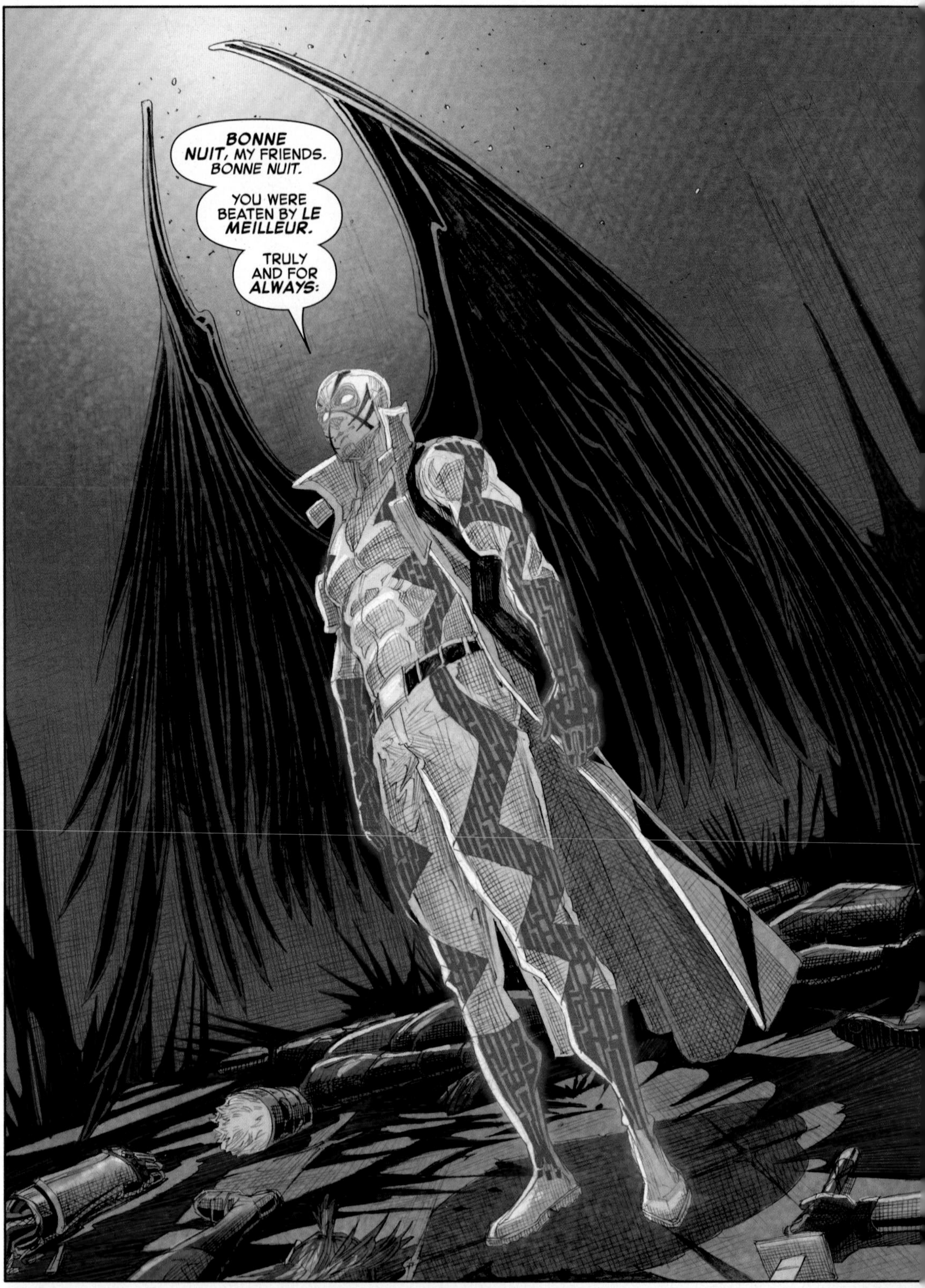
BONNE NUIT, MY FRIENDS. BONNE NUIT.
YOU WERE BEATEN BY LE MEILLEUR.
TRULY AND FOR ALWAYS:

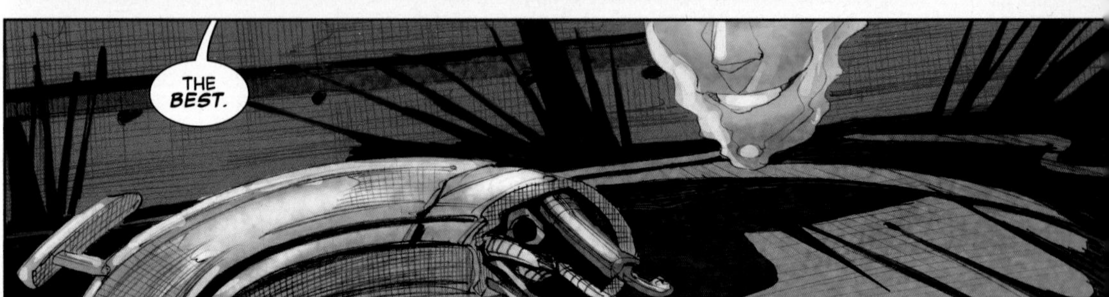
THE BEST.

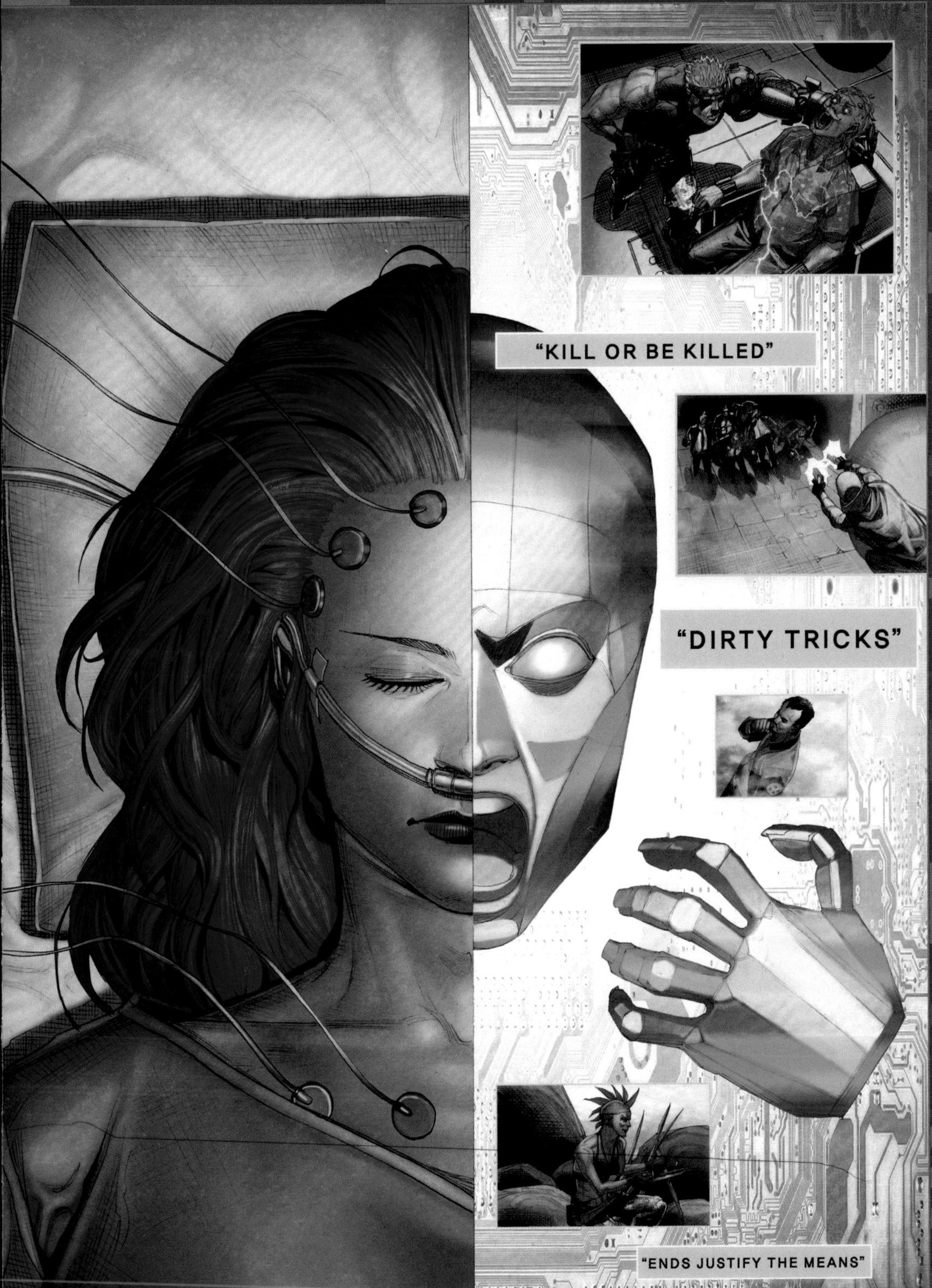
"KILL OR BE KILLED"
"DIRTY TRICKS"
"ENDS JUSTIFY THE MEANS"

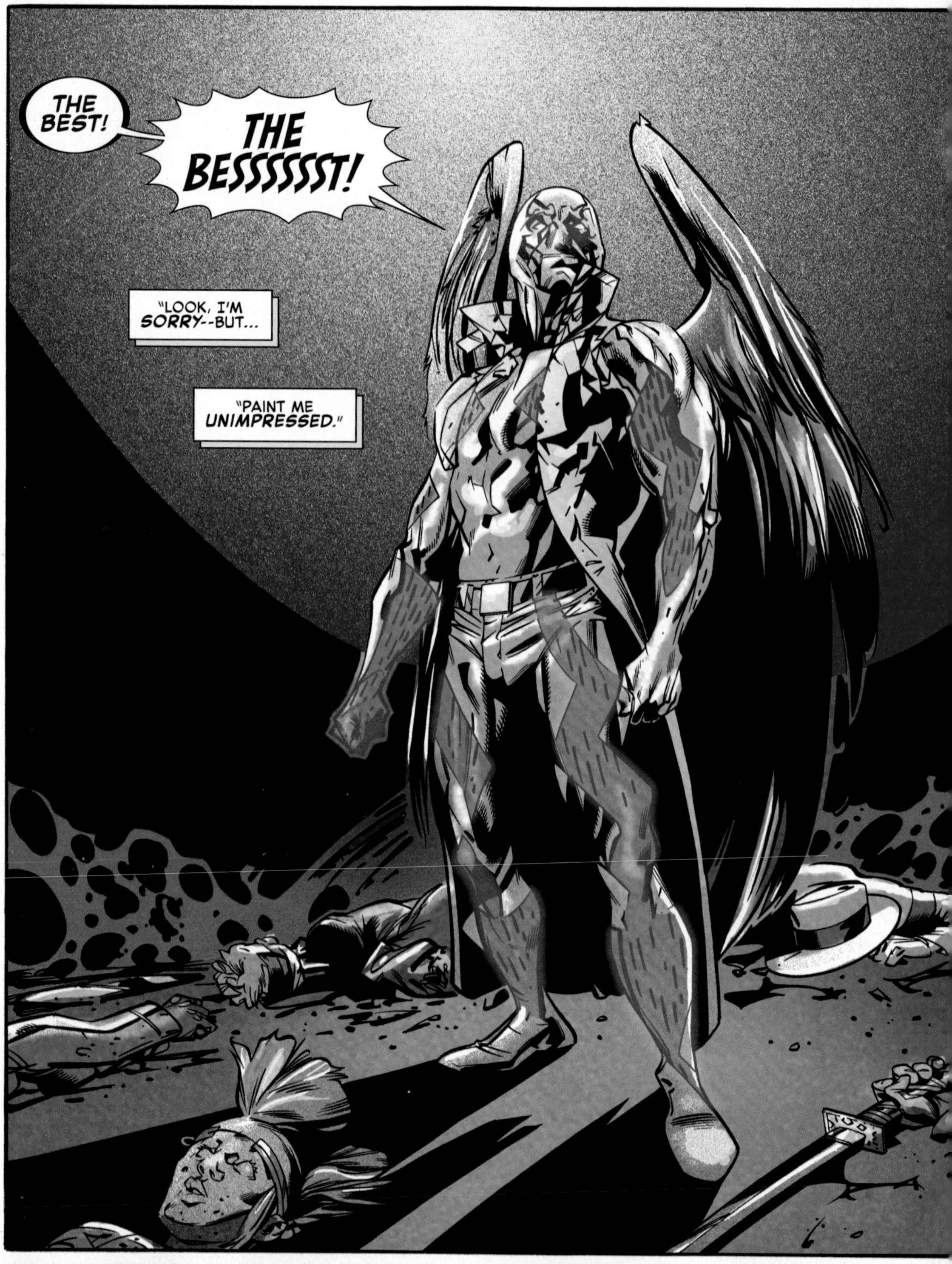
THE BEST!
THE BESSSSSST!
"LOOK, I'M SORRY--BUT...
"PAINT ME UNIMPRESSED."

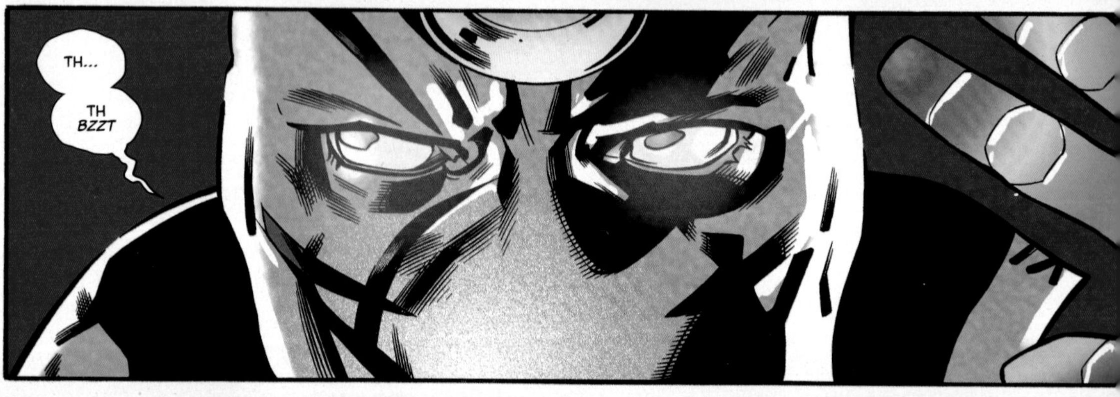
TH...
TH BZZT

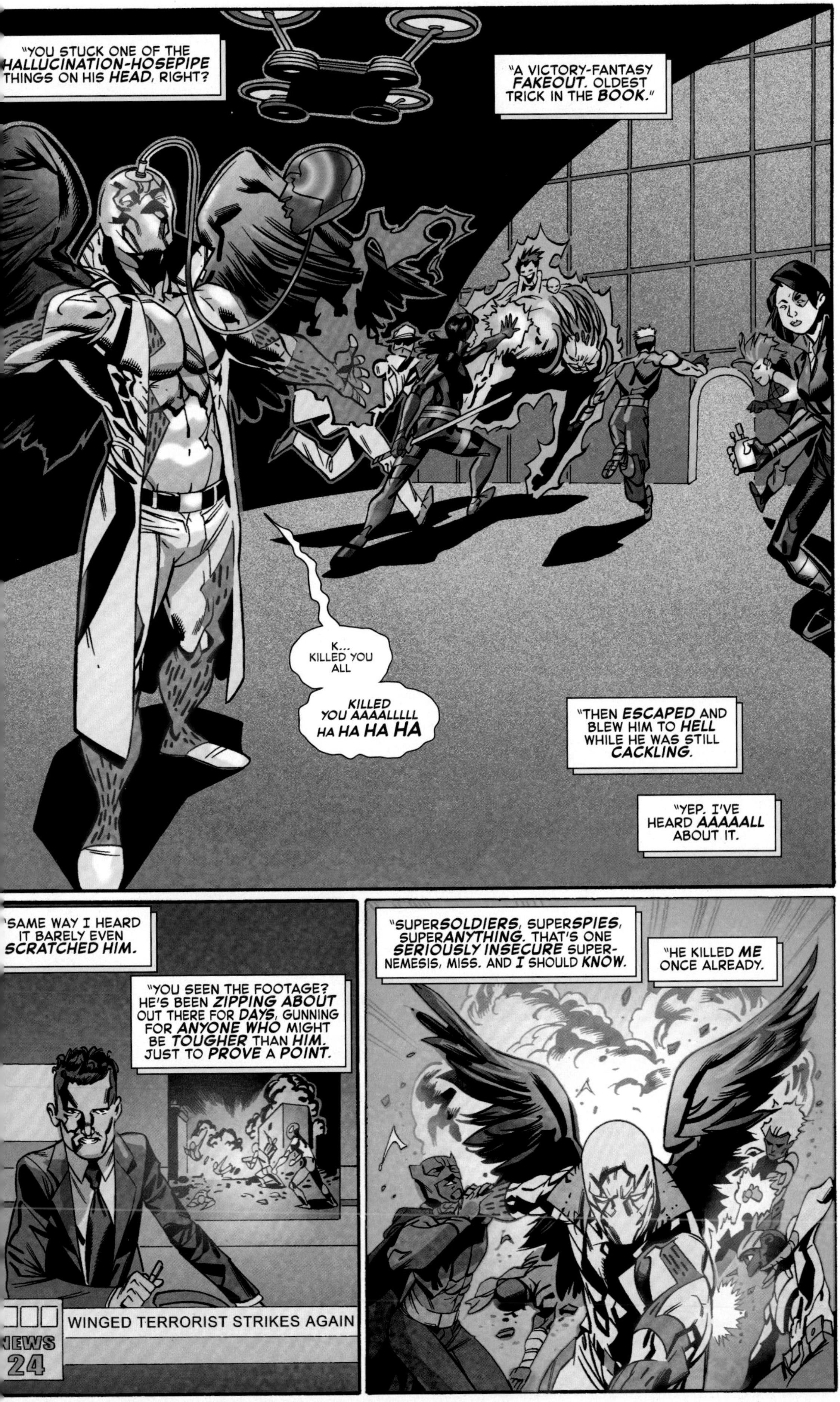
"YOU STUCK ONE OF THE HALLUCINATION-HOSEPIPE THINGS ON HIS HEAD, RIGHT?
"A VICTORY-FANTASY FAKEOUT. OLDEST TRICK IN THE BOOK."
K... KILLED YOU ALL
KILLED YOU AAAALLLLL HA HA HA HA
"THEN ESCAPED AND BLEW HIM TO HELL WHILE HE WAS STILL CACKLING.
"YEP. I'VE HEARD AAAAALL ABOUT IT.
"SAME WAY I HEARD IT BARELY EVEN SCRATCHED HIM.
"YOU SEEN THE FOOTAGE? HE'S BEEN ZIPPING ABOUT OUT THERE FOR DAYS, GUNNING FOR ANYONE WHO MIGHT BE TOUGHER THAN HIM. JUST TO PROVE A POINT.
WINGED TERRORIST STRIKES AGAIN
NEWS 24
"SUPERSOLDIERS, SUPERSPIES, SUPERANYTHING. THAT'S ONE SERIOUSLY INSECURE SUPER-NEMESIS, MISS. AND I SHOULD KNOW.
"HE KILLED ME ONCE ALREADY.

"I KNOW ABOUT THE *REST* OF IT, TOO. LIKE...YOU GOT THAT GROSS *ALIEN GUY* UPSTAIRS ON *OVERWATCH.* 'KEEP YOUR ENEMIES CLOSE,' RIGHT?"

"HE'S IN *BANGKOK*... LOOKS LIKE ANOTHER *COVERT MILITARY GROUP.* A-AT LEAST *THREE* NEW POWERS DEMONSTRATED. *FOUR* IF YOU COUNT THE *MIGHTY MORPHING ACCENT.*"

C-CAN I HAVE A *BISCOTTI* NOW?

FORMAT'S THE KEY. THAT CHEESE-GOBBLING PETRI-ERROR *FANTOMEX* NOT ONLY COPIED THE *VOLGA EFFECT* FROM *HOPE*-- BUT *DIGITIZED* IT.

AND THANKS TO THE GLORIFIED *ARCADE-MACHINE* HE CALLS A *BRAIN* HE'S BEEN ABLE TO *REWRITE* IT, TOO. HENCE THE ANNOYING LACK OF *EXPLODO FATALITY SIDE EFFECTS.*

HE'S ESSENTIALLY RUNNING A *PIRATE COPY* OF *SUPER-MUTANTISM* WITH THE *DRMS* FILED OFF. SOMEONE MAY NOW BRING ME MY MEDAL FOR *SPLENDID METAPHORS.*

AND NO, MOJO, YOU MAY *NOT.*

THIS BISCOTTI IS *MY* BISCOTTI.

"*YEEEEHP,* TRUTH *IS* I KNOW PRETTY MUCH *EVERYTHING* ABOUT THIS PLACE."

"I KNOW WE *RELOCATED* BY A COUPLA THOUSAND *MILES*...I KNOW YOU'RE ALL *TWITCHY* IN CASE *PEPE LE POWERMAD* FINDS YOU..."

"...AND I KNOW YOUR *GLORIOUS LEADER* HAS A *SINGLE MULTIFUNCTIONAL* SOLUTION TO *ALL* THESE *PROBLEMS.* BY WHICH I *MEAN:*"

VOLGA.

THE *BIGBAD* WHO *STARTED* IT ALL. MINCING RUSSIAN *BASTARD* WITH THE SECRET FORMULA TO THE BIOTECH WHICH *CAUSED* ALL THIS CRAP.

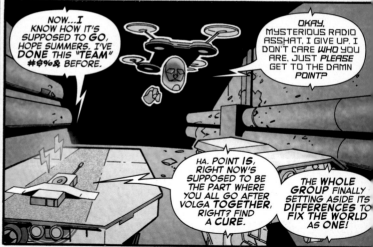

NOW...I KNOW HOW IT'S SUPPOSED TO GO, HOPE SUMMERS. I'VE DONE THIS "TEAM" #$%& BEFORE.

OKAY, MYSTERIOUS RADIO *ASSHAT,* I GIVE UP. I DON'T CARE *WHO* YOU ARE, JUST *PLEASE* GET TO THE DAMN *POINT?*

HA. POINT *IS,* RIGHT NOW'S *SUPPOSED* TO BE THE PART WHERE YOU ALL GO AFTER VOLGA *TOGETHER,* RIGHT? FIND A *CURE.*

THE *WHOLE GROUP* FINALLY SETTING ASIDE ITS *DIFFERENCES* TO FIX THE WORLD AS ONE!

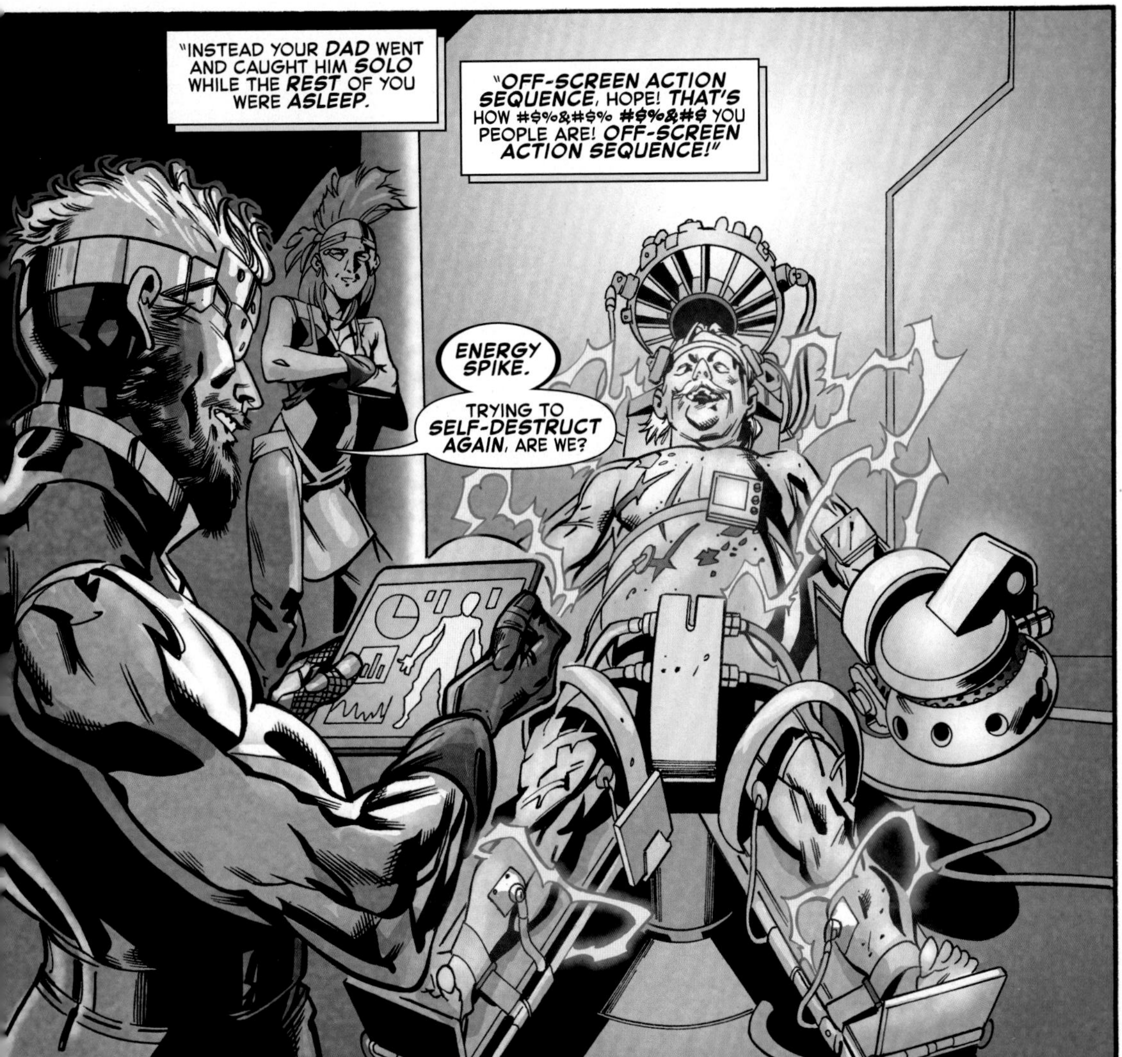
"INSTEAD YOUR DAD WENT AND CAUGHT HIM SOLO WHILE THE REST OF YOU WERE ASLEEP.
"OFF-SCREEN ACTION SEQUENCE, HOPE! THAT'S HOW #$%&#$% #$%&#$ YOU PEOPLE ARE! OFF-SCREEN ACTION SEQUENCE!"
ENERGY SPIKE.
TRYING TO SELF-DESTRUCT AGAIN, ARE WE?

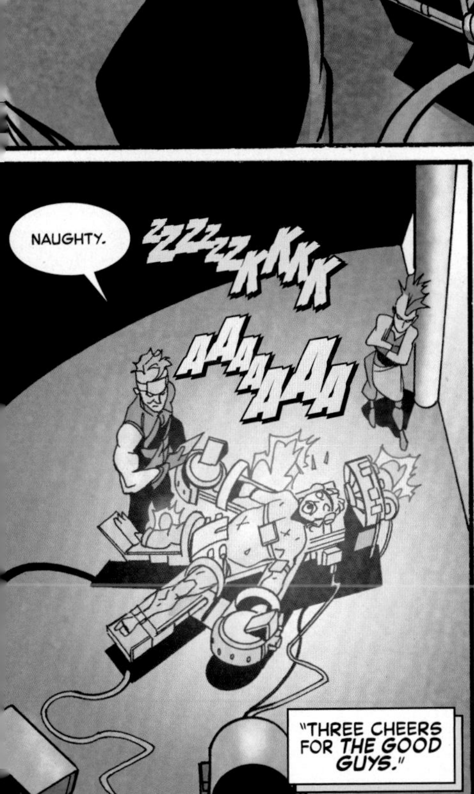
NAUGHTY.
ZZZZZKKKK
AAAAAAAA
"THREE CHEERS FOR THE GOOD GUYS."

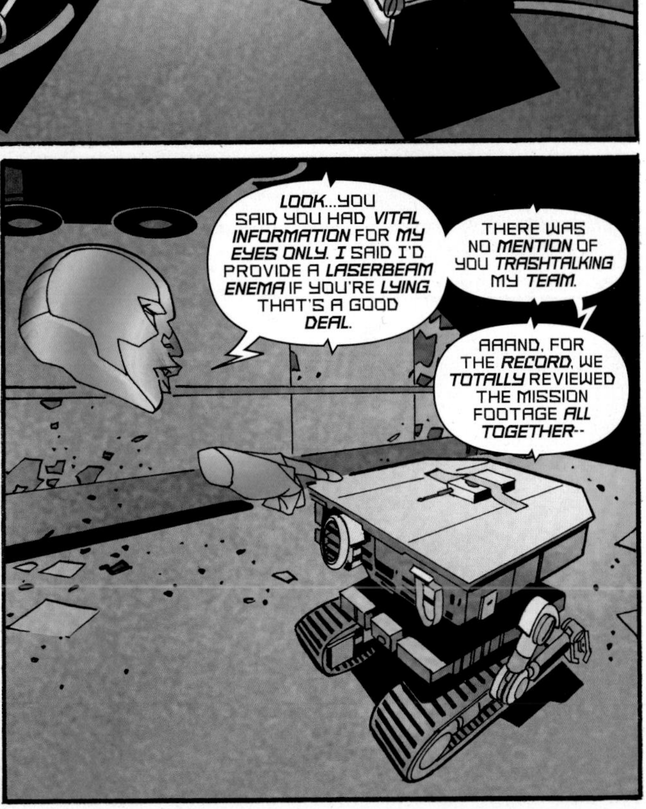
LOOK...YOU SAID YOU HAD VITAL INFORMATION FOR MY EYES ONLY. I SAID I'D PROVIDE A LASERBEAM ENEMA IF YOU'RE LYING. THAT'S A GOOD DEAL.
THERE WAS NO MENTION OF YOU TRASHTALKING MY TEAM.
AAAND, FOR THE RECORD, WE TOTALLY REVIEWED THE MISSION FOOTAGE ALL TOGETHER--

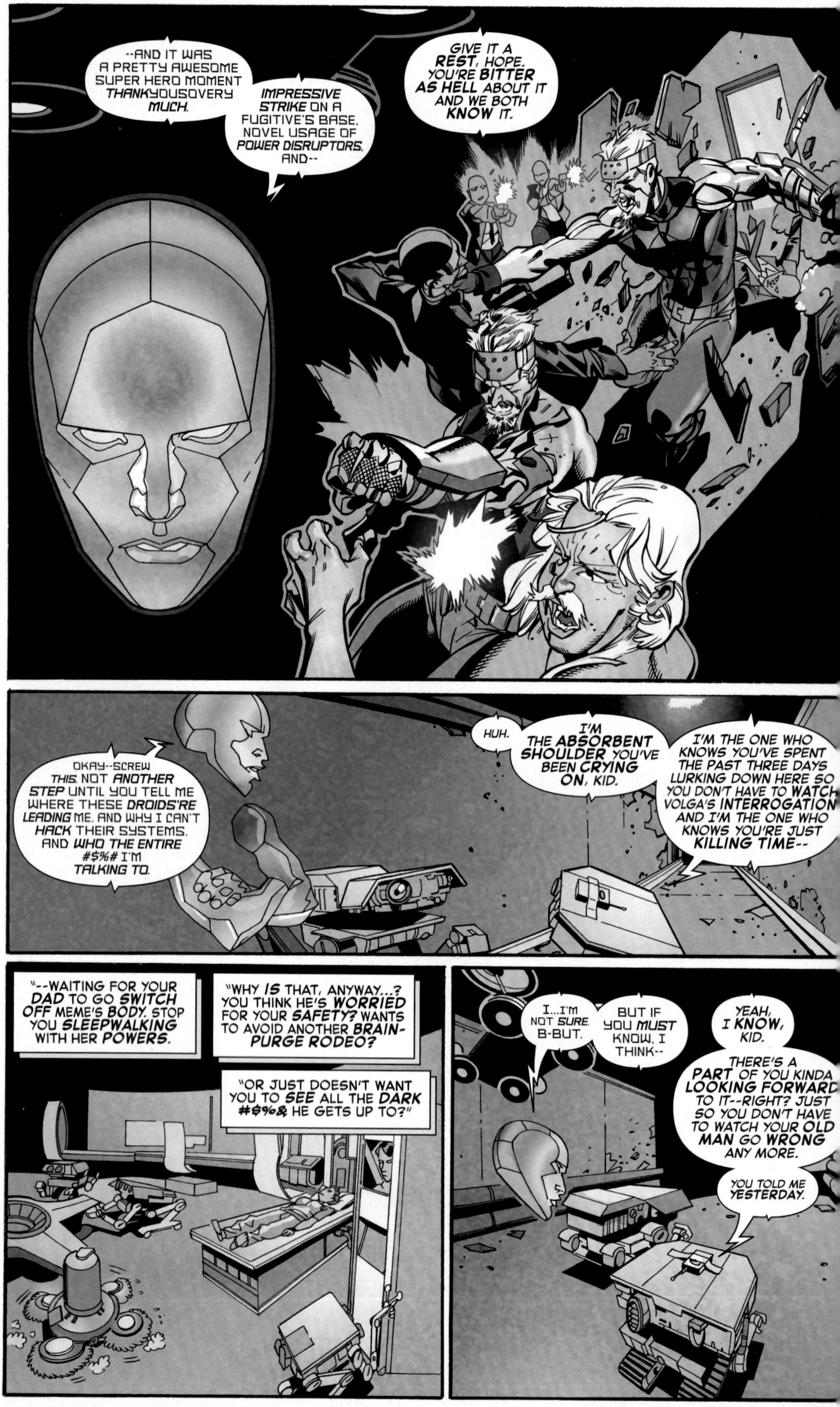
--AND IT WAS A PRETTY AWESOME SUPER HERO MOMENT THANKYOUSOVERY MUCH.
IMPRESSIVE STRIKE ON A FUGITIVE'S BASE, NOVEL USAGE OF POWER DISRUPTORS, AND--
GIVE IT A REST, HOPE. YOU'RE BITTER AS HELL ABOUT IT AND WE BOTH KNOW IT.
OKAY--SCREW THIS. NOT ANOTHER STEP UNTIL YOU TELL ME WHERE THESE DROIDS'RE LEADING ME. AND WHY I CAN'T HACK THEIR SYSTEMS. AND WHO THE ENTIRE #$%# I'M TALKING TO.
HUH.
I'M THE ABSORBENT SHOULDER YOU'VE BEEN CRYING ON, KID.
I'M THE ONE WHO KNOWS YOU'VE SPENT THE PAST THREE DAYS LURKING DOWN HERE SO YOU DON'T HAVE TO WATCH VOLGA'S INTERROGATION AND I'M THE ONE WHO KNOWS YOU'RE JUST KILLING TIME--
"--WAITING FOR YOUR DAD TO GO SWITCH OFF MEME'S BODY. STOP YOU SLEEPWALKING WITH HER POWERS.
"WHY IS THAT, ANYWAY...? YOU THINK HE'S WORRIED FOR YOUR SAFETY? WANTS TO AVOID ANOTHER BRAIN-PURGE RODEO?
"OR JUST DOESN'T WANT YOU TO SEE ALL THE DARK #$%& HE GETS UP TO?"
I...I'M NOT SURE. B-BUT.
BUT IF YOU MUST KNOW, I THINK--
YEAH, I KNOW, KID.
THERE'S A PART OF YOU KINDA LOOKING FORWARD TO IT--RIGHT? JUST SO YOU DON'T HAVE TO WATCH YOUR OLD MAN GO WRONG ANY MORE.
YOU TOLD ME YESTERDAY.

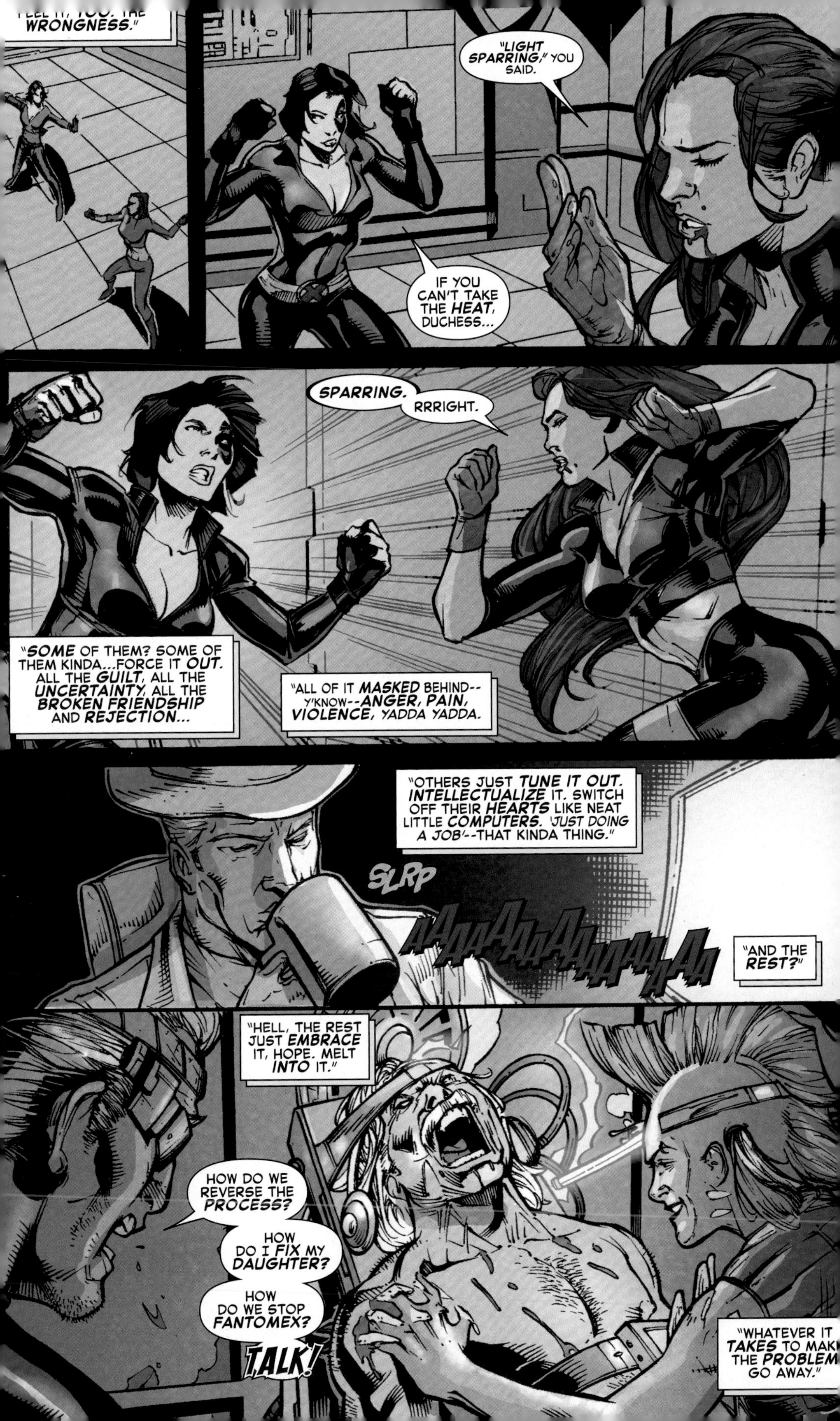

WRONGNESS."
"LIGHT SPARRING," YOU SAID.
IF YOU CAN'T TAKE THE HEAT, DUCHESS...
SPARRING. RRRIGHT.
"SOME OF THEM? SOME OF THEM KINDA...FORCE IT OUT. ALL THE GUILT, ALL THE UNCERTAINTY, ALL THE BROKEN FRIENDSHIP AND REJECTION...
"ALL OF IT MASKED BEHIND--Y'KNOW--ANGER, PAIN, VIOLENCE, YADDA YADDA.
"OTHERS JUST TUNE IT OUT. INTELLECTUALIZE IT. SWITCH OFF THEIR HEARTS LIKE NEAT LITTLE COMPUTERS. 'JUST DOING A JOB'--THAT KINDA THING."
SLRP
AAAAAAAAAAAAAAAAAA
"AND THE REST?"
"HELL, THE REST JUST EMBRACE IT, HOPE. MELT INTO IT."
HOW DO WE REVERSE THE PROCESS?
HOW DO I FIX MY DAUGHTER?
HOW DO WE STOP FANTOMEX?
TALK!
"WHATEVER IT TAKES TO MAK THE PROBLEM GO AWAY."

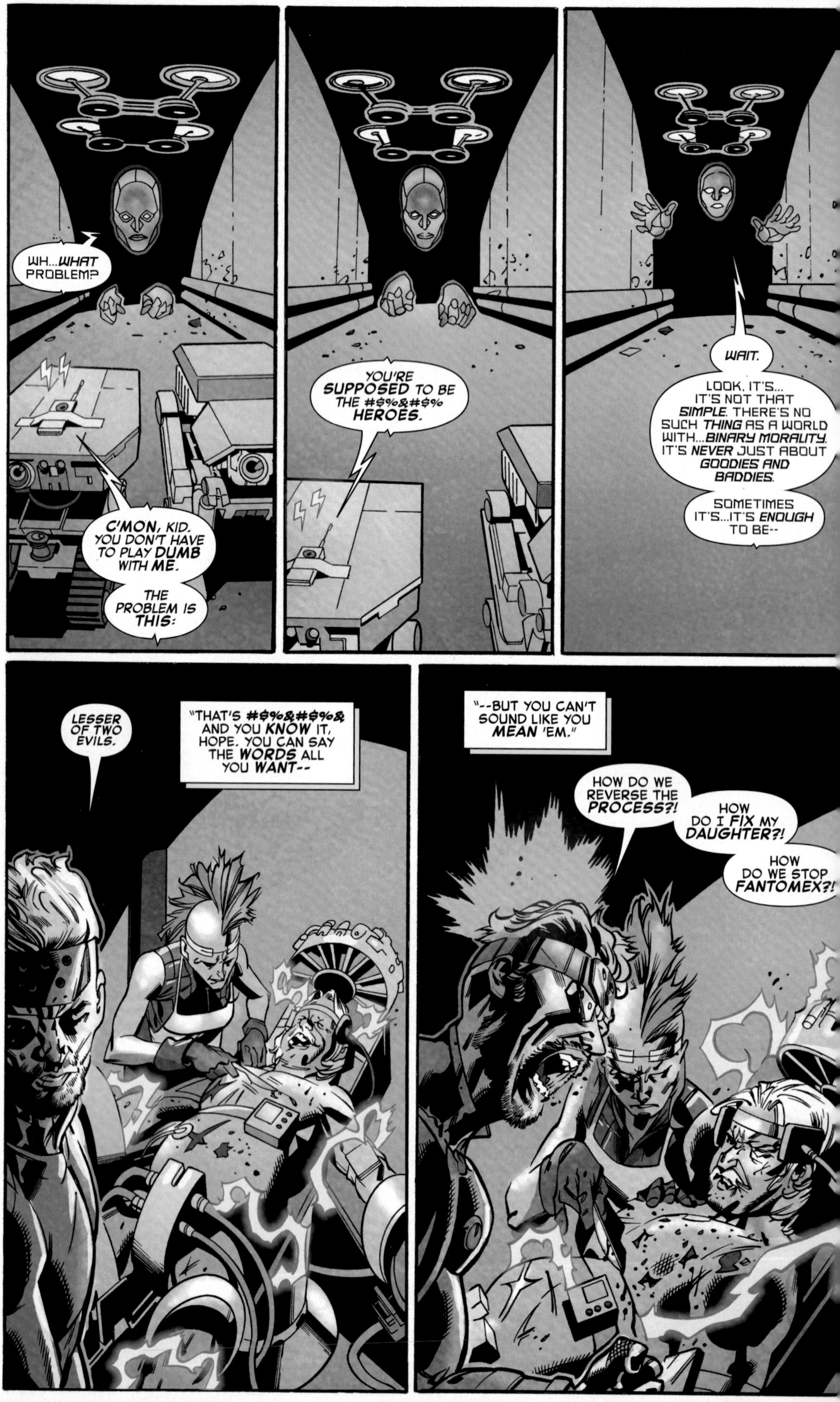

WH...WHAT PROBLEM?
C'MON, KID. YOU DON'T HAVE TO PLAY DUMB WITH ME.
THE PROBLEM IS THIS:
YOU'RE SUPPOSED TO BE THE #$%&#$% HEROES.
WAIT.
LOOK, IT'S... IT'S NOT THAT SIMPLE. THERE'S NO SUCH THING AS A WORLD WITH...BINARY MORALITY. IT'S NEVER JUST ABOUT GOODIES AND BADDIES.
SOMETIMES IT'S...IT'S ENOUGH TO BE--
LESSER OF TWO EVILS.
"THAT'S #$%&#$%& AND YOU KNOW IT, HOPE. YOU CAN SAY THE WORDS ALL YOU WANT--
"--BUT YOU CAN'T SOUND LIKE YOU MEAN 'EM."
HOW DO WE REVERSE THE PROCESS?!
HOW DO I FIX MY DAUGHTER?!
HOW DO WE STOP FANTOMEX?!

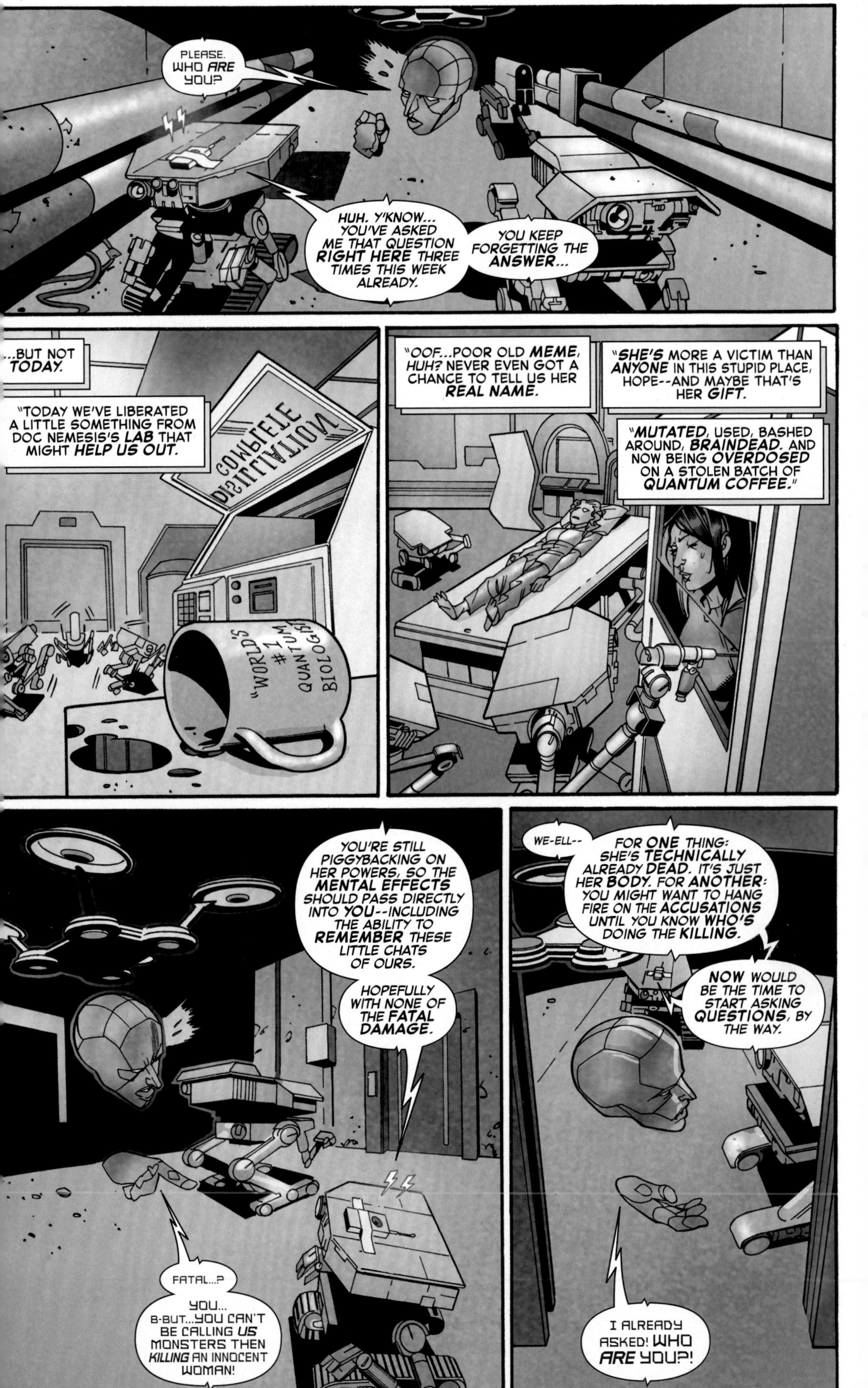
PLEASE. WHO *ARE* YOU?
HUH. Y'KNOW... YOU'VE ASKED ME THAT QUESTION **RIGHT HERE** THREE TIMES THIS WEEK ALREADY.
YOU KEEP FORGETTING THE **ANSWER**...
...BUT NOT **TODAY.**
"TODAY WE'VE LIBERATED A LITTLE SOMETHING FROM DOC NEMESIS'S **LAB** THAT MIGHT **HELP US OUT.**
COMPLETE DISTILLATION
"WORLD'S #1 QUANTUM BIOLOGIST"
"OOF...POOR OLD **MEME,** HUH? NEVER EVEN GOT A CHANCE TO TELL US HER **REAL NAME.**
"**SHE'S** MORE A VICTIM THAN **ANYONE** IN THIS STUPID PLACE, HOPE--AND MAYBE THAT'S HER **GIFT.**
"**MUTATED,** USED, BASHED AROUND, **BRAINDEAD.** AND NOW BEING **OVERDOSED** ON A STOLEN BATCH OF **QUANTUM COFFEE.**"
YOU'RE STILL PIGGYBACKING ON HER POWERS, SO THE **MENTAL EFFECTS** SHOULD PASS DIRECTLY INTO **YOU**--INCLUDING THE ABILITY TO **REMEMBER** THESE LITTLE CHATS OF OURS.
HOPEFULLY WITH NONE OF THE **FATAL DAMAGE.**
FATAL...?
YOU... B-BUT...YOU CAN'T BE CALLING *US* MONSTERS THEN *KILLING* AN INNOCENT WOMAN!
WE-ELL--
FOR **ONE** THING: SHE'S **TECHNICALLY** ALREADY **DEAD.** IT'S JUST HER **BODY.** FOR **ANOTHER:** YOU MIGHT WANT TO HANG FIRE ON THE **ACCUSATIONS** UNTIL YOU KNOW **WHO'S** DOING THE **KILLING.**
NOW WOULD BE THE TIME TO START ASKING **QUESTIONS,** BY THE WAY.
I ALREADY ASKED! **WHO *ARE* YOU?!**

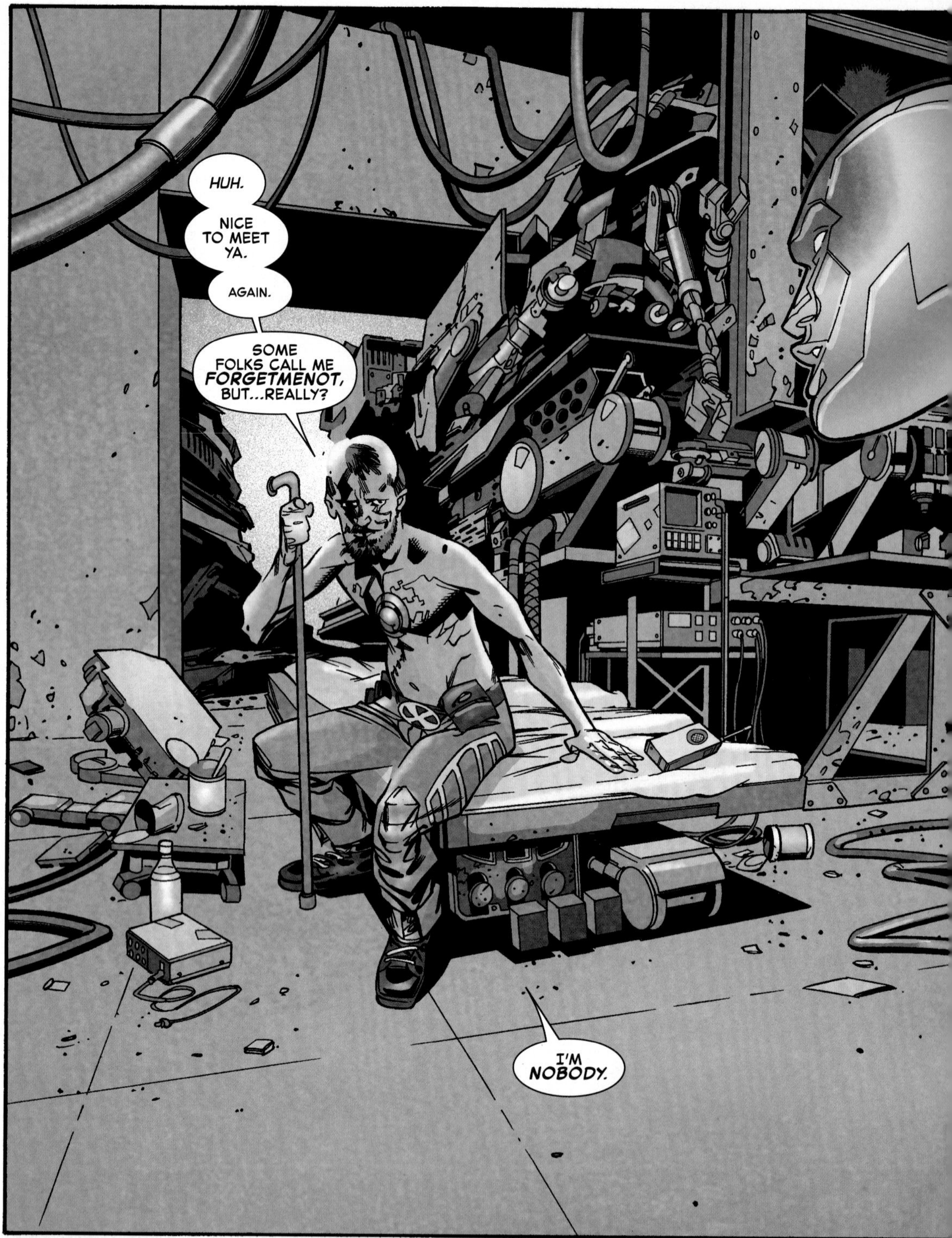
HUH.
NICE TO MEET YA.
AGAIN.
SOME FOLKS CALL ME FORGETMENOT, BUT...REALLY?
I'M NOBODY.

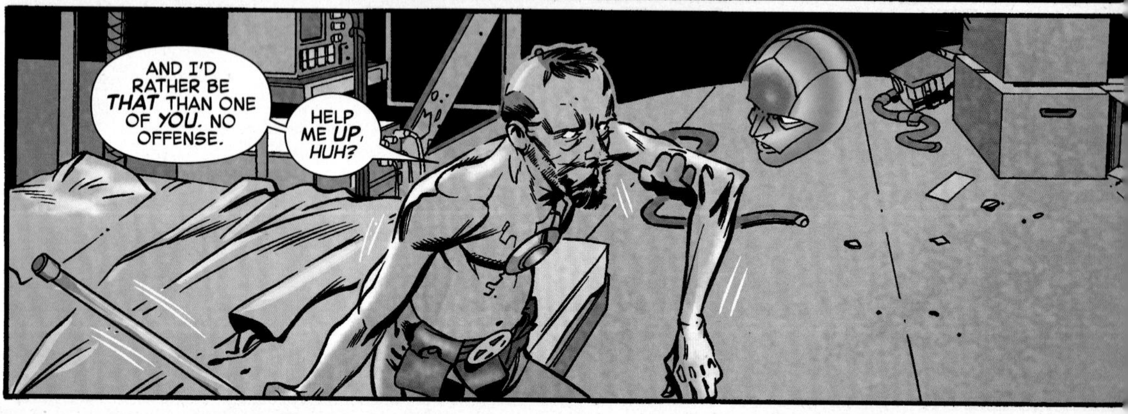
AND I'D RATHER BE THAT THAN ONE OF YOU. NO OFFENSE.
HELP ME UP, HUH?

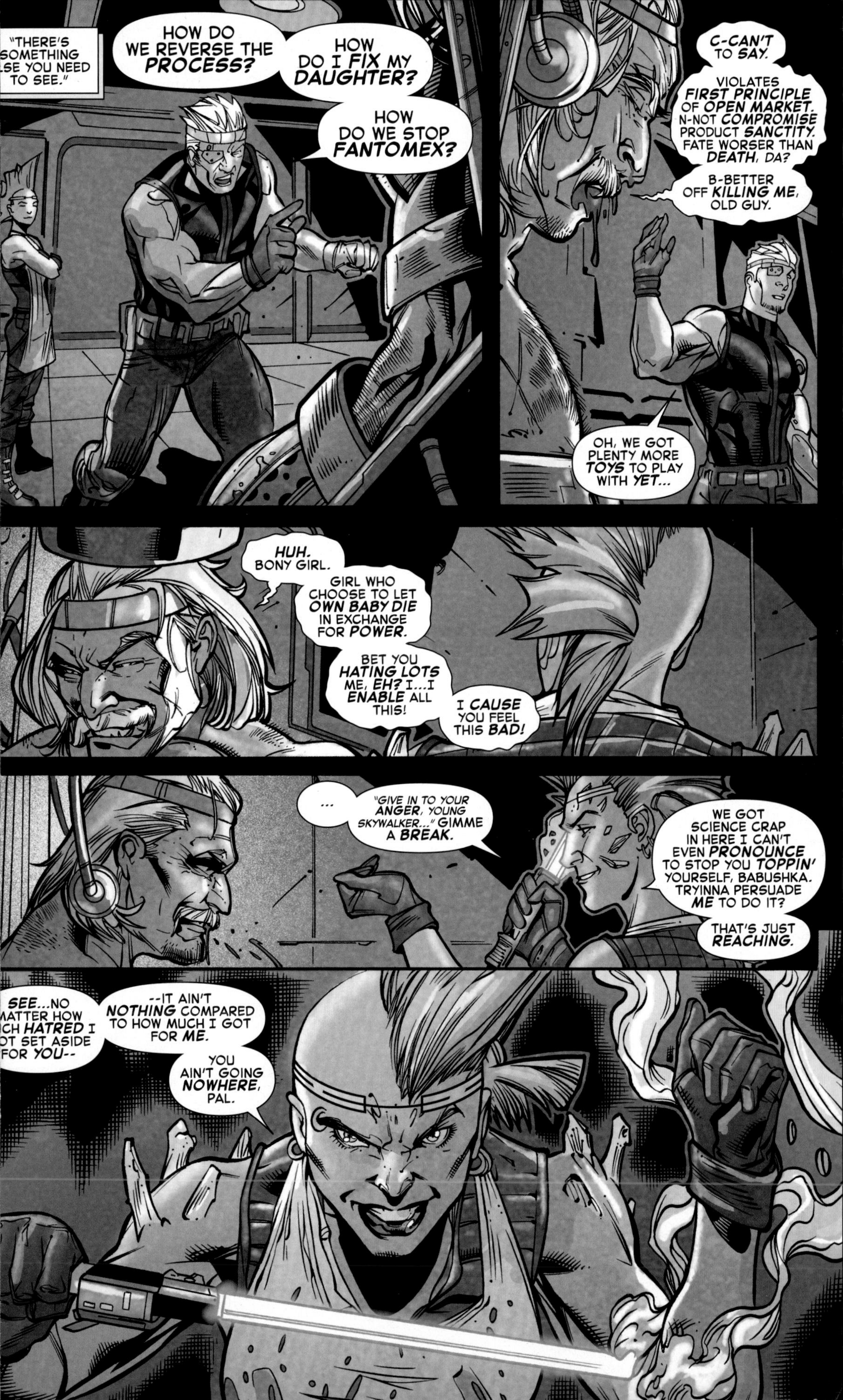
"THERE'S SOMETHING ELSE YOU NEED TO SEE."
HOW DO WE REVERSE THE PROCESS?
HOW DO I FIX MY DAUGHTER?
HOW DO WE STOP FANTOMEX?
C-CAN'T TO SAY.
VIOLATES FIRST PRINCIPLE OF OPEN MARKET. N-NOT COMPROMISE PRODUCT SANCTITY. FATE WORSER THAN DEATH, DA?
B-BETTER OFF KILLING ME, OLD GUY.
OH, WE GOT PLENTY MORE TOYS TO PLAY WITH YET...
HUH. BONY GIRL.
GIRL WHO CHOOSE TO LET OWN BABY DIE IN EXCHANGE FOR POWER.
BET YOU HATING LOTS ME, EH? I...I ENABLE ALL THIS!
I CAUSE YOU FEEL THIS BAD!
...
"GIVE IN TO YOUR ANGER, YOUNG SKYWALKER..." GIMME A BREAK.
WE GOT SCIENCE CRAP IN HERE I CAN'T EVEN PRONOUNCE TO STOP YOU TOPPIN' YOURSELF, BABUSHKA. TRYINNA PERSUADE ME TO DO IT?
THAT'S JUST REACHING.
SEE...NO MATTER HOW ...CH HATRED I ...OT SET ASIDE FOR YOU--
--IT AIN'T NOTHING COMPARED TO HOW MUCH I GOT FOR ME.
YOU AIN'T GOING NOWHERE, PAL.

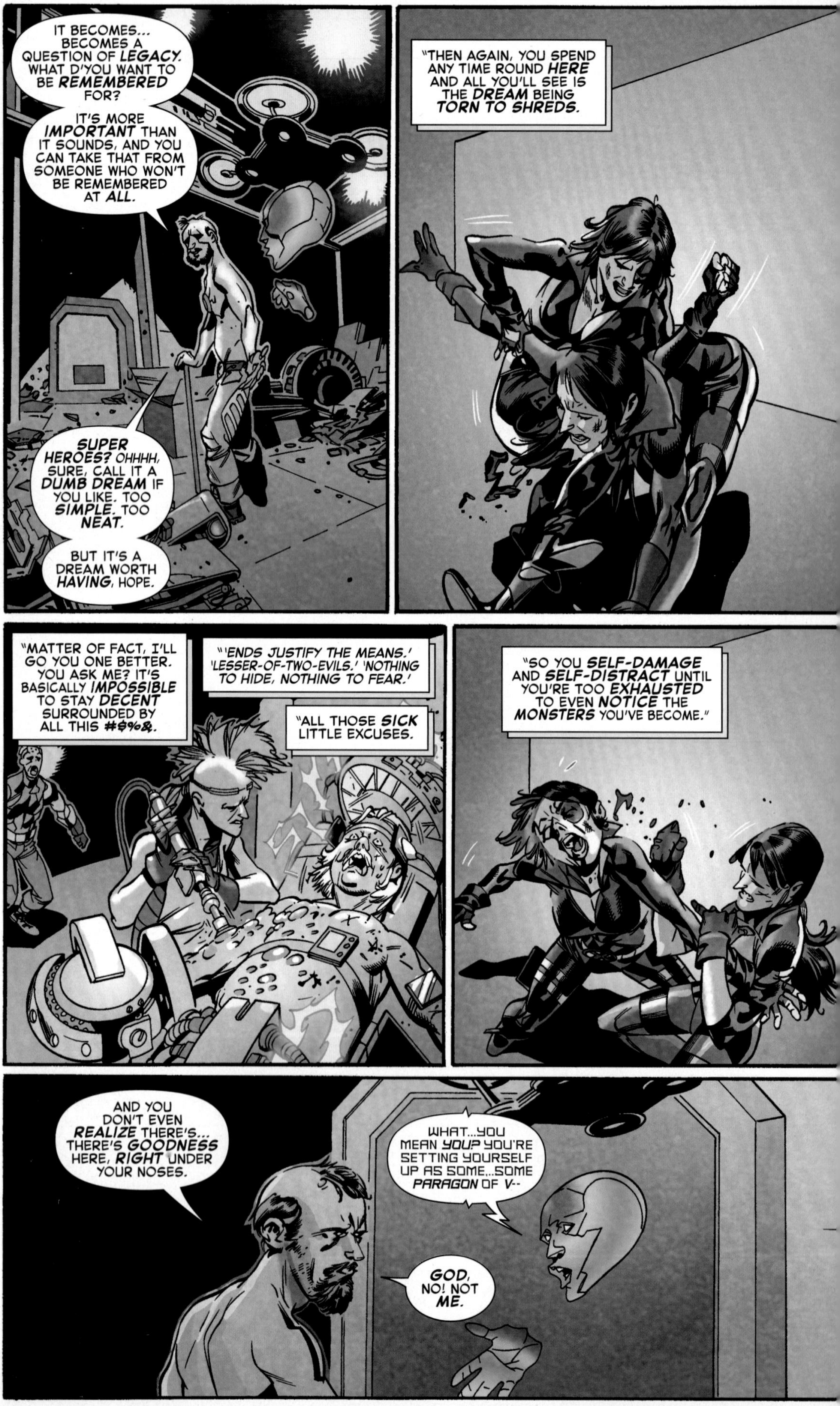
IT BECOMES... BECOMES A QUESTION OF LEGACY. WHAT D'YOU WANT TO BE REMEMBERED FOR?
IT'S MORE IMPORTANT THAN IT SOUNDS, AND YOU CAN TAKE THAT FROM SOMEONE WHO WON'T BE REMEMBERED AT ALL.
SUPER HEROES? OHHHH, SURE, CALL IT A DUMB DREAM IF YOU LIKE. TOO SIMPLE. TOO NEAT.
BUT IT'S A DREAM WORTH HAVING, HOPE.
"THEN AGAIN, YOU SPEND ANY TIME ROUND HERE AND ALL YOU'LL SEE IS THE DREAM BEING TORN TO SHREDS.
"MATTER OF FACT, I'LL GO YOU ONE BETTER. YOU ASK ME? IT'S BASICALLY IMPOSSIBLE TO STAY DECENT SURROUNDED BY ALL THIS #$%&.
"'ENDS JUSTIFY THE MEANS.' 'LESSER-OF-TWO-EVILS.' 'NOTHING TO HIDE, NOTHING TO FEAR.'
"ALL THOSE SICK LITTLE EXCUSES.
"SO YOU SELF-DAMAGE AND SELF-DISTRACT UNTIL YOU'RE TOO EXHAUSTED TO EVEN NOTICE THE MONSTERS YOU'VE BECOME."
AND YOU DON'T EVEN REALIZE THERE'S... THERE'S GOODNESS HERE, RIGHT UNDER YOUR NOSES.
WHAT...YOU MEAN YOU? YOU'RE SETTING YOURSELF UP AS SOME...SOME PARAGON OF V--
GOD, NO! NOT ME.

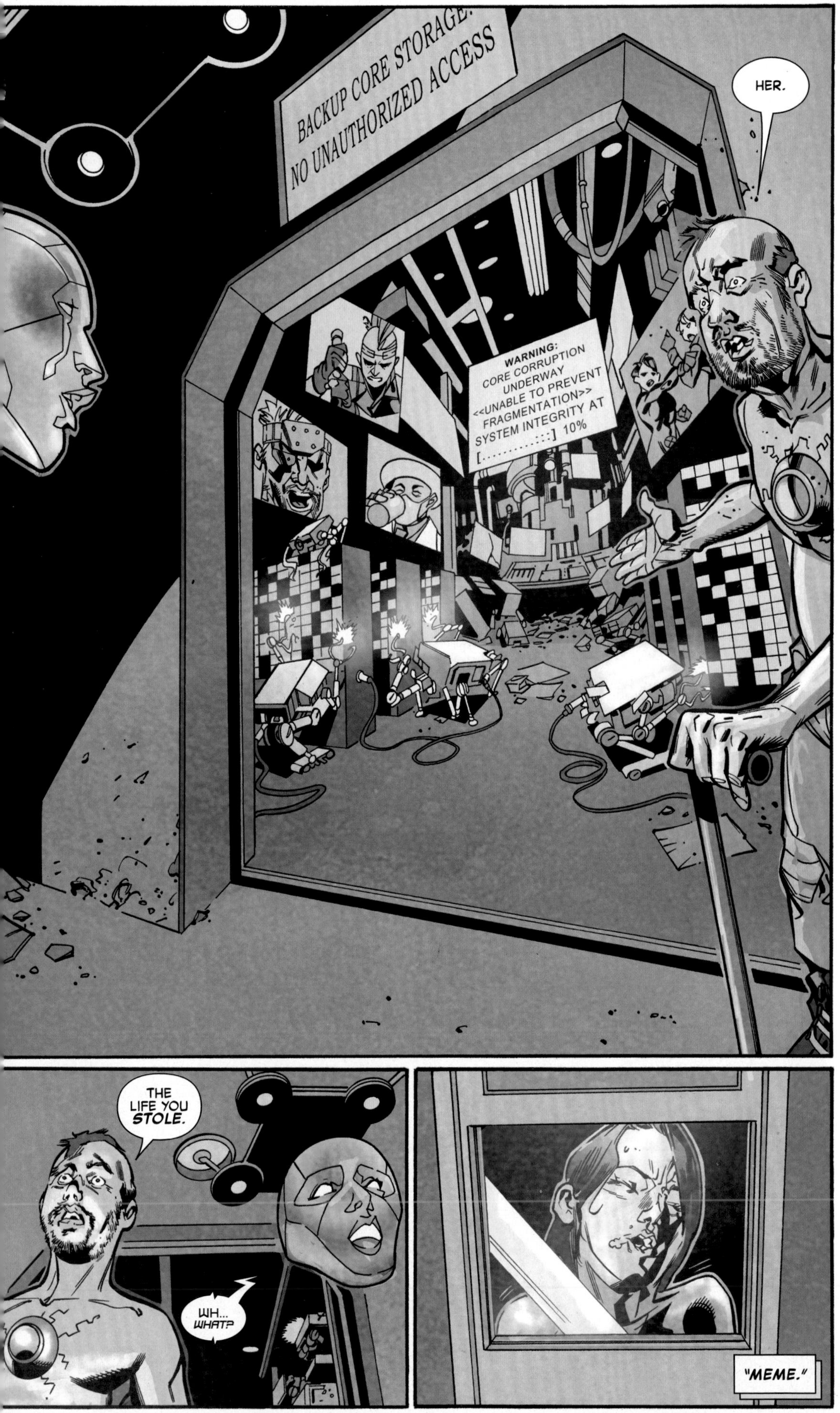
BACKUP CORE STORAGE.
NO UNAUTHORIZED ACCESS
HER.
WARNING:
CORE CORRUPTION
UNDERWAY
<<UNABLE TO PREVENT
FRAGMENTATION>>
SYSTEM INTEGRITY AT
[............:::] 10%
THE LIFE YOU STOLE.
WH... WHAT?
"MEME."

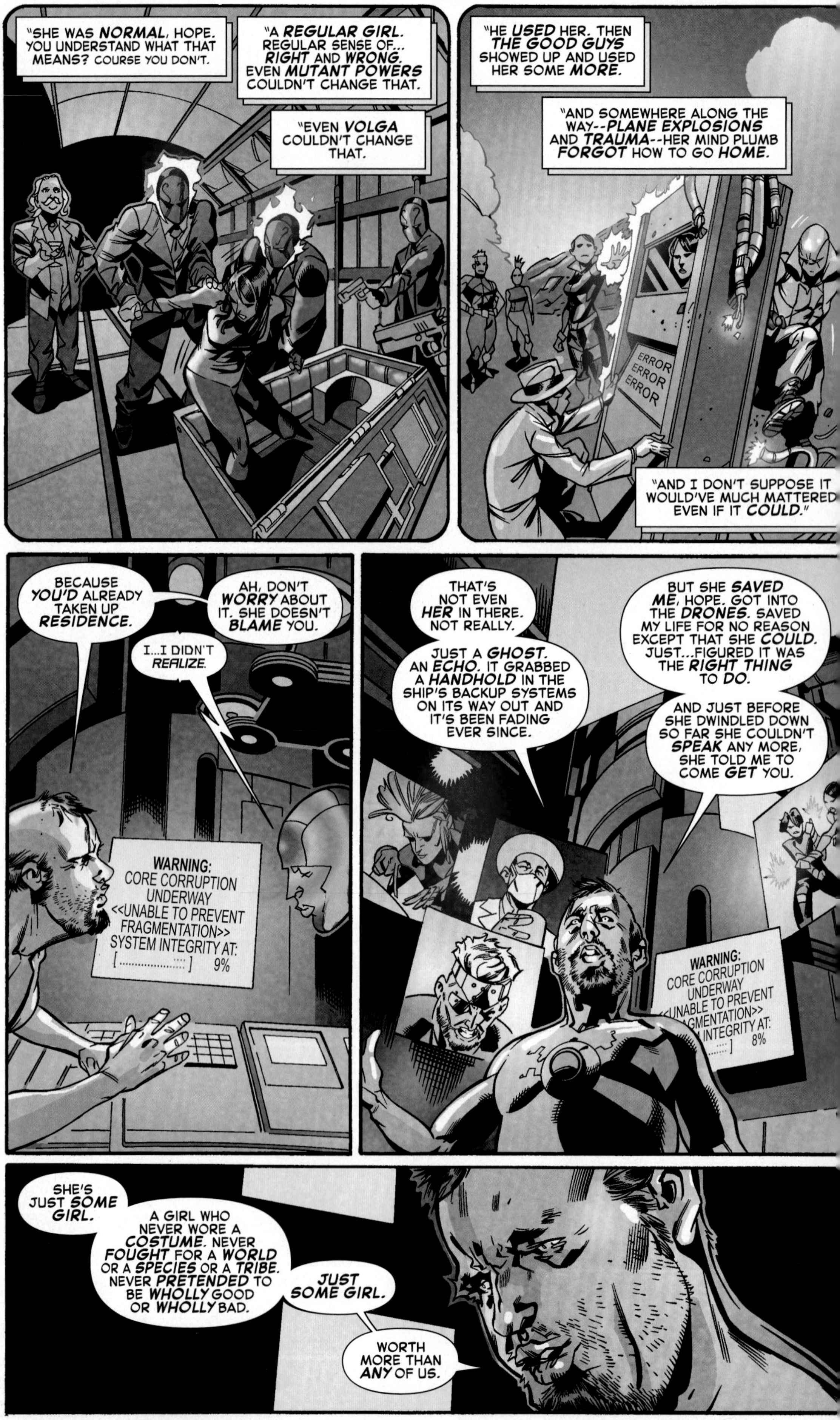
"SHE WAS NORMAL, HOPE. YOU UNDERSTAND WHAT THAT MEANS? COURSE YOU DON'T.
"A REGULAR GIRL. REGULAR SENSE OF... RIGHT AND WRONG. EVEN MUTANT POWERS COULDN'T CHANGE THAT.
"EVEN VOLGA COULDN'T CHANGE THAT.
"HE USED HER. THEN THE GOOD GUYS SHOWED UP AND USED HER SOME MORE.
"AND SOMEWHERE ALONG THE WAY--PLANE EXPLOSIONS AND TRAUMA--HER MIND PLUMB FORGOT HOW TO GO HOME.
ERROR ERROR ERROR
"AND I DON'T SUPPOSE IT WOULD'VE MUCH MATTERED EVEN IF IT COULD."
AH, DON'T WORRY ABOUT IT. SHE DOESN'T BLAME YOU.
I...I DIDN'T REALIZE.
BECAUSE YOU'D ALREADY TAKEN UP RESIDENCE.
WARNING: CORE CORRUPTION UNDERWAY <<UNABLE TO PREVENT FRAGMENTATION>> SYSTEM INTEGRITY AT: 9%
THAT'S NOT EVEN HER IN THERE. NOT REALLY.
JUST A GHOST. AN ECHO. IT GRABBED A HANDHOLD IN THE SHIP'S BACKUP SYSTEMS ON ITS WAY OUT AND IT'S BEEN FADING EVER SINCE.
BUT SHE SAVED ME, HOPE. GOT INTO THE DRONES. SAVED MY LIFE FOR NO REASON EXCEPT THAT SHE COULD. JUST...FIGURED IT WAS THE RIGHT THING TO DO.
AND JUST BEFORE SHE DWINDLED DOWN SO FAR SHE COULDN'T SPEAK ANY MORE, SHE TOLD ME TO COME GET YOU.
WARNING: CORE CORRUPTION UNDERWAY
8%
SHE'S JUST SOME GIRL.
A GIRL WHO NEVER WORE A COSTUME. NEVER FOUGHT FOR A WORLD OR A SPECIES OR A TRIBE. NEVER PRETENDED TO BE WHOLLY GOOD OR WHOLLY BAD.
JUST SOME GIRL.
WORTH MORE THAN ANY OF US.

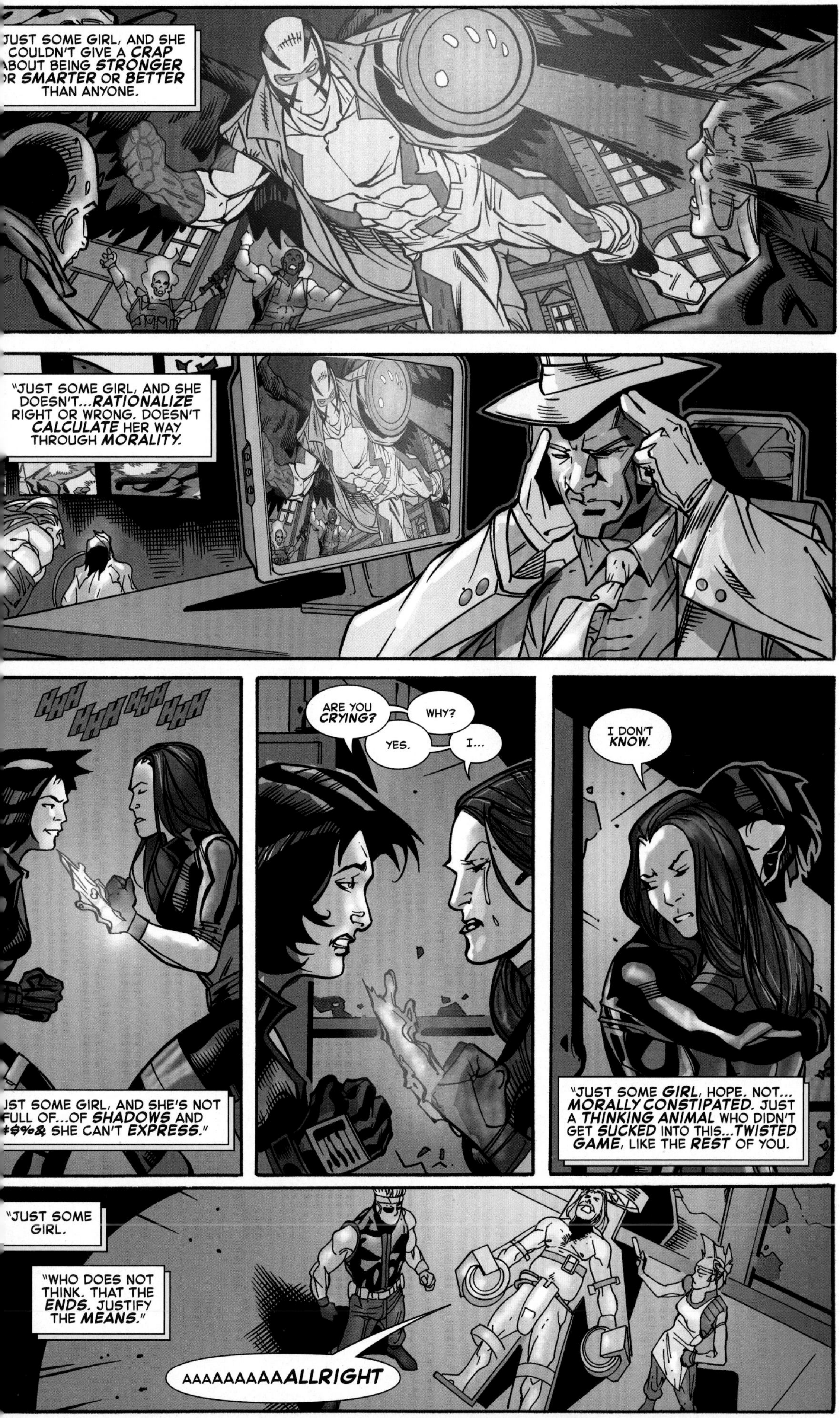
JUST SOME GIRL, AND SHE COULDN'T GIVE A CRAP ABOUT BEING STRONGER OR SMARTER OR BETTER THAN ANYONE.
"JUST SOME GIRL, AND SHE DOESN'T...RATIONALIZE RIGHT OR WRONG. DOESN'T CALCULATE HER WAY THROUGH MORALITY.
HHH HHH HHH HHH
JUST SOME GIRL, AND SHE'S NOT FULL OF...OF SHADOWS AND #$%& SHE CAN'T EXPRESS."
ARE YOU CRYING?
WHY?
YES.
I...
I DON'T KNOW.
"JUST SOME GIRL, HOPE. NOT... MORALLY CONSTIPATED. JUST A THINKING ANIMAL WHO DIDN'T GET SUCKED INTO THIS...TWISTED GAME, LIKE THE REST OF YOU.
"JUST SOME GIRL.
"WHO DOES NOT THINK. THAT THE ENDS. JUSTIFY THE MEANS."
AAAAAAAAAALLRIGHT

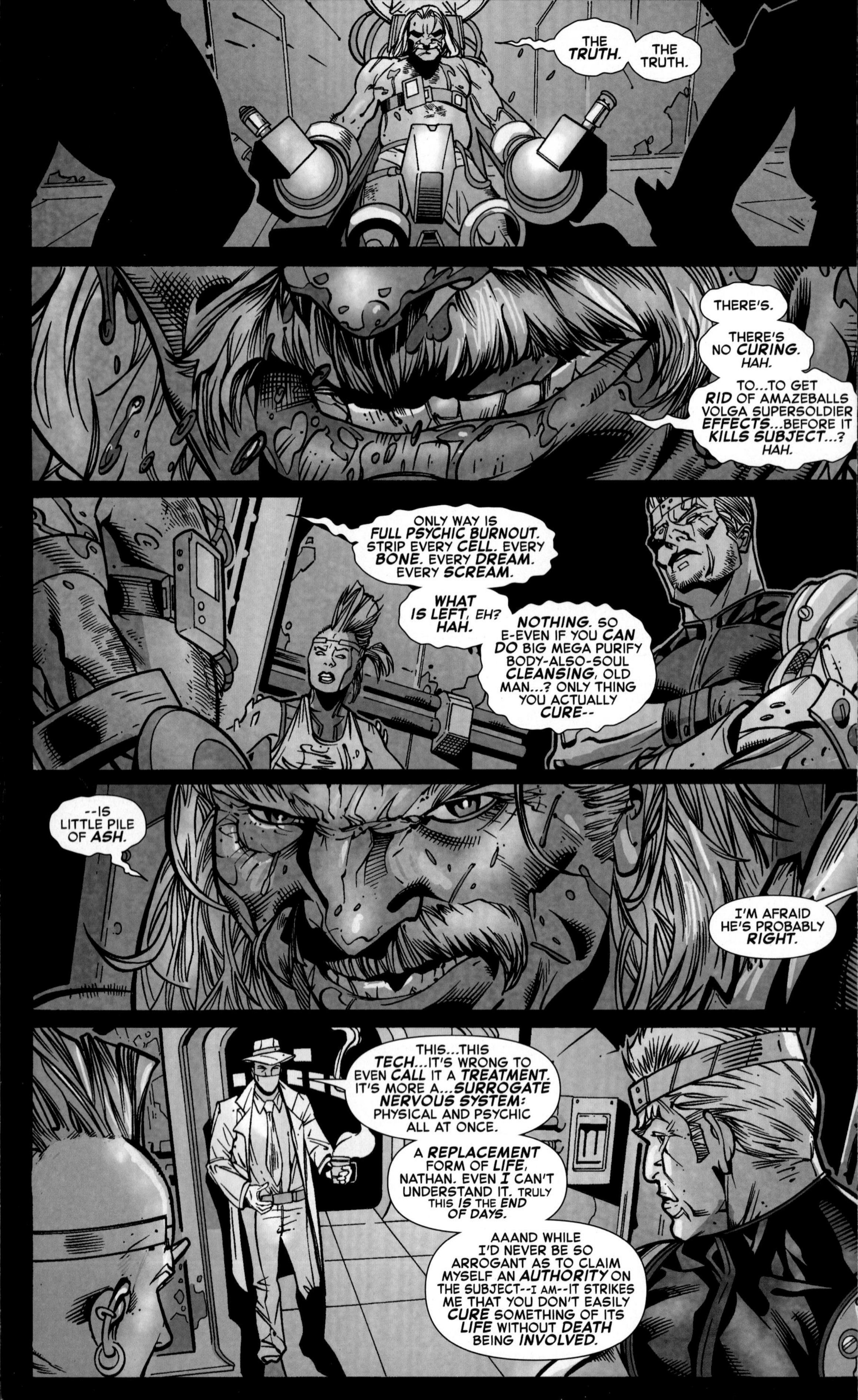

THE TRUTH.
THE TRUTH.
THERE'S.
THERE'S NO CURING. HAH.
TO...TO GET RID OF AMAZEBALLS VOLGA SUPERSOLDIER EFFECTS...BEFORE IT KILLS SUBJECT...? HAH.
ONLY WAY IS FULL PSYCHIC BURNOUT. STRIP EVERY CELL. EVERY BONE. EVERY DREAM. EVERY SCREAM.
WHAT IS LEFT, EH? HAH.
NOTHING. SO E-EVEN IF YOU CAN DO BIG MEGA PURIFY BODY-ALSO-SOUL CLEANSING, OLD MAN...? ONLY THING YOU ACTUALLY CURE--
--IS LITTLE PILE OF ASH.
I'M AFRAID HE'S PROBABLY RIGHT.
THIS...THIS TECH...IT'S WRONG TO EVEN CALL IT A TREATMENT. IT'S MORE A...SURROGATE NERVOUS SYSTEM: PHYSICAL AND PSYCHIC ALL AT ONCE.
A REPLACEMENT FORM OF LIFE, NATHAN. EVEN I CAN'T UNDERSTAND IT. TRULY THIS IS THE END OF DAYS.
AAAND WHILE I'D NEVER BE SO ARROGANT AS TO CLAIM MYSELF AN AUTHORITY ON THE SUBJECT--I AM--IT STRIKES ME THAT YOU DON'T EASILY CURE SOMETHING OF ITS LIFE WITHOUT DEATH BEING INVOLVED.

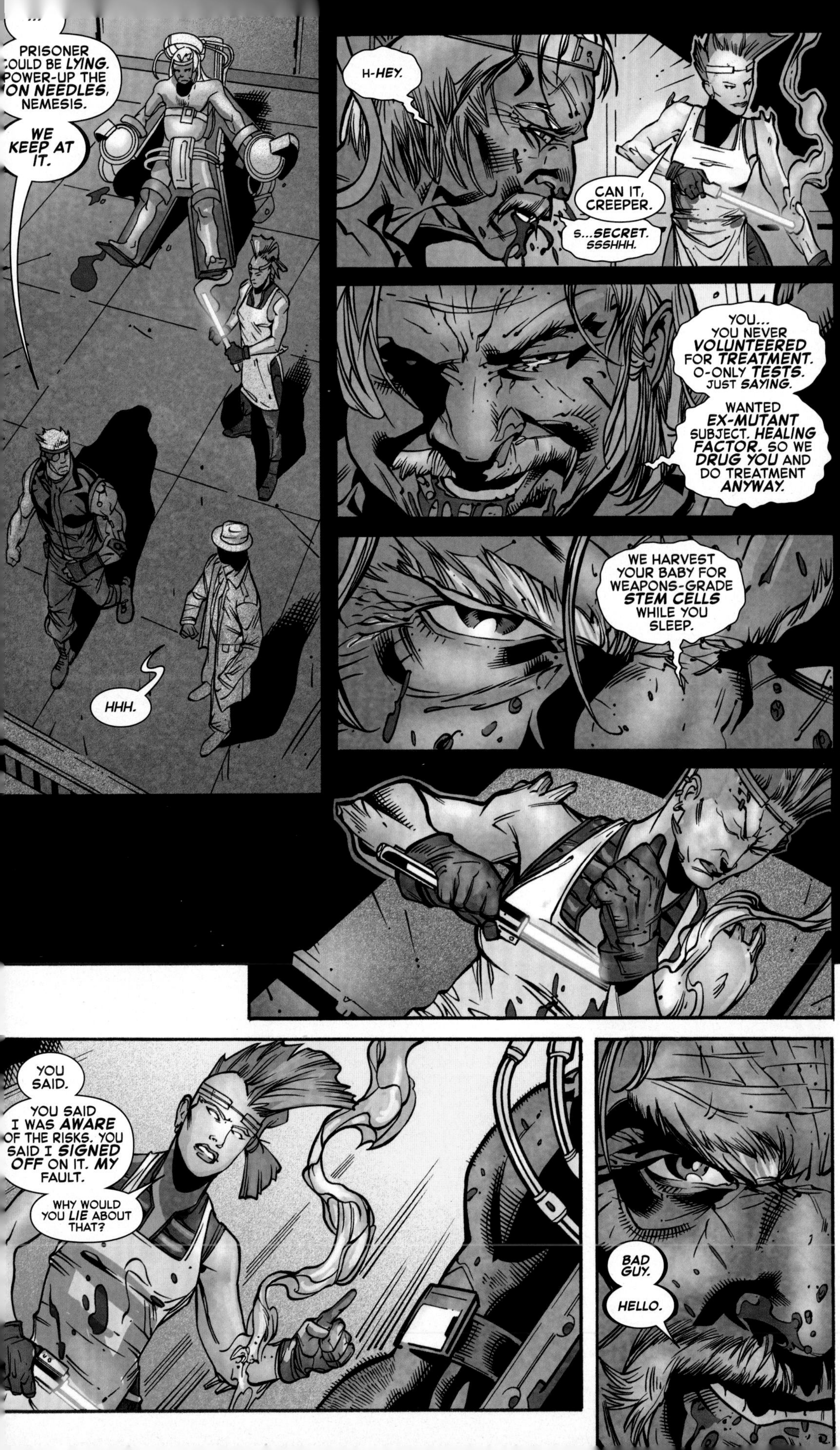
...
PRISONER COULD BE LYING. POWER-UP THE ON NEEDLES, NEMESIS.
WE KEEP AT IT.
HHH.
H-HEY.
CAN IT, CREEPER.
S...SECRET. SSSHHH.
YOU... YOU NEVER VOLUNTEERED FOR TREATMENT. O-ONLY TESTS. JUST SAYING.
WANTED EX-MUTANT SUBJECT. HEALING FACTOR. SO WE DRUG YOU AND DO TREATMENT ANYWAY.
WE HARVEST YOUR BABY FOR WEAPONS-GRADE STEM CELLS WHILE YOU SLEEP.
YOU SAID.
YOU SAID I WAS AWARE OF THE RISKS. YOU SAID I SIGNED OFF ON IT. MY FAULT.
WHY WOULD YOU LIE ABOUT THAT?
BAD GUY.
HELLO.

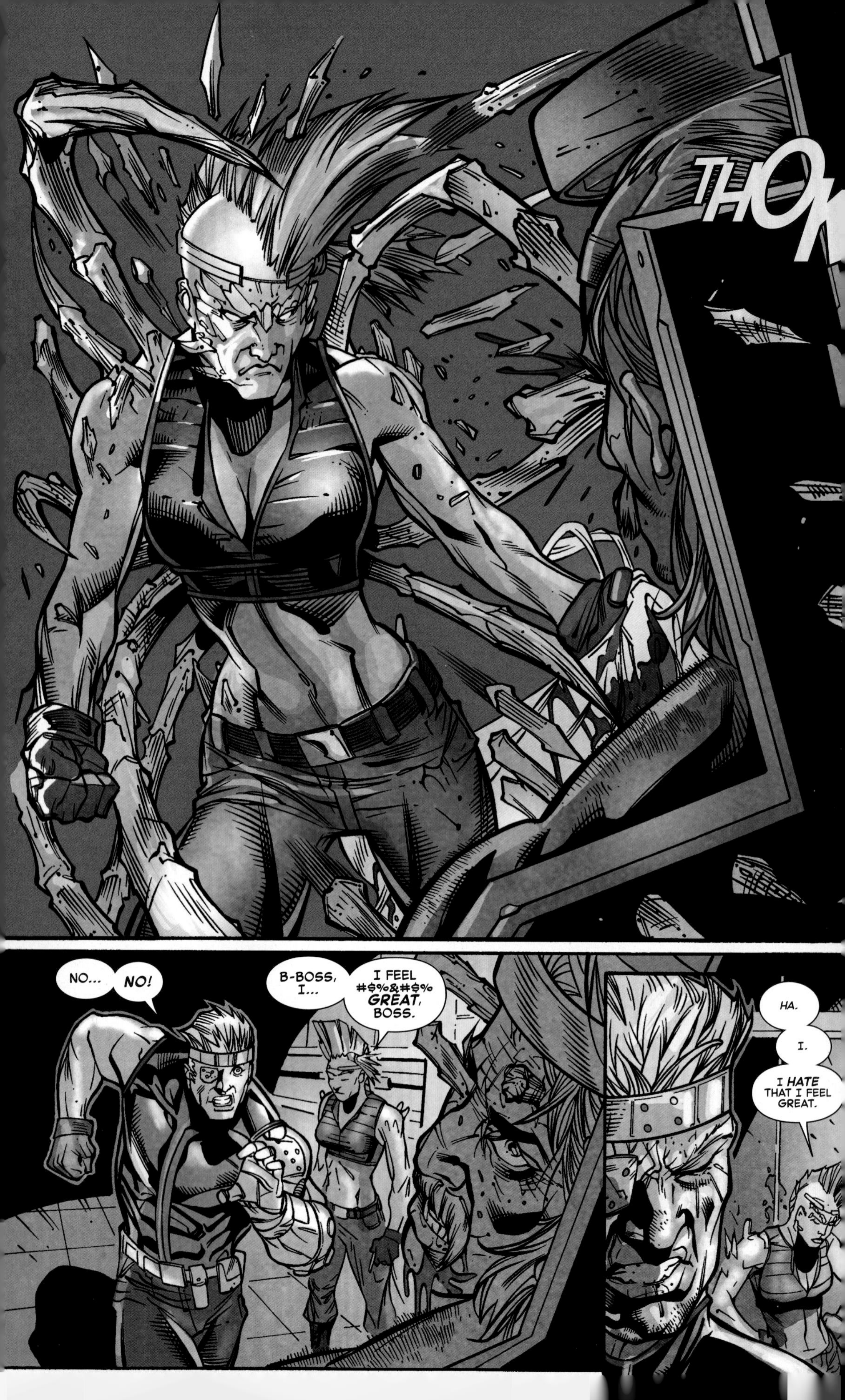
THOK
NO...
NO!
B-BOSS, I...
I FEEL #$%&#$% GREAT, BOSS.
HA.
I.
I HATE THAT I FEEL GREAT.

GEEZ...

EVERYONE'S *GUILTY PLEASURE*, RIGHT? CHEERING ON THE *GRIMDARK HEROES.*

WARNING:
CORE CORRUPTION
UNDERWAY
<<UNABLE TO PREVENT
FRAGMENTATION>>
SYSTEM INTEGRITY AT:
[::::::::::::::::] 7%

EXCEPT-- *WHOOPS*--NOW AND THEN THERE'S A MISSION WITH *NO OUTCOME* AT *ALL.*

AND THAT'S WHEN YOU HAVE TO HOPE THAT PEOPLE-- *NORMAL* PEOPLE, I MEAN--START TO *WONDER:*

WERE THEY SECRETLY CHEERING FOR THE *NASTY #$%&* ALL ALONG?

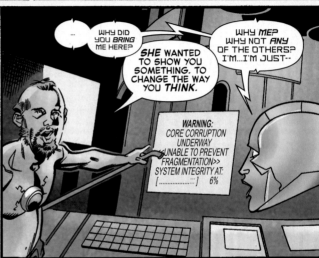

... WHY DID YOU *BRING* ME HERE?

SHE WANTED TO SHOW YOU SOMETHING. TO CHANGE THE WAY YOU *THINK.*

WHY *ME?* WHY NOT *ANY* OF THE OTHERS? I'M...I'M JUST--

WARNING:
CORE CORRUPTION
UNDERWAY
<<UNABLE TO PREVENT
FRAGMENTATION>>
SYSTEM INTEGRITY AT:
[::::::::::::::::] 6%

OPENING VIDEO FILE
[334:DD:217]

OPENING VIDEO FILE
[334:DD:217]

JST

=KK=

S-S-S-SOME... ZZZK.

GIRL.

WARNING:
CORE CORRUPTION
UNDERWAY
<<UNABLE TO PREVENT
FRAGMENTATION>>
SYSTEM INTEGRITY AT:
5%
[::::::::::::::::]

HA. YEAH.

WATCH *CLOSE*, KID.

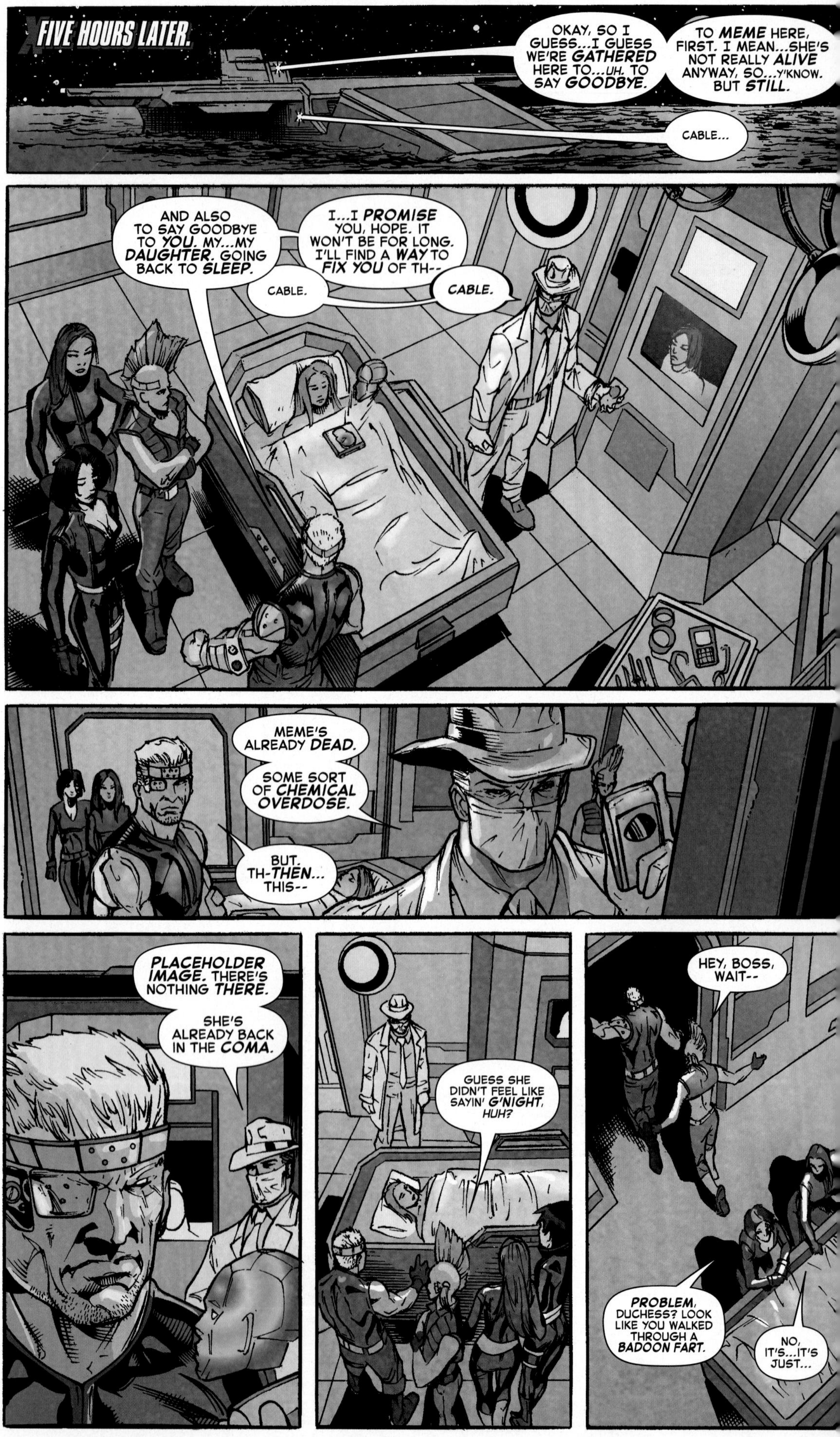
FIVE HOURS LATER.
OKAY, SO I GUESS...I GUESS WE'RE GATHERED HERE TO...UH. TO SAY GOODBYE.
TO MEME HERE, FIRST. I MEAN...SHE'S NOT REALLY ALIVE ANYWAY, SO...Y'KNOW. BUT STILL.
CABLE...
AND ALSO TO SAY GOODBYE TO YOU. MY...MY DAUGHTER. GOING BACK TO SLEEP.
I...I PROMISE YOU, HOPE. IT WON'T BE FOR LONG. I'LL FIND A WAY TO FIX YOU OF TH--
CABLE.
CABLE.
MEME'S ALREADY DEAD.
SOME SORT OF CHEMICAL OVERDOSE.
BUT. TH-THEN... THIS--
PLACEHOLDER IMAGE. THERE'S NOTHING THERE.
SHE'S ALREADY BACK IN THE COMA.
GUESS SHE DIDN'T FEEL LIKE SAYIN' G'NIGHT, HUH?
HEY, BOSS, WAIT--
PROBLEM, DUCHESS? LOOK LIKE YOU WALKED THROUGH A BADOON FART.
NO, IT'S...IT'S JUST...

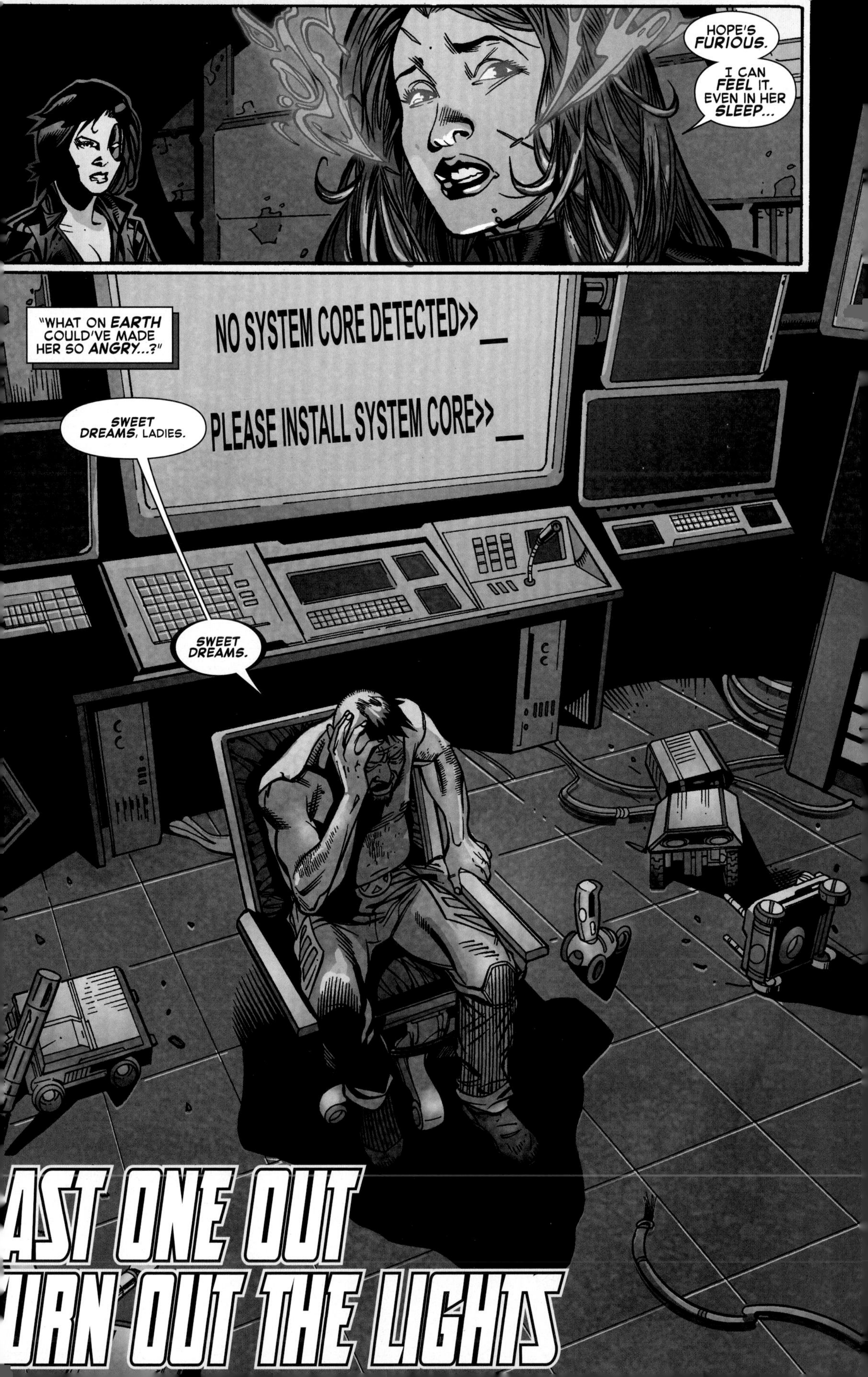

HOPE'S FURIOUS.
I CAN FEEL IT. EVEN IN HER SLEEP...
"WHAT ON EARTH COULD'VE MADE HER SO ANGRY...?"
NO SYSTEM CORE DETECTED>> _
PLEASE INSTALL SYSTEM CORE>> _
SWEET DREAMS, LADIES.
SWEET DREAMS.
AST ONE OUT
URN OUT THE LIGHTS

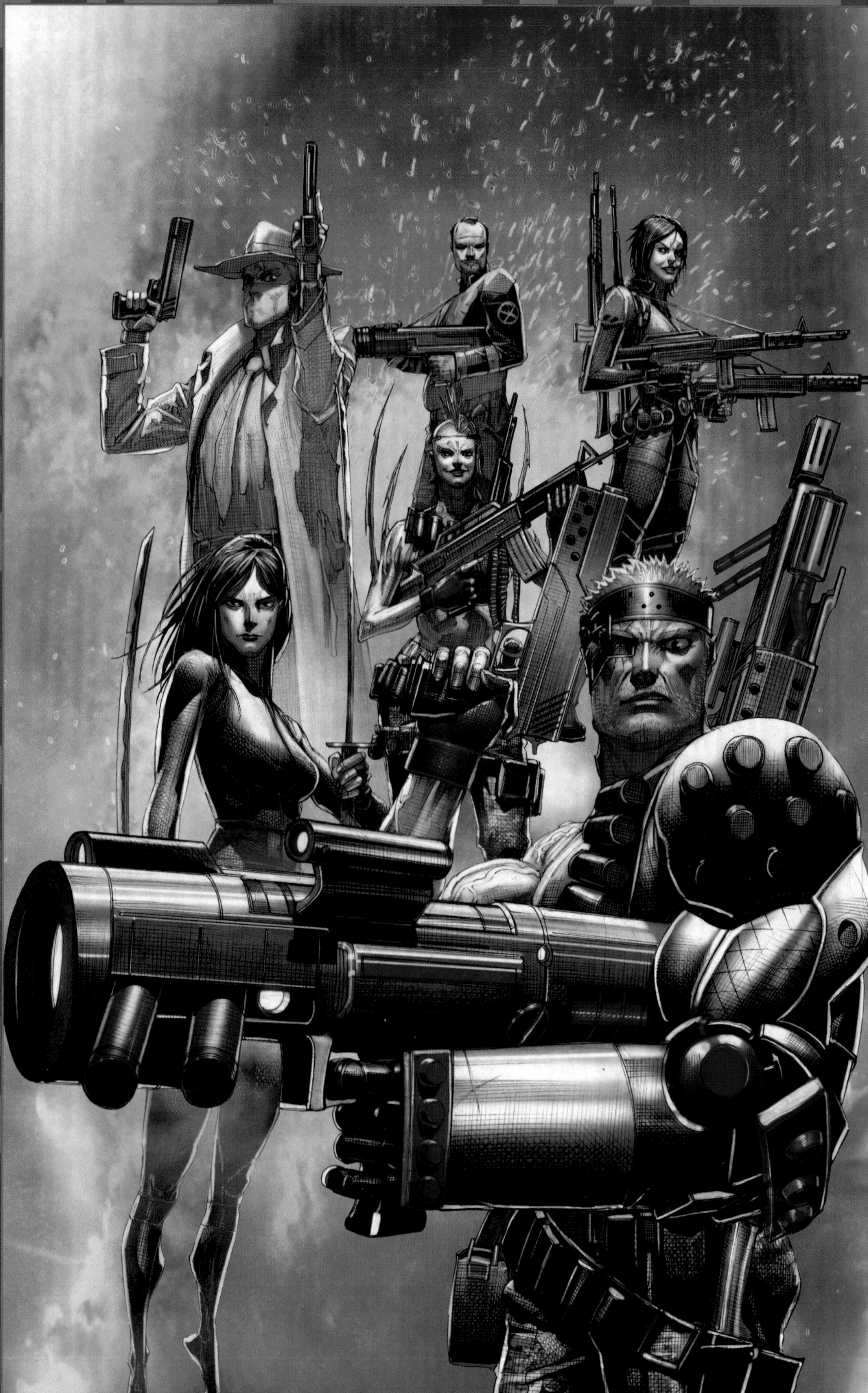

›› 14 ‹‹

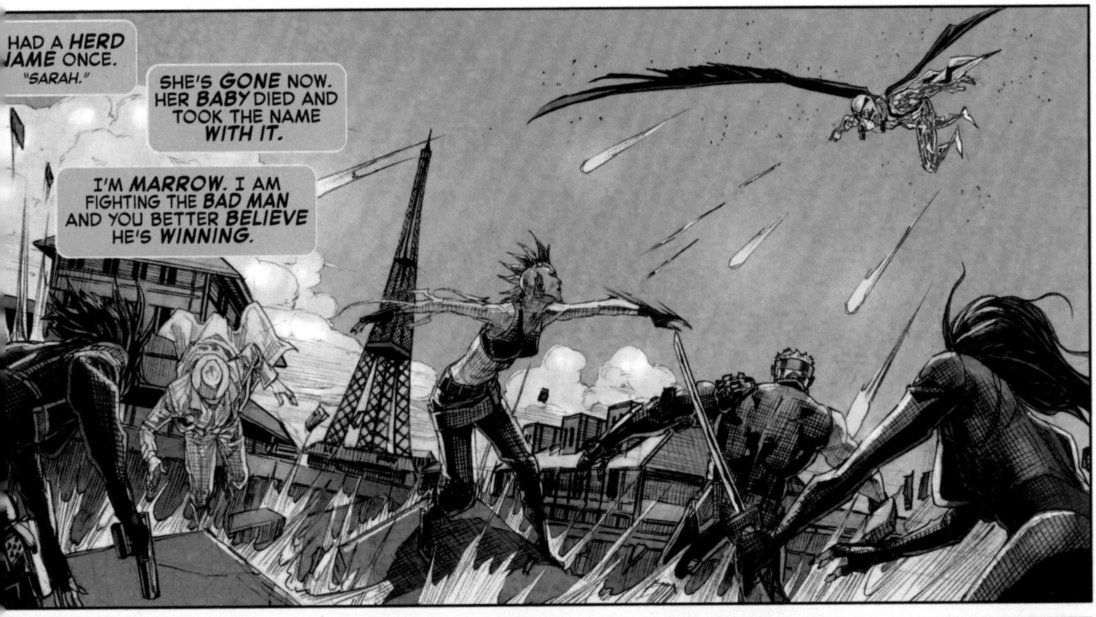
HAD A HERD
NAME ONCE.
"SARAH."
SHE'S GONE NOW. HER BABY DIED AND TOOK THE NAME WITH IT.
I'M MARROW. I AM FIGHTING THE BAD MAN AND YOU BETTER BELIEVE HE'S WINNING.
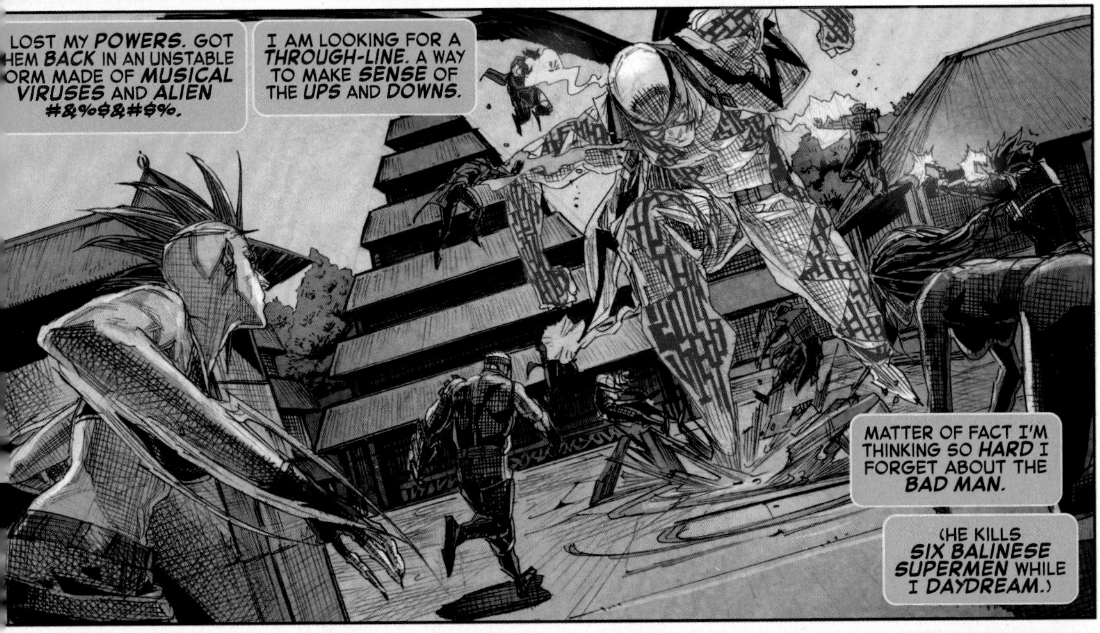
LOST MY POWERS. GOT
HEM BACK IN AN UNSTABLE
ORM MADE OF MUSICAL
VIRUSES AND ALIEN
#&%$&#$%.
I AM LOOKING FOR A THROUGH-LINE. A WAY TO MAKE SENSE OF THE UPS AND DOWNS.
MATTER OF FACT I'M THINKING SO HARD I FORGET ABOUT THE BAD MAN.
(HE KILLS SIX BALINESE SUPERMEN WHILE I DAYDREAM.)
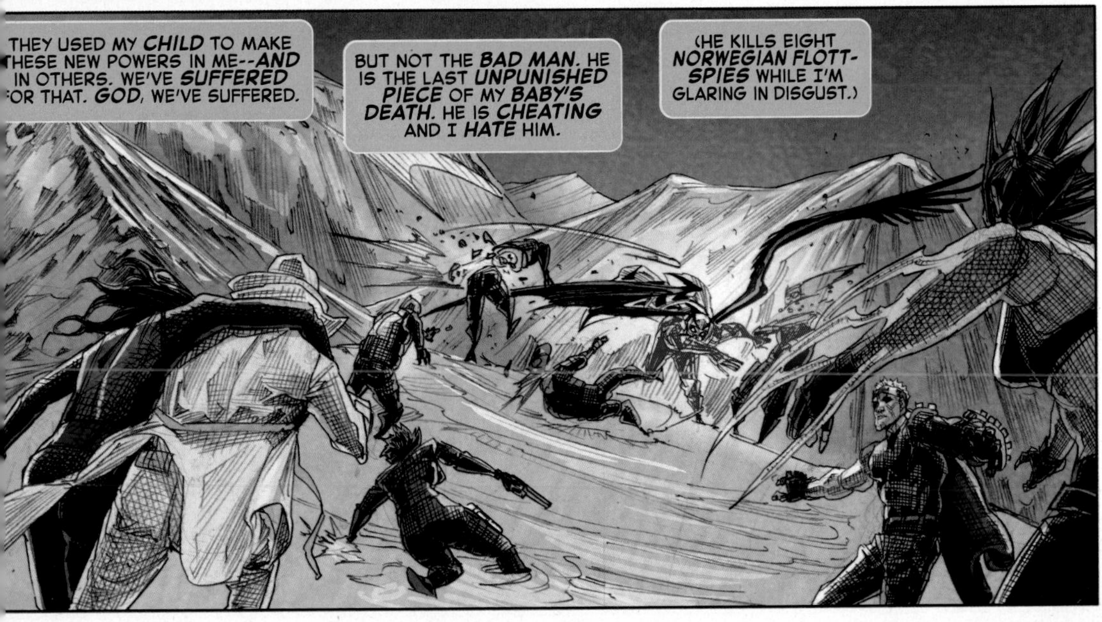
THEY USED MY CHILD TO MAKE
THESE NEW POWERS IN ME--AND
IN OTHERS. WE'VE SUFFERED
FOR THAT. GOD, WE'VE SUFFERED.
BUT NOT THE BAD MAN. HE IS THE LAST UNPUNISHED PIECE OF MY BABY'S DEATH. HE IS CHEATING AND I HATE HIM.
(HE KILLS EIGHT NORWEGIAN FLOTT-SPIES WHILE I'M GLARING IN DISGUST.)

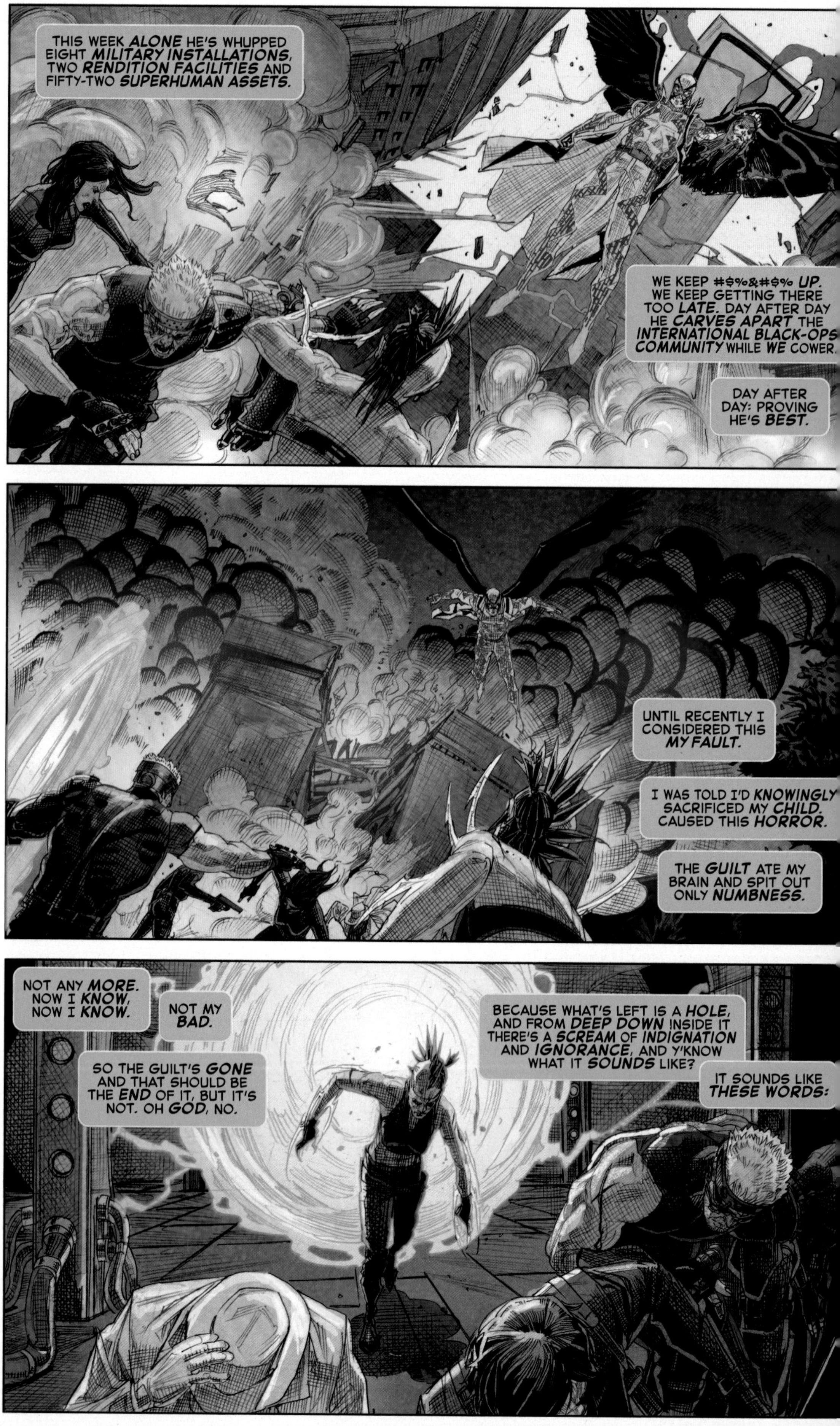
THIS WEEK ALONE HE'S WHUPPED EIGHT MILITARY INSTALLATIONS, TWO RENDITION FACILITIES AND FIFTY-TWO SUPERHUMAN ASSETS.
WE KEEP #$%&#$% UP. WE KEEP GETTING THERE TOO LATE. DAY AFTER DAY HE CARVES APART THE INTERNATIONAL BLACK-OPS COMMUNITY WHILE WE COWER.
DAY AFTER DAY: PROVING HE'S BEST.
UNTIL RECENTLY I CONSIDERED THIS MY FAULT.
I WAS TOLD I'D KNOWINGLY SACRIFICED MY CHILD. CAUSED THIS HORROR.
THE GUILT ATE MY BRAIN AND SPIT OUT ONLY NUMBNESS.
NOT ANY MORE. NOW I KNOW, NOW I KNOW.
NOT MY BAD.
SO THE GUILT'S GONE AND THAT SHOULD BE THE END OF IT, BUT IT'S NOT. OH GOD, NO.
BECAUSE WHAT'S LEFT IS A HOLE, AND FROM DEEP DOWN INSIDE IT THERE'S A SCREAM OF INDIGNATION AND IGNORANCE, AND Y'KNOW WHAT IT SOUNDS LIKE?
IT SOUNDS LIKE THESE WORDS:

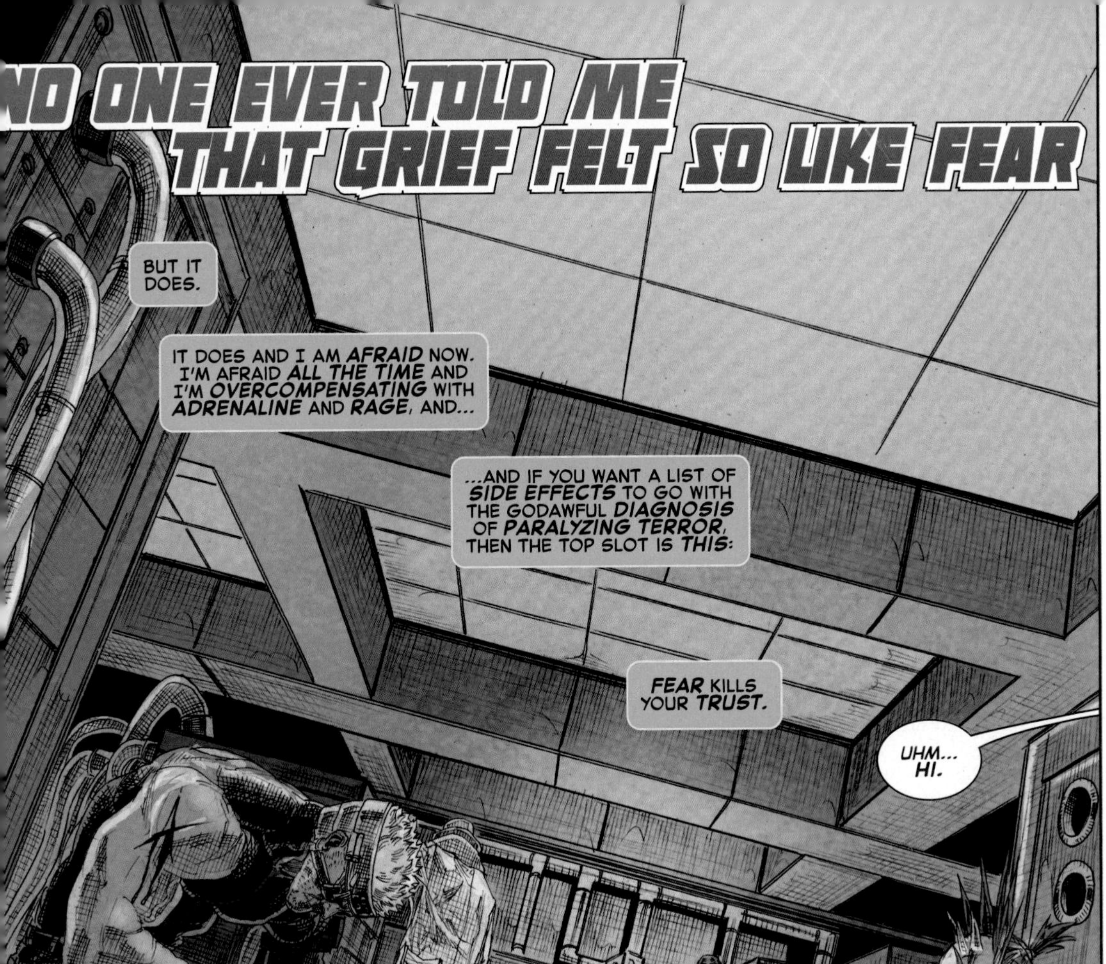
NO ONE EVER TOLD ME THAT GRIEF FELT SO LIKE FEAR
BUT IT DOES.
IT DOES AND I AM AFRAID NOW. I'M AFRAID ALL THE TIME AND I'M OVERCOMPENSATING WITH ADRENALINE AND RAGE, AND...
...AND IF YOU WANT A LIST OF SIDE EFFECTS TO GO WITH THE GODAWFUL DIAGNOSIS OF PARALYZING TERROR, THEN THE TOP SLOT IS THIS:
FEAR KILLS YOUR TRUST.
UHM... HI.
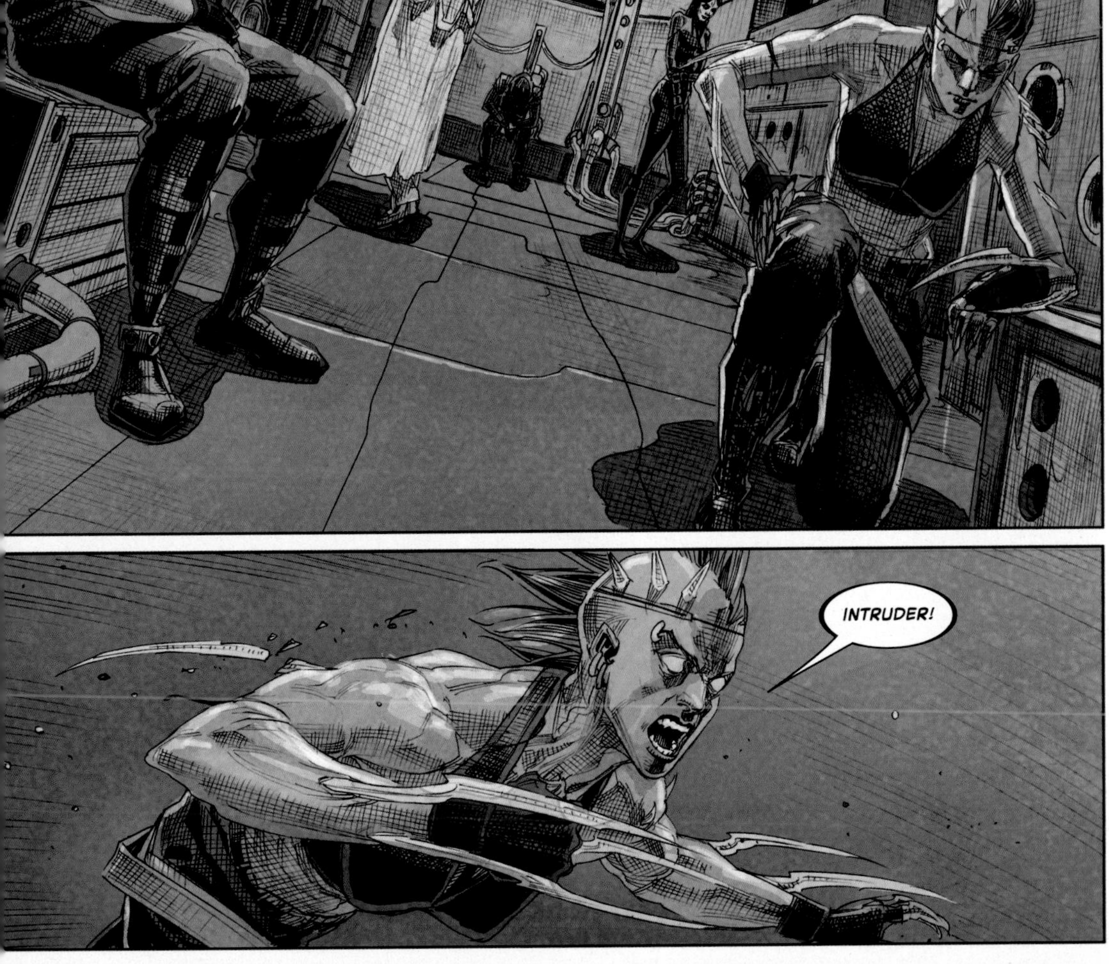
INTRUDER!

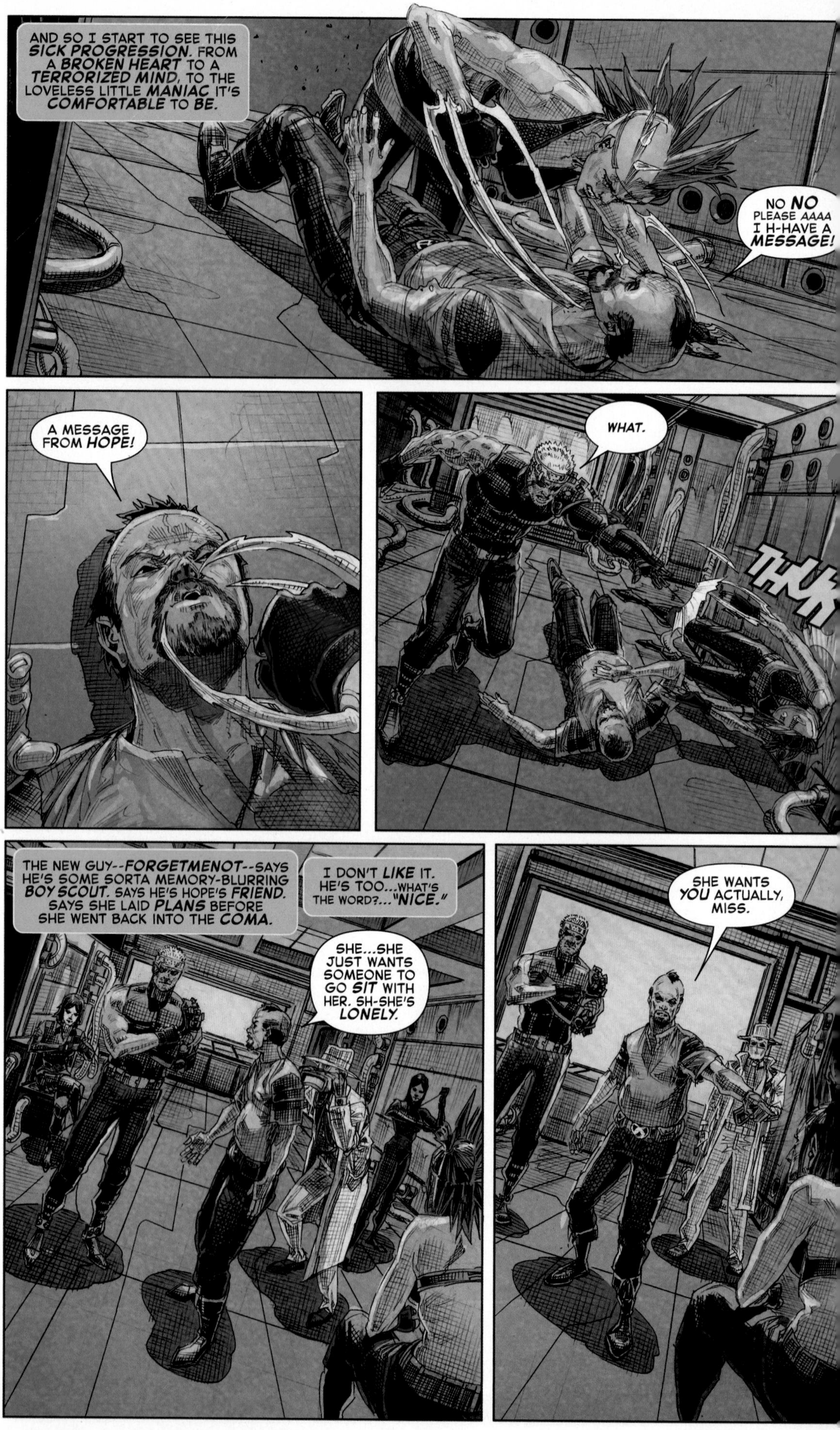
AND SO I START TO SEE THIS SICK PROGRESSION. FROM A BROKEN HEART TO A TERRORIZED MIND, TO THE LOVELESS LITTLE MANIAC IT'S COMFORTABLE TO BE.
NO NO PLEASE AAAA I H-HAVE A MESSAGE!
A MESSAGE FROM HOPE!
WHAT.
THUK
THE NEW GUY--FORGETMENOT--SAYS HE'S SOME SORTA MEMORY-BLURRING BOY SCOUT. SAYS HE'S HOPE'S FRIEND. SAYS SHE LAID PLANS BEFORE SHE WENT BACK INTO THE COMA.
I DON'T LIKE IT. HE'S TOO...WHAT'S THE WORD?..."NICE."
SHE...SHE JUST WANTS SOMEONE TO GO SIT WITH HER. SH-SHE'S LONELY.
SHE WANTS YOU ACTUALLY, MISS.

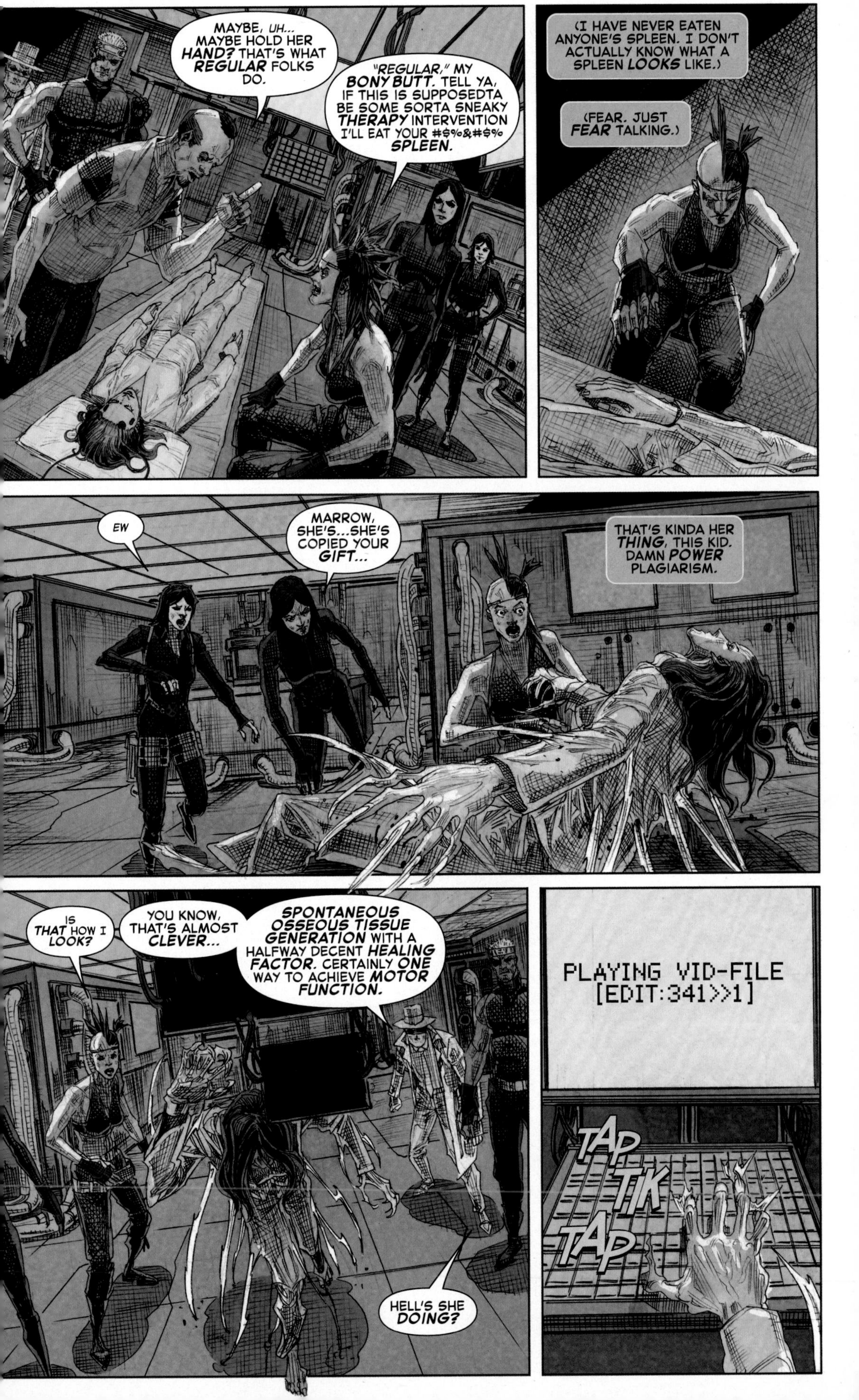

MAYBE, UH... MAYBE HOLD HER HAND? THAT'S WHAT REGULAR FOLKS DO.
"REGULAR," MY BONY BUTT. TELL YA, IF THIS IS SUPPOSEDTA BE SOME SORTA SNEAKY THERAPY INTERVENTION I'LL EAT YOUR #$%&#$% SPLEEN.
(I HAVE NEVER EATEN ANYONE'S SPLEEN. I DON'T ACTUALLY KNOW WHAT A SPLEEN LOOKS LIKE.)
(FEAR. JUST FEAR TALKING.)
EW
MARROW, SHE'S...SHE'S COPIED YOUR GIFT...
THAT'S KINDA HER THING, THIS KID. DAMN POWER PLAGIARISM.
IS THAT HOW I LOOK?
YOU KNOW, THAT'S ALMOST CLEVER...
SPONTANEOUS OSSEOUS TISSUE GENERATION WITH A HALFWAY DECENT HEALING FACTOR. CERTAINLY ONE WAY TO ACHIEVE MOTOR FUNCTION.
HELL'S SHE DOING?
PLAYING VID-FILE [EDIT:341>>1]
TAP
TIK
TAP

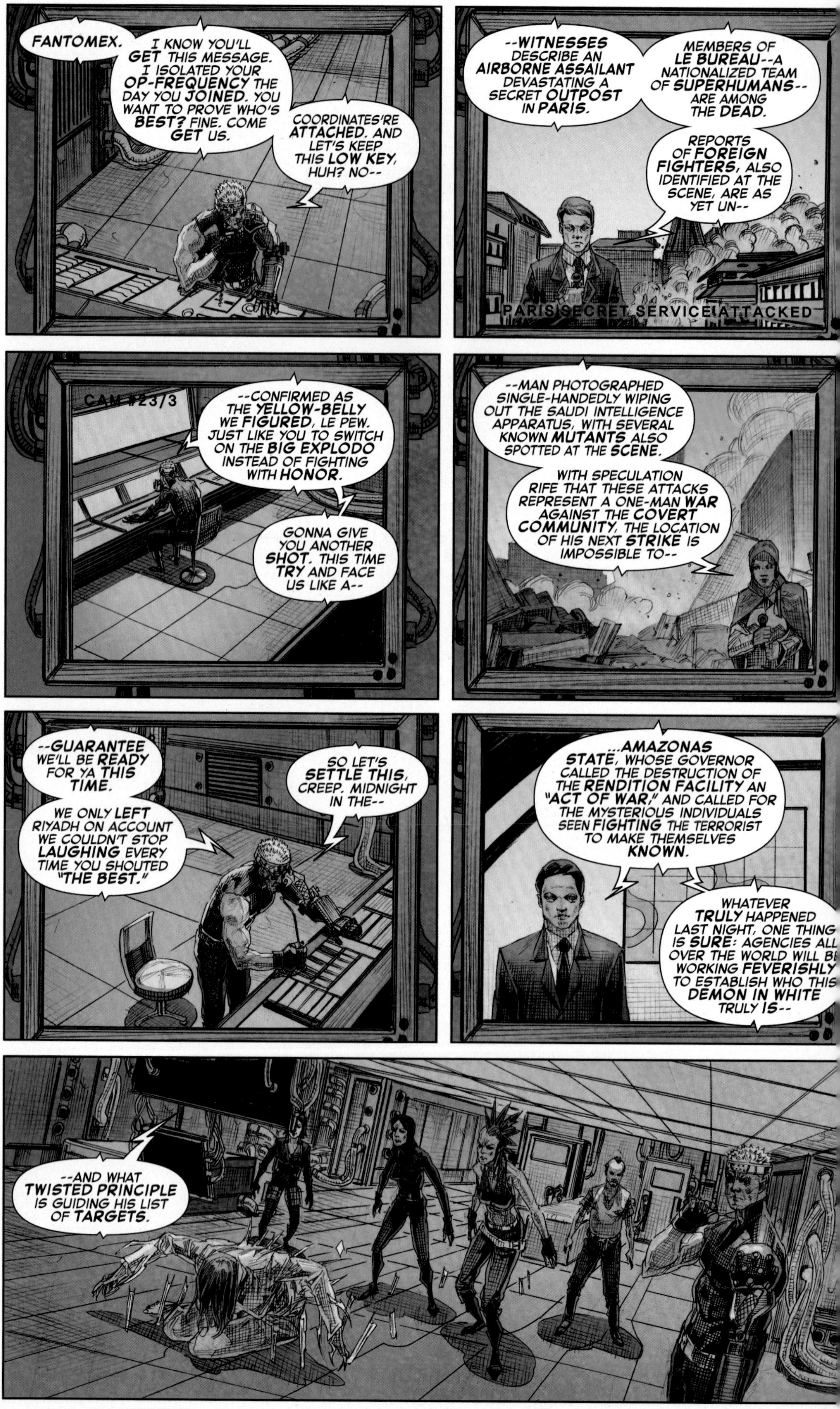
FANTOMEX.
I KNOW YOU'LL GET THIS MESSAGE. I ISOLATED YOUR OP-FREQUENCY THE DAY YOU JOINED. YOU WANT TO PROVE WHO'S BEST? FINE. COME GET US.
COORDINATES'RE ATTACHED. AND LET'S KEEP THIS LOW KEY, HUH? NO--
--WITNESSES DESCRIBE AN AIRBORNE ASSAILANT DEVASTATING A SECRET OUTPOST IN PARIS.
MEMBERS OF LE BUREAU--A NATIONALIZED TEAM OF SUPERHUMANS--ARE AMONG THE DEAD.
REPORTS OF FOREIGN FIGHTERS, ALSO IDENTIFIED AT THE SCENE, ARE AS YET UN--
PARIS SECRET SERVICE ATTACKED
CAM #23/3
--CONFIRMED AS THE YELLOW-BELLY WE FIGURED, LE PEW. JUST LIKE YOU TO SWITCH ON THE BIG EXPLODO INSTEAD OF FIGHTING WITH HONOR.
GONNA GIVE YOU ANOTHER SHOT. THIS TIME TRY AND FACE US LIKE A--
--MAN PHOTOGRAPHED SINGLE-HANDEDLY WIPING OUT THE SAUDI INTELLIGENCE APPARATUS, WITH SEVERAL KNOWN MUTANTS ALSO SPOTTED AT THE SCENE.
WITH SPECULATION RIFE THAT THESE ATTACKS REPRESENT A ONE-MAN WAR AGAINST THE COVERT COMMUNITY, THE LOCATION OF HIS NEXT STRIKE IS IMPOSSIBLE TO--
--GUARANTEE WE'LL BE READY FOR YA THIS TIME.
WE ONLY LEFT RIYADH ON ACCOUNT WE COULDN'T STOP LAUGHING EVERY TIME YOU SHOUTED "THE BEST."
SO LET'S SETTLE THIS, CREEP. MIDNIGHT IN THE--
...AMAZONAS STATE, WHOSE GOVERNOR CALLED THE DESTRUCTION OF THE RENDITION FACILITY AN "ACT OF WAR," AND CALLED FOR THE MYSTERIOUS INDIVIDUALS SEEN FIGHTING THE TERRORIST TO MAKE THEMSELVES KNOWN.
WHATEVER TRULY HAPPENED LAST NIGHT, ONE THING IS SURE: AGENCIES ALL OVER THE WORLD WILL BE WORKING FEVERISHLY TO ESTABLISH WHO THIS DEMON IN WHITE TRULY IS--
--AND WHAT TWISTED PRINCIPLE IS GUIDING HIS LIST OF TARGETS.

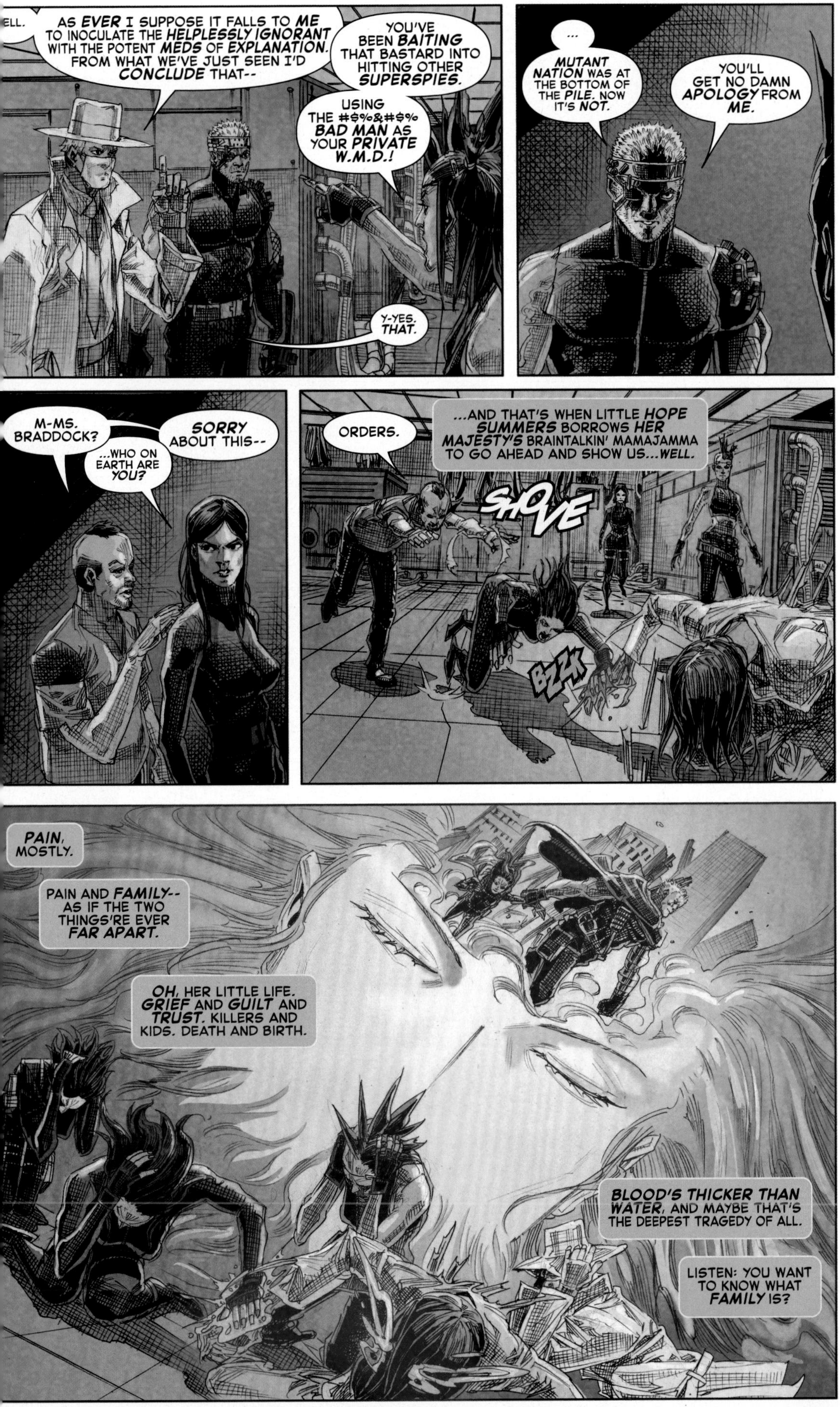
ELL.
AS EVER I SUPPOSE IT FALLS TO ME TO INOCULATE THE HELPLESSLY IGNORANT WITH THE POTENT MEDS OF EXPLANATION. FROM WHAT WE'VE JUST SEEN I'D CONCLUDE THAT--
YOU'VE BEEN BAITING THAT BASTARD INTO HITTING OTHER SUPERSPIES.
USING THE #$%&#$% BAD MAN AS YOUR PRIVATE W.M.D.!
Y-YES. THAT.
...
MUTANT NATION WAS AT THE BOTTOM OF THE PILE. NOW IT'S NOT.
YOU'LL GET NO DAMN APOLOGY FROM ME.
M-MS. BRADDOCK?
SORRY ABOUT THIS--
...WHO ON EARTH ARE YOU?
ORDERS.
...AND THAT'S WHEN LITTLE HOPE SUMMERS BORROWS HER MAJESTY'S BRAINTALKIN' MAMAJAMMA TO GO AHEAD AND SHOW US...WELL.
SHOVE
BZZK
PAIN, MOSTLY.
PAIN AND FAMILY-- AS IF THE TWO THINGS'RE EVER FAR APART.
OH, HER LITTLE LIFE. GRIEF AND GUILT AND TRUST. KILLERS AND KIDS. DEATH AND BIRTH.
BLOOD'S THICKER THAN WATER, AND MAYBE THAT'S THE DEEPEST TRAGEDY OF ALL.
LISTEN: YOU WANT TO KNOW WHAT FAMILY IS?

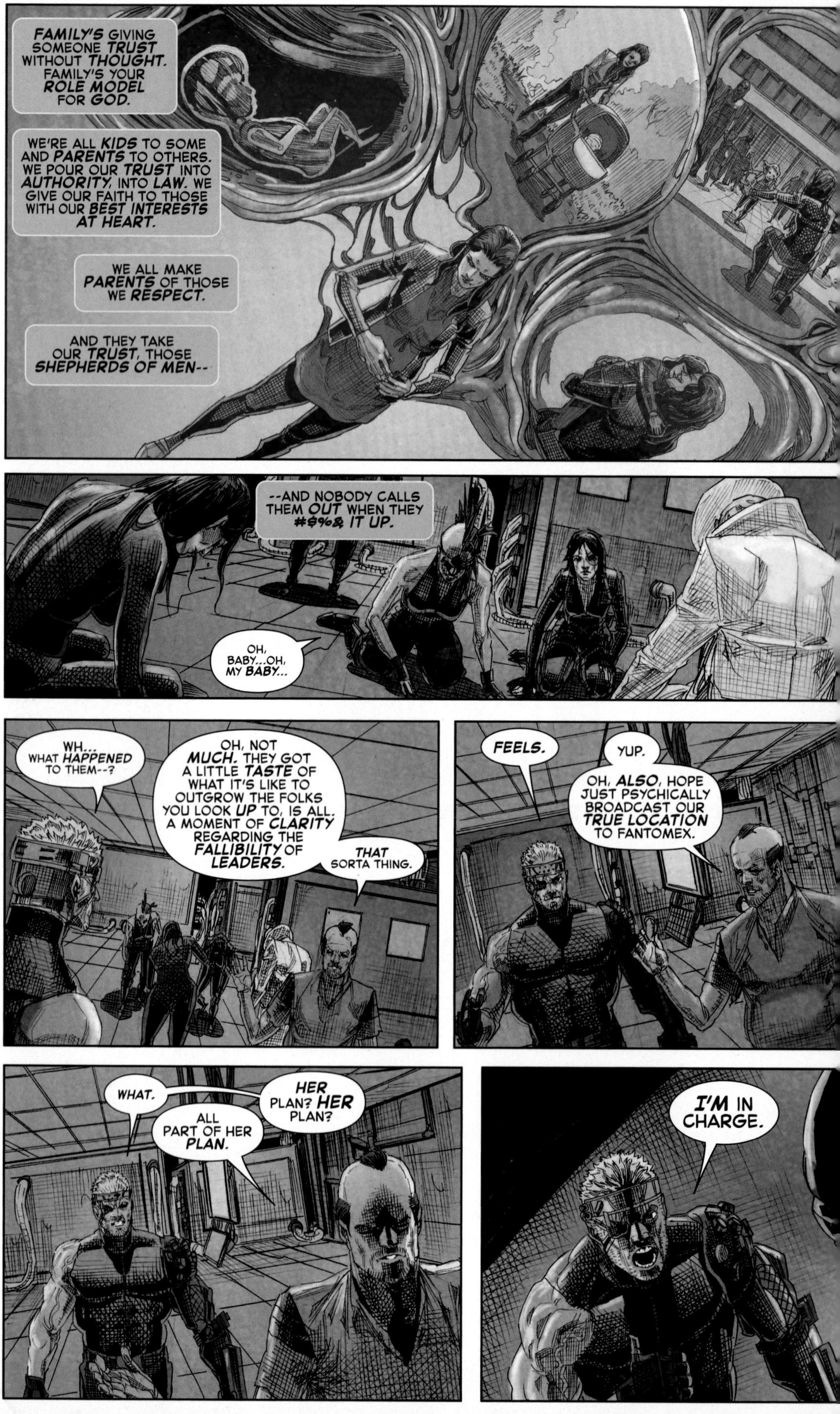
FAMILY'S GIVING SOMEONE TRUST WITHOUT THOUGHT. FAMILY'S YOUR ROLE MODEL FOR GOD.
WE'RE ALL KIDS TO SOME AND PARENTS TO OTHERS. WE POUR OUR TRUST INTO AUTHORITY, INTO LAW. WE GIVE OUR FAITH TO THOSE WITH OUR BEST INTERESTS AT HEART.
WE ALL MAKE PARENTS OF THOSE WE RESPECT.
AND THEY TAKE OUR TRUST, THOSE SHEPHERDS OF MEN--
--AND NOBODY CALLS THEM OUT WHEN THEY #$%& IT UP.
OH, BABY...OH, MY BABY...
WH... WHAT HAPPENED TO THEM--?
OH, NOT MUCH. THEY GOT A LITTLE TASTE OF WHAT IT'S LIKE TO OUTGROW THE FOLKS YOU LOOK UP TO, IS ALL. A MOMENT OF CLARITY REGARDING THE FALLIBILITY OF LEADERS.
THAT SORTA THING.
FEELS.
YUP.
OH, ALSO, HOPE JUST PSYCHICALLY BROADCAST OUR TRUE LOCATION TO FANTOMEX.
WHAT.
ALL PART OF HER PLAN.
HER PLAN? HER PLAN?
I'M IN CHARGE.

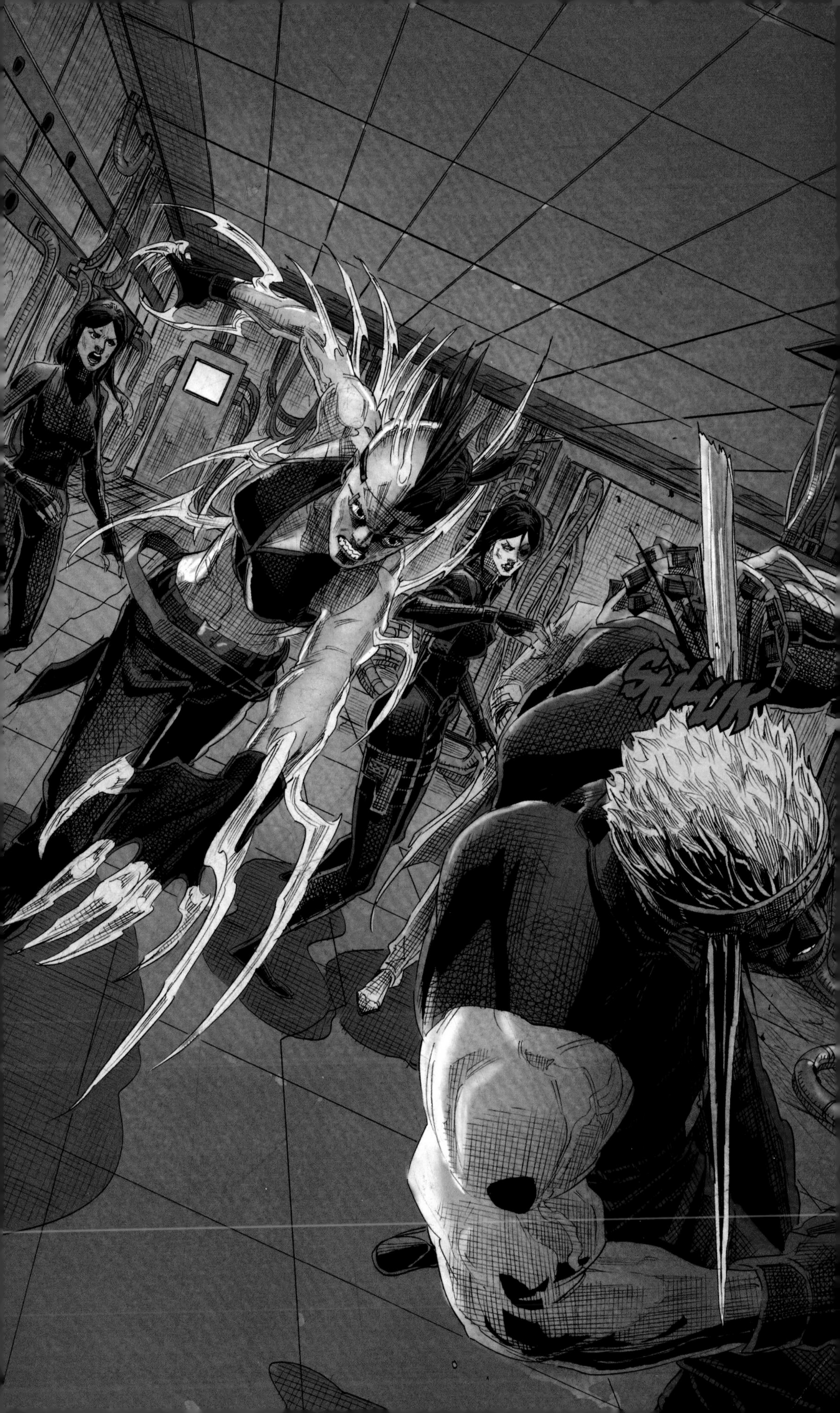
SHLUK

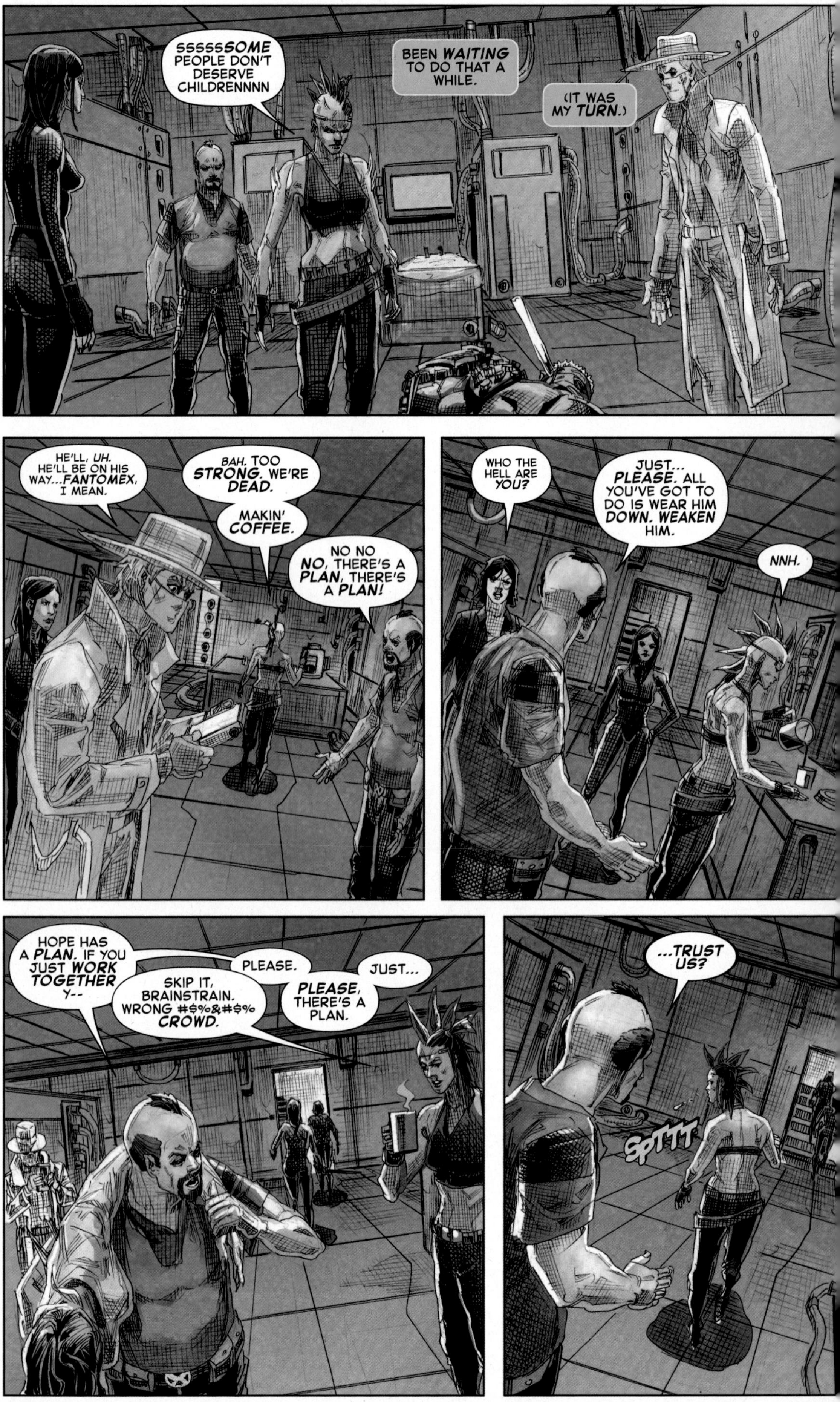
SSSSSSOME PEOPLE DON'T DESERVE CHILDRENNNN
BEEN WAITING TO DO THAT A WHILE.
(IT WAS MY TURN.)
HE'LL, UH. HE'LL BE ON HIS WAY...FANTOMEX, I MEAN.
BAH. TOO STRONG. WE'RE DEAD.
MAKIN' COFFEE.
NO NO NO, THERE'S A PLAN, THERE'S A PLAN!
WHO THE HELL ARE YOU?
JUST... PLEASE. ALL YOU'VE GOT TO DO IS WEAR HIM DOWN. WEAKEN HIM.
NNH.
HOPE HAS A PLAN. IF YOU JUST WORK TOGETHER Y--
PLEASE.
SKIP IT, BRAINSTRAIN. WRONG #$%&#$% CROWD.
JUST...
PLEASE, THERE'S A PLAN.
...TRUST US?
SPTTT

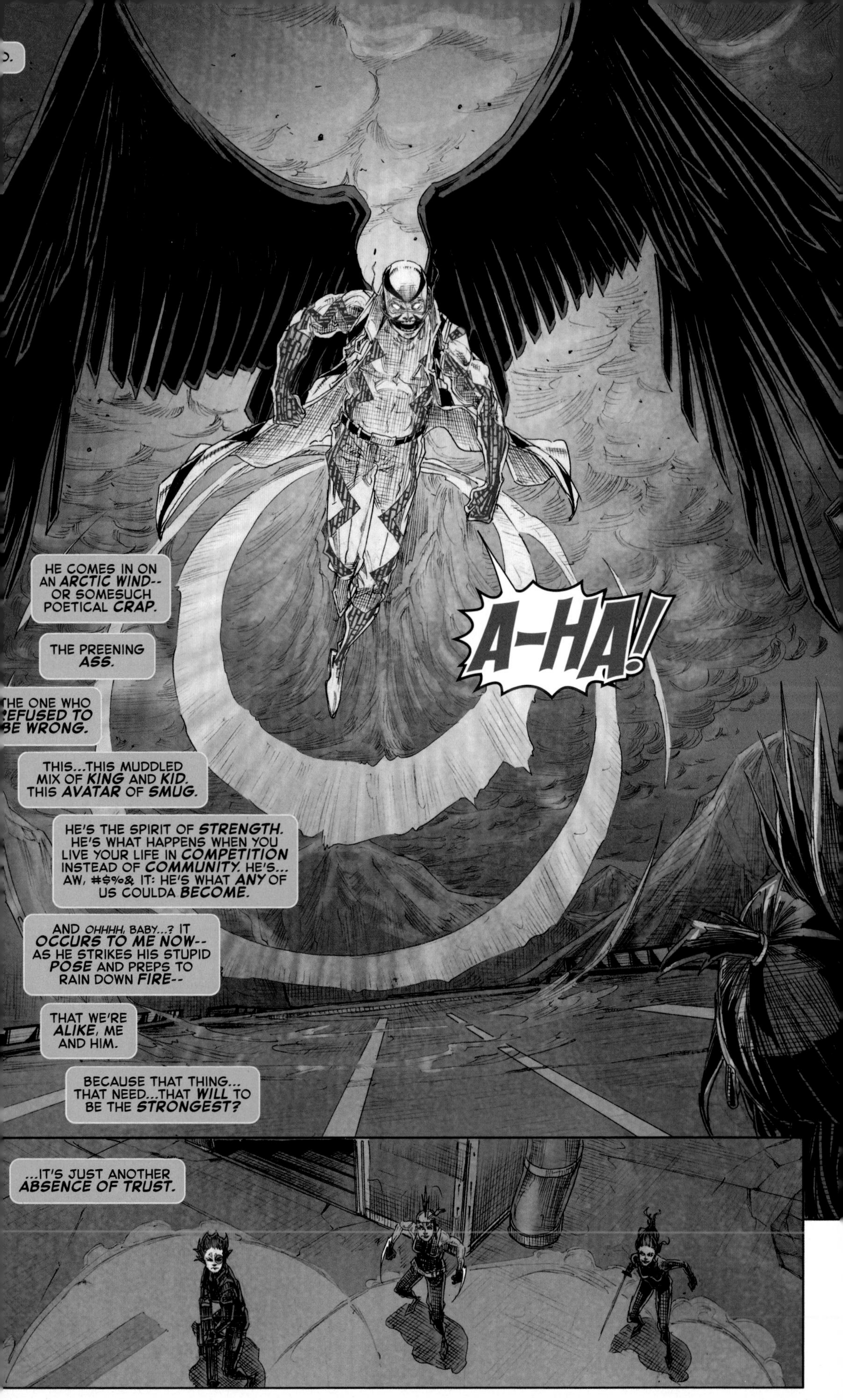
HE COMES IN ON AN ARCTIC WIND-- OR SOMESUCH POETICAL CRAP.
A-HA!
THE PREENING ASS.
THE ONE WHO REFUSED TO BE WRONG.
THIS...THIS MUDDLED MIX OF KING AND KID. THIS AVATAR OF SMUG.
HE'S THE SPIRIT OF STRENGTH. HE'S WHAT HAPPENS WHEN YOU LIVE YOUR LIFE IN COMPETITION INSTEAD OF COMMUNITY. HE'S... AW, #$%& IT: HE'S WHAT ANY OF US COULDA BECOME.
AND OHHHH, BABY...? IT OCCURS TO ME NOW-- AS HE STRIKES HIS STUPID POSE AND PREPS TO RAIN DOWN FIRE--
THAT WE'RE ALIKE, ME AND HIM.
BECAUSE THAT THING... THAT NEED...THAT WILL TO BE THE STRONGEST?
...IT'S JUST ANOTHER ABSENCE OF TRUST.

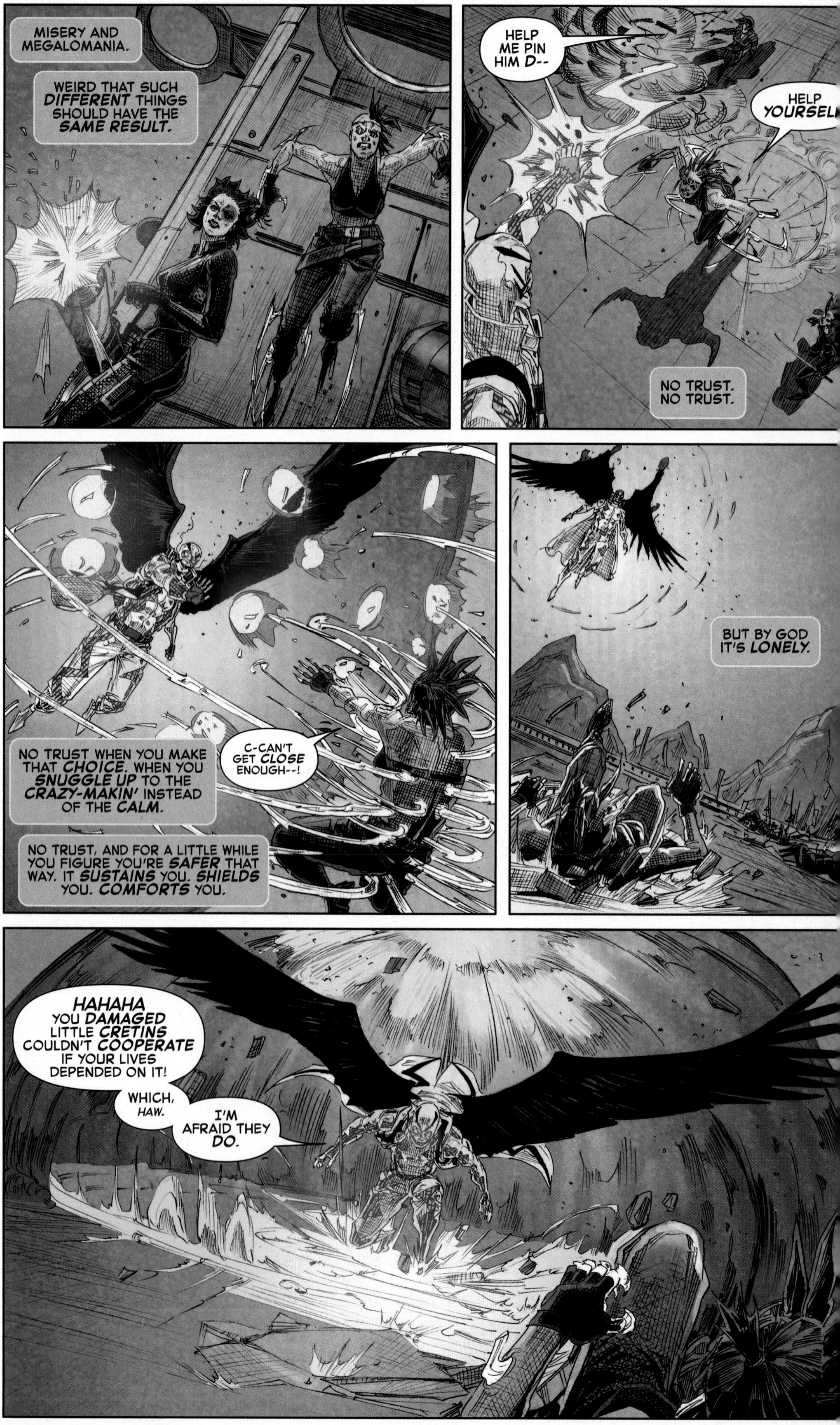
MISERY AND MEGALOMANIA.
WEIRD THAT SUCH DIFFERENT THINGS SHOULD HAVE THE SAME RESULT.
HELP ME PIN HIM D--
HELP YOURSEL
NO TRUST. NO TRUST.
NO TRUST WHEN YOU MAKE THAT CHOICE. WHEN YOU SNUGGLE UP TO THE CRAZY-MAKIN' INSTEAD OF THE CALM.
C-CAN'T GET CLOSE ENOUGH--!
NO TRUST, AND FOR A LITTLE WHILE YOU FIGURE YOU'RE SAFER THAT WAY. IT SUSTAINS YOU. SHIELDS YOU. COMFORTS YOU.
BUT BY GOD IT'S LONELY.
HAHAHA YOU DAMAGED LITTLE CRETINS COULDN'T COOPERATE IF YOUR LIVES DEPENDED ON IT!
WHICH, HAW.
I'M AFRAID THEY DO.

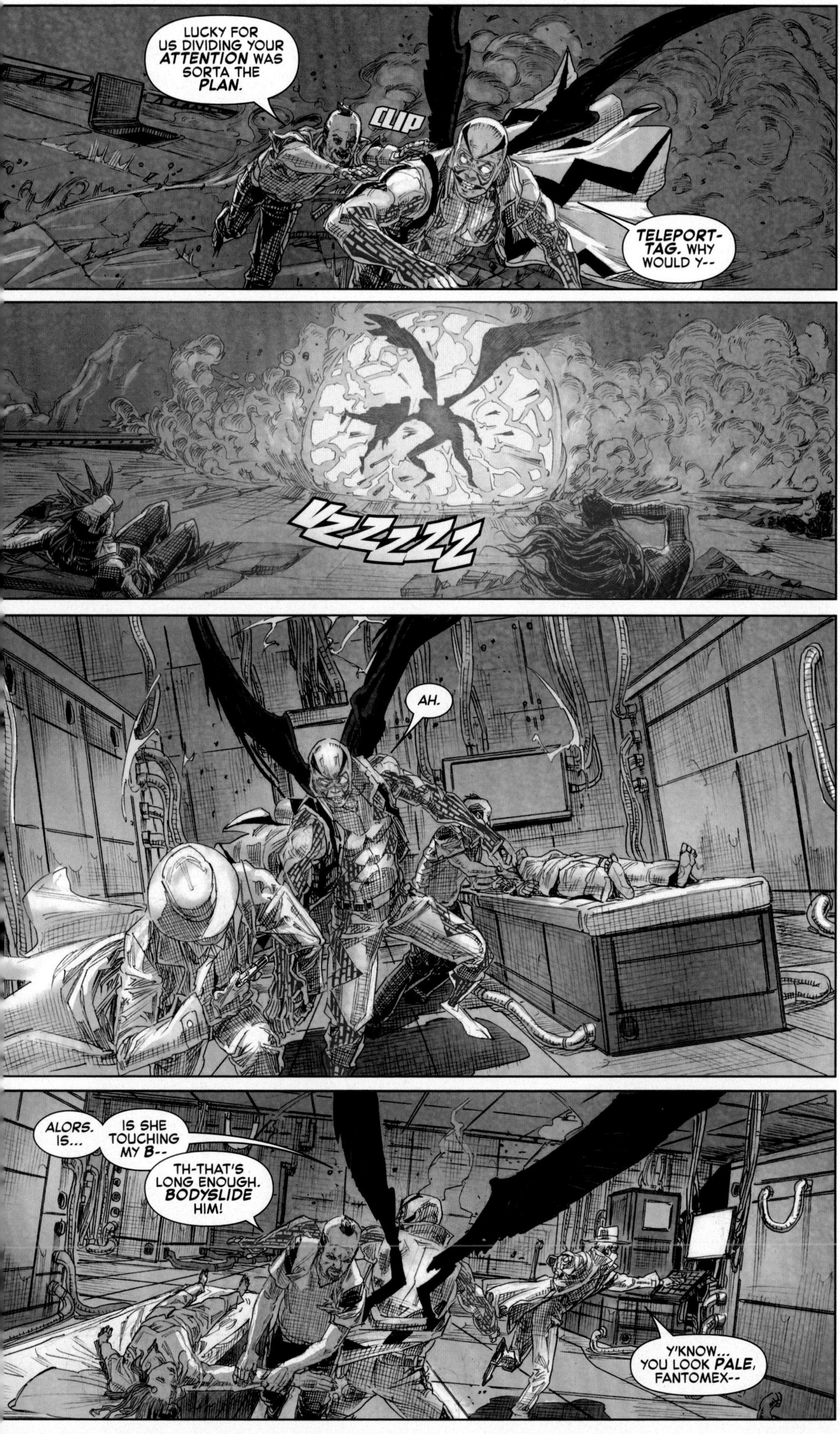
LUCKY FOR US DIVIDING YOUR ATTENTION WAS SORTA THE PLAN.
CLIP
TELEPORT-TAG. WHY WOULD Y--
VZZZZZ
AH.
ALORS. IS...
IS SHE TOUCHING MY B--
TH-THAT'S LONG ENOUGH. BODYSLIDE HIM!
Y'KNOW... YOU LOOK PALE, FANTOMEX--

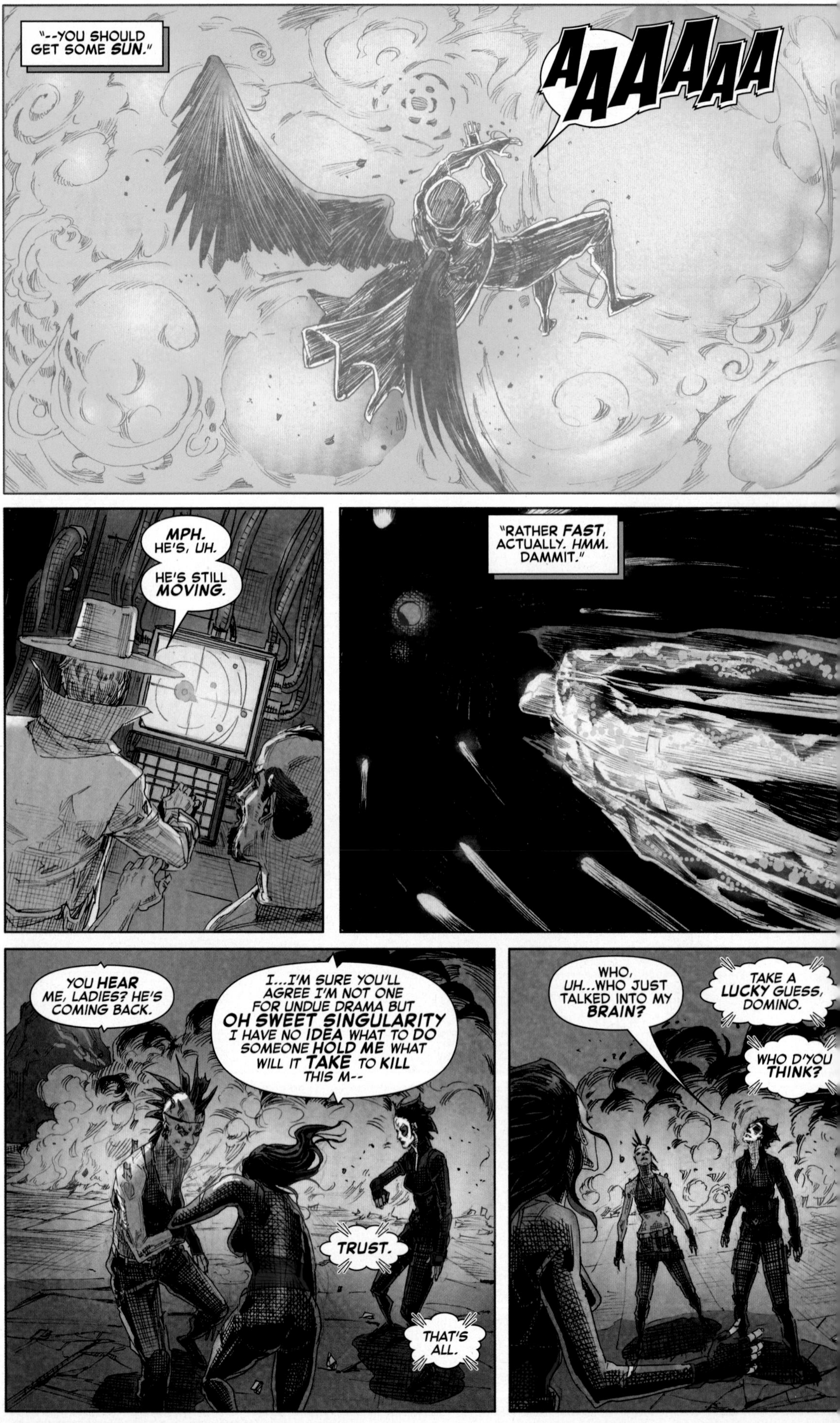
"--YOU SHOULD GET SOME SUN."
AAAAAA
MPH. HE'S, UH.
HE'S STILL MOVING.
"RATHER FAST, ACTUALLY. HMM. DAMMIT."
YOU HEAR ME, LADIES? HE'S COMING BACK.
I...I'M SURE YOU'LL AGREE I'M NOT ONE FOR UNDUE DRAMA BUT OH SWEET SINGULARITY I HAVE NO IDEA WHAT TO DO SOMEONE HOLD ME WHAT WILL IT TAKE TO KILL THIS M--
TRUST.
THAT'S ALL.
WHO, UH...WHO JUST TALKED INTO MY BRAIN?
TAKE A LUCKY GUESS, DOMINO.
WHO D'YOU THINK?

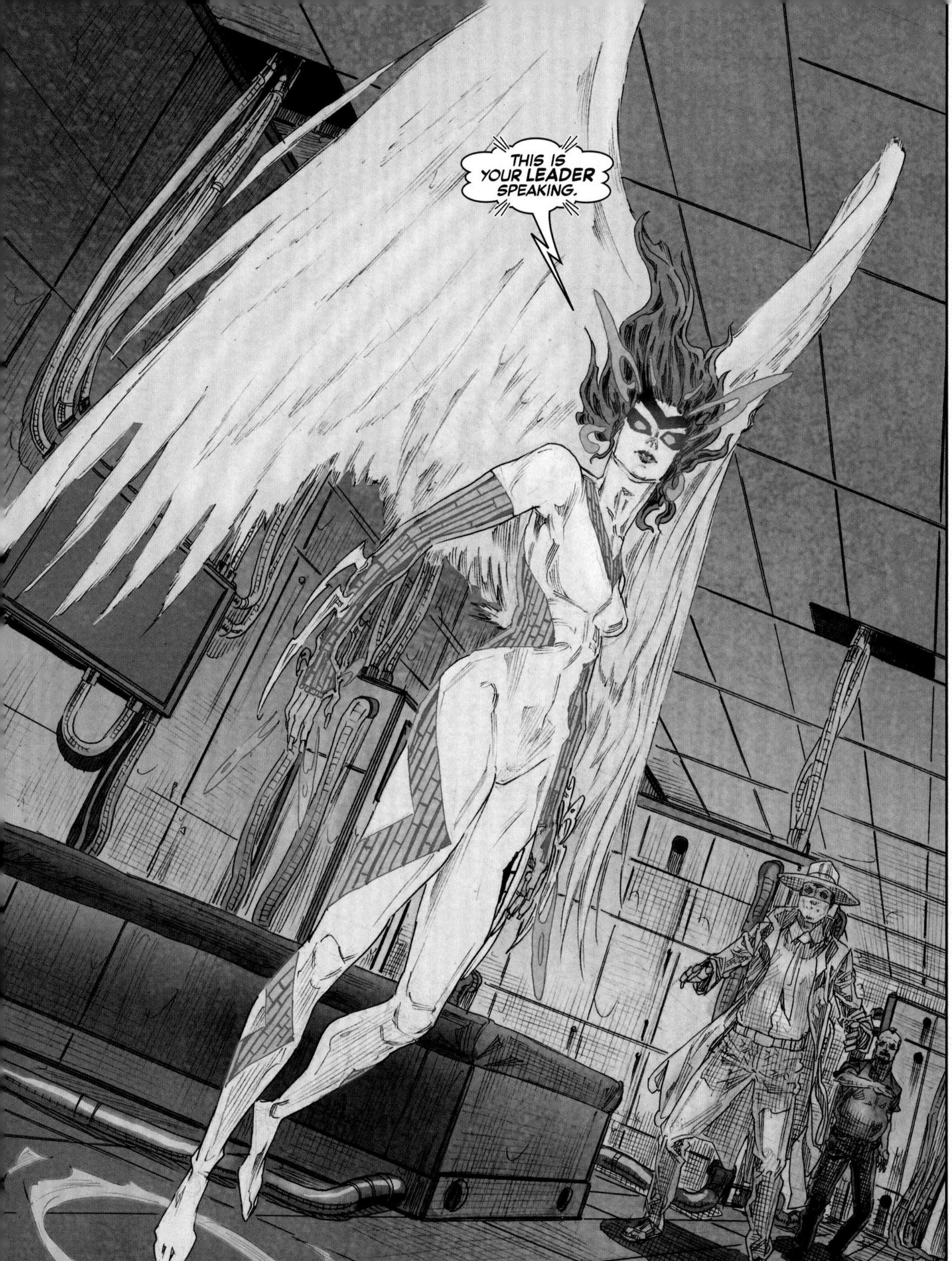
THIS IS YOUR LEADER SPEAKING.

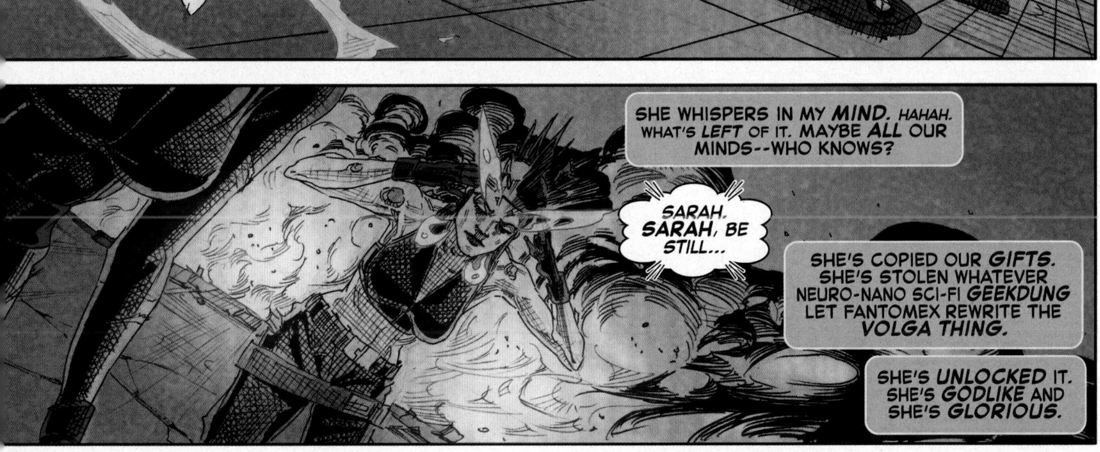
SHE WHISPERS IN MY MIND. HAHAH. WHAT'S LEFT OF IT. MAYBE ALL OUR MINDS--WHO KNOWS?
SARAH. SARAH, BE STILL...
SHE'S COPIED OUR GIFTS. SHE'S STOLEN WHATEVER NEURO-NANO SCI-FI GEEKDUNG LET FANTOMEX REWRITE THE VOLGA THING.
SHE'S UNLOCKED IT. SHE'S GODLIKE AND SHE'S GLORIOUS.

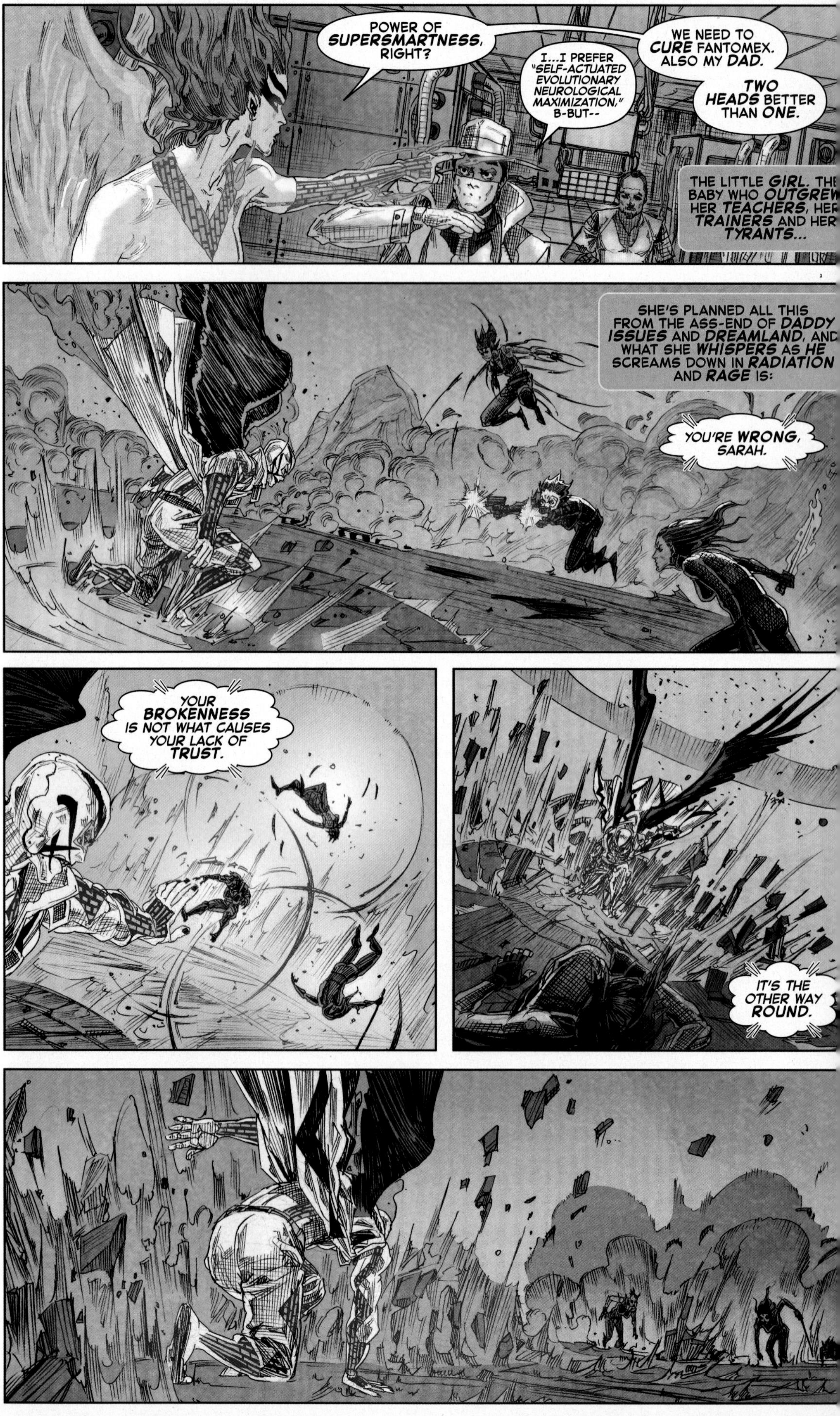
POWER OF SUPERSMARTNESS, RIGHT?
I...I PREFER "SELF-ACTUATED EVOLUTIONARY NEUROLOGICAL MAXIMIZATION," B-BUT--
WE NEED TO CURE FANTOMEX. ALSO MY DAD.
TWO HEADS BETTER THAN ONE.
THE LITTLE GIRL. THE BABY WHO OUTGREW HER TEACHERS, HER TRAINERS AND HER TYRANTS...
SHE'S PLANNED ALL THIS FROM THE ASS-END OF DADDY ISSUES AND DREAMLAND, AND WHAT SHE WHISPERS AS HE SCREAMS DOWN IN RADIATION AND RAGE IS:
YOU'RE WRONG, SARAH.
YOUR BROKENNESS IS NOT WHAT CAUSES YOUR LACK OF TRUST.
IT'S THE OTHER WAY ROUND.

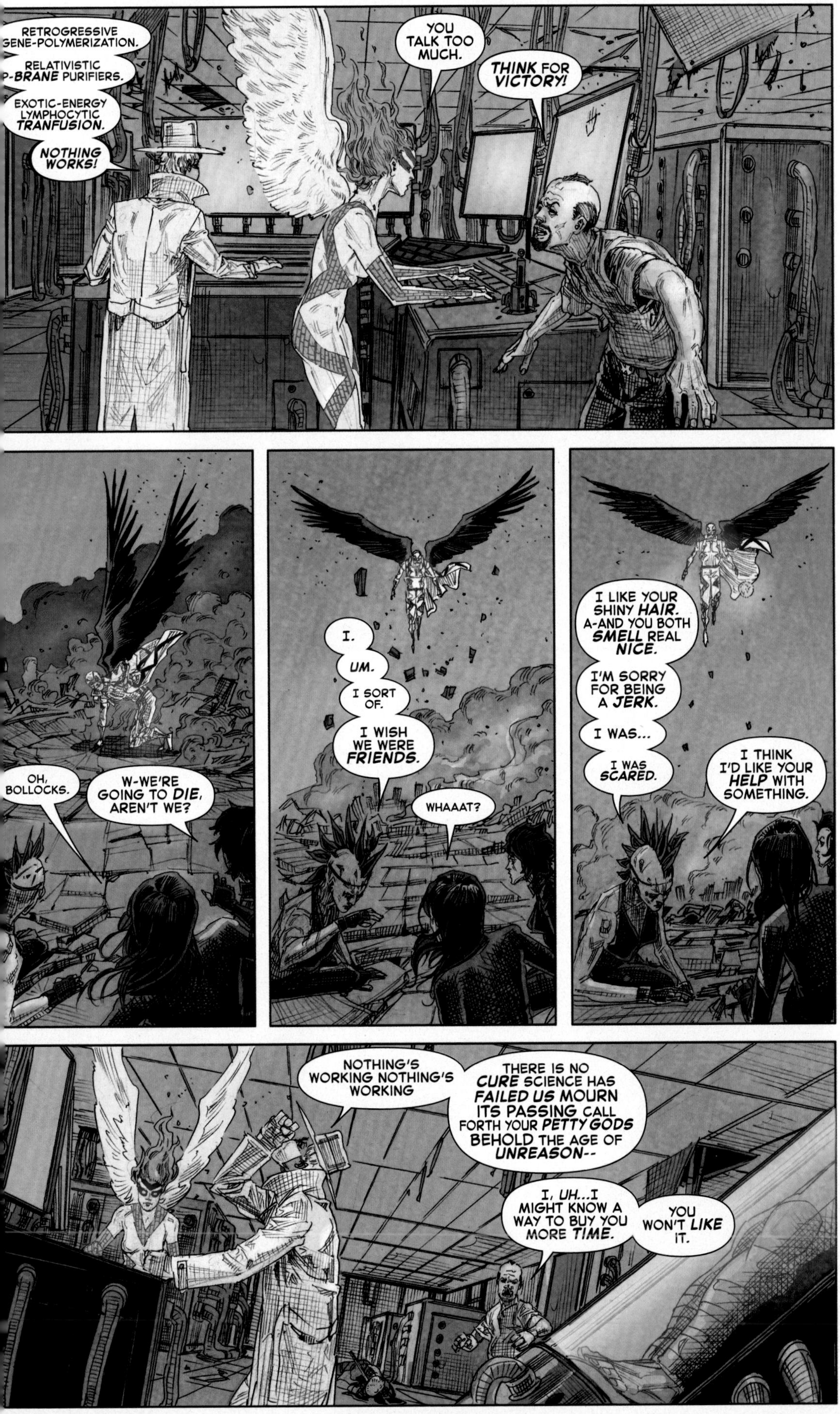
RETROGRESSIVE GENE-POLYMERIZATION.
RELATIVISTIC P-BRANE PURIFIERS.
EXOTIC-ENERGY LYMPHOCYTIC TRANFUSION.
NOTHING WORKS!
YOU TALK TOO MUCH.
THINK FOR VICTORY!
OH, BOLLOCKS.
W-WE'RE GOING TO DIE, AREN'T WE?
I.
UM.
I SORT OF.
I WISH WE WERE FRIENDS.
WHAAAT?
I LIKE YOUR SHINY HAIR. A-AND YOU BOTH SMELL REAL NICE.
I'M SORRY FOR BEING A JERK.
I WAS...
I WAS SCARED.
I THINK I'D LIKE YOUR HELP WITH SOMETHING.
NOTHING'S WORKING NOTHING'S WORKING
THERE IS NO CURE SCIENCE HAS FAILED US MOURN ITS PASSING CALL FORTH YOUR PETTY GODS BEHOLD THE AGE OF UNREASON--
I, UH...I MIGHT KNOW A WAY TO BUY YOU MORE TIME.
YOU WON'T LIKE IT.

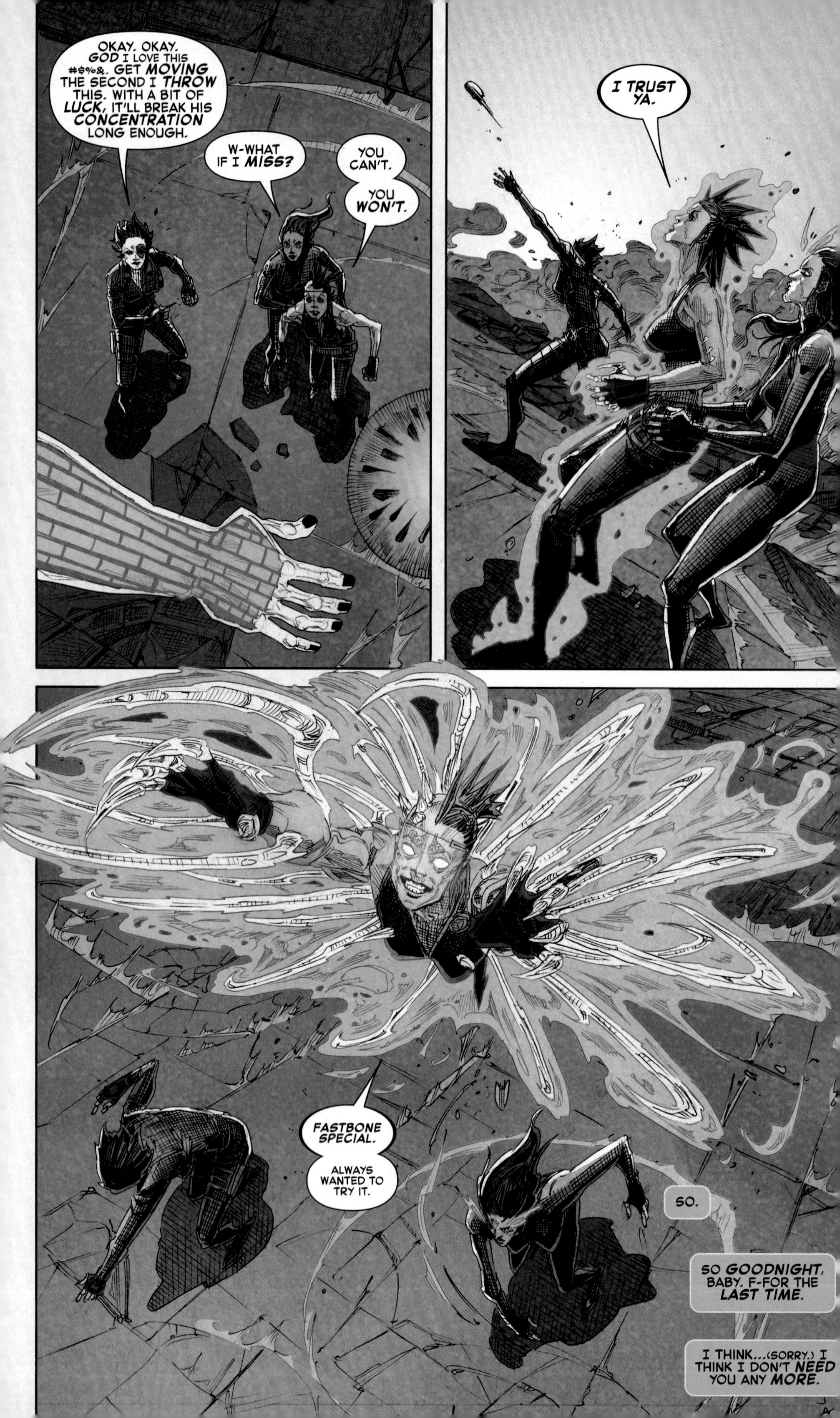
OKAY. OKAY. GOD I LOVE THIS #$%&. GET MOVING THE SECOND I THROW THIS. WITH A BIT OF LUCK, IT'LL BREAK HIS CONCENTRATION LONG ENOUGH.
W-WHAT IF I MISS?
YOU CAN'T.
YOU WON'T.
I TRUST YA.
FASTBONE SPECIAL.
ALWAYS WANTED TO TRY IT.
SO.
SO GOODNIGHT, BABY. F-FOR THE LAST TIME.
I THINK...(SORRY.) I THINK I DON'T NEED YOU ANY MORE.

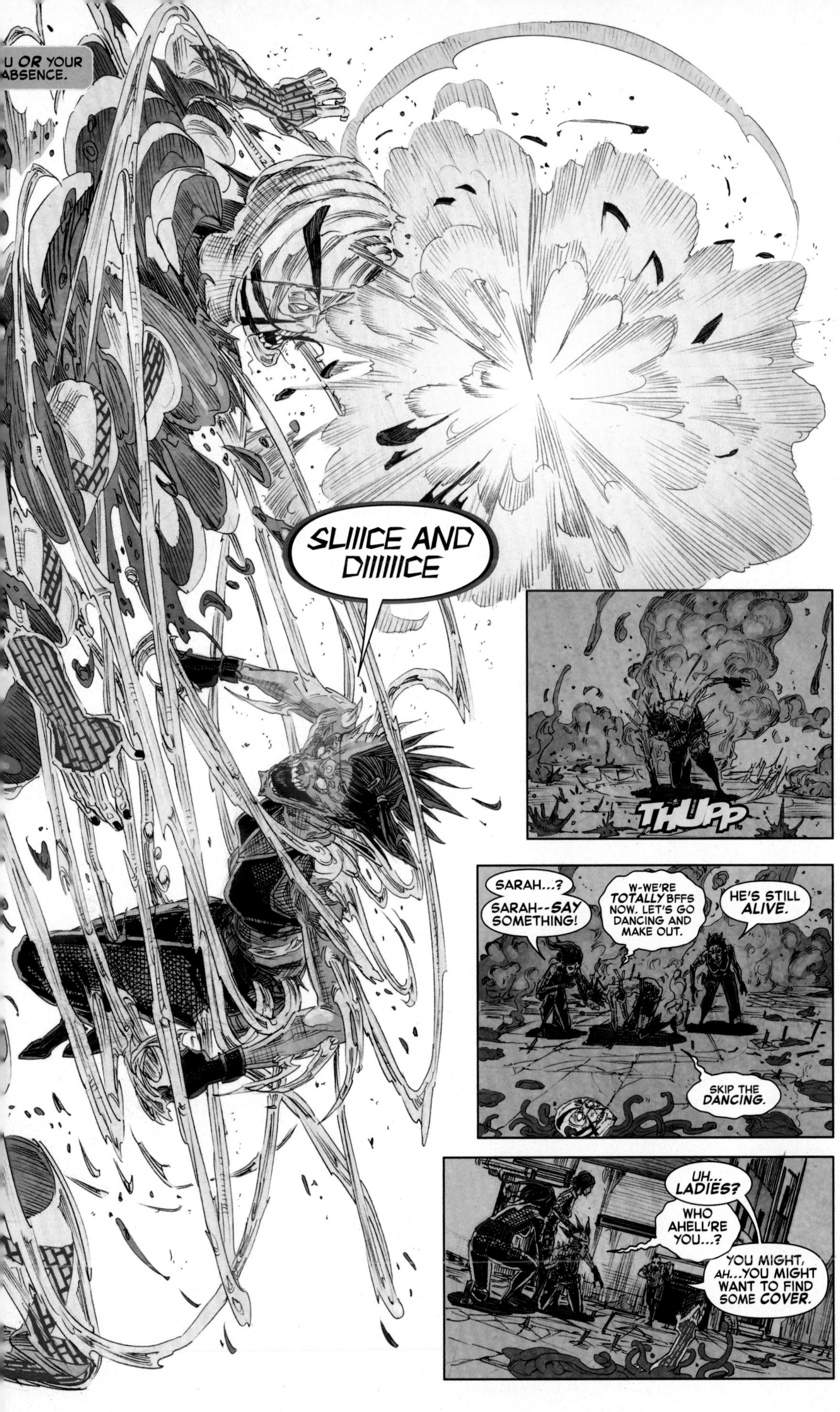
U OR YOUR
ABSENCE.
SLIIICE AND DIIIIIICE
THUPP
SARAH...?
SARAH--SAY SOMETHING!
W-WE'RE TOTALLY BFFS NOW. LET'S GO DANCING AND MAKE OUT.
HE'S STILL ALIVE.
SKIP THE DANCING.
UH... LADIES?
WHO AHELL'RE YOU...?
YOU MIGHT, AH...YOU MIGHT WANT TO FIND SOME COVER.

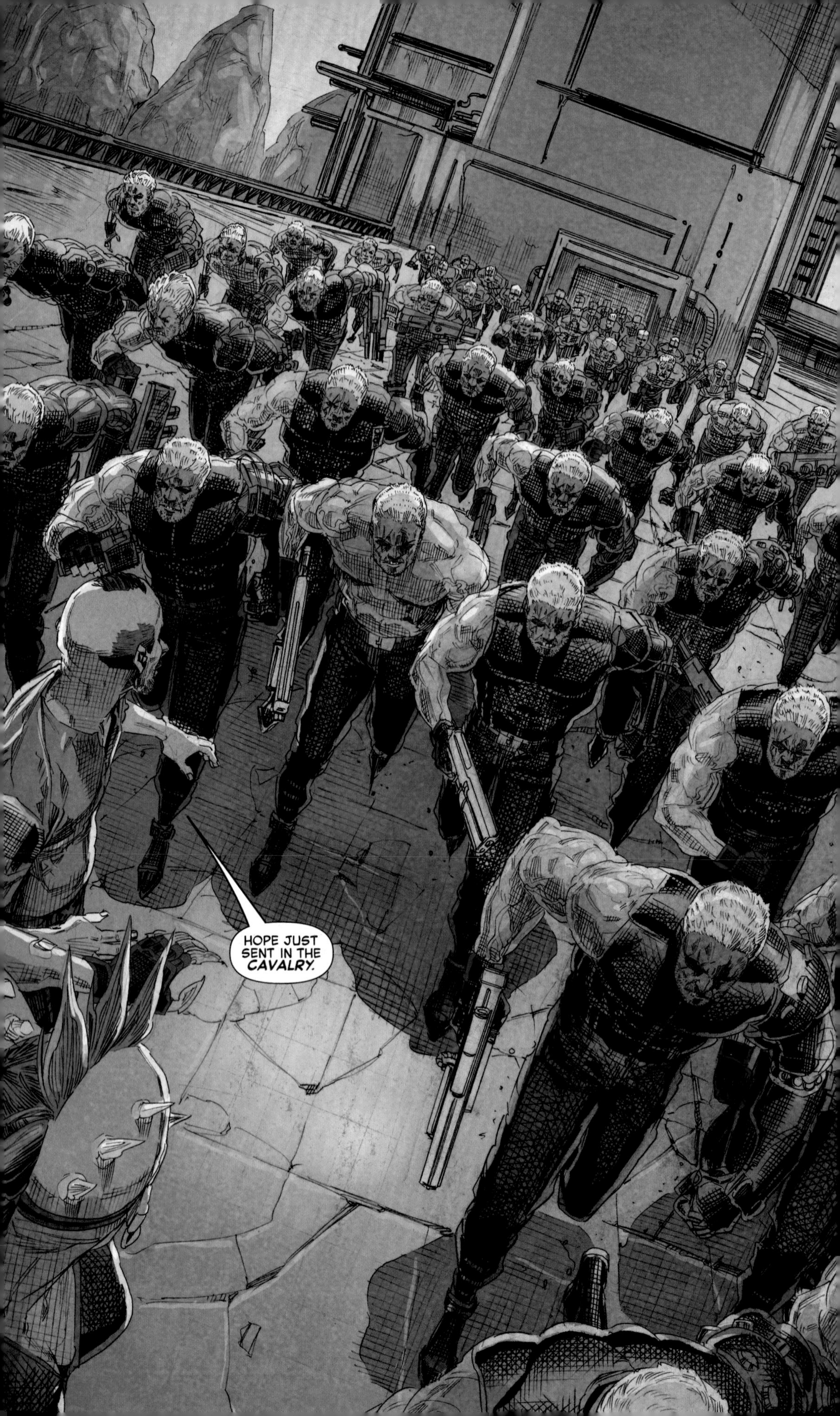
HOPE JUST SENT IN THE CAVALRY.

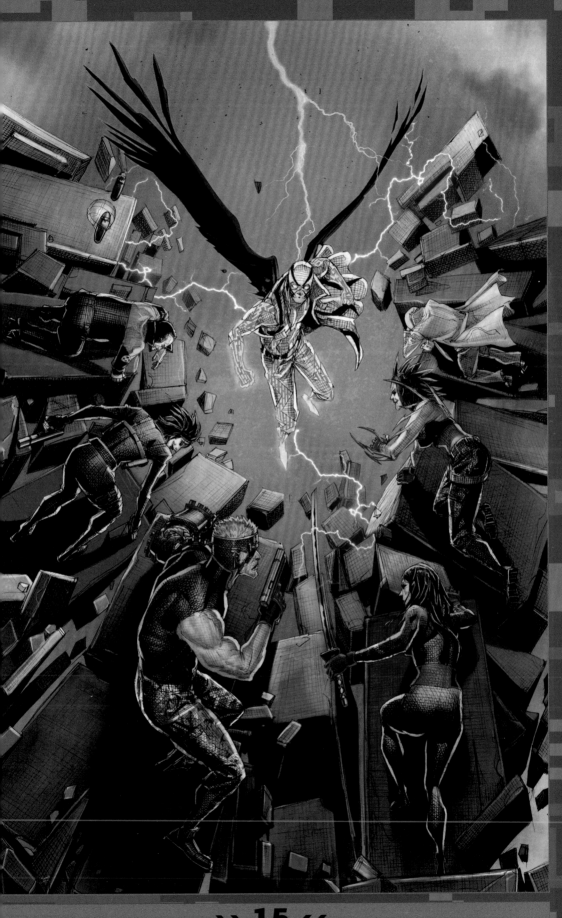

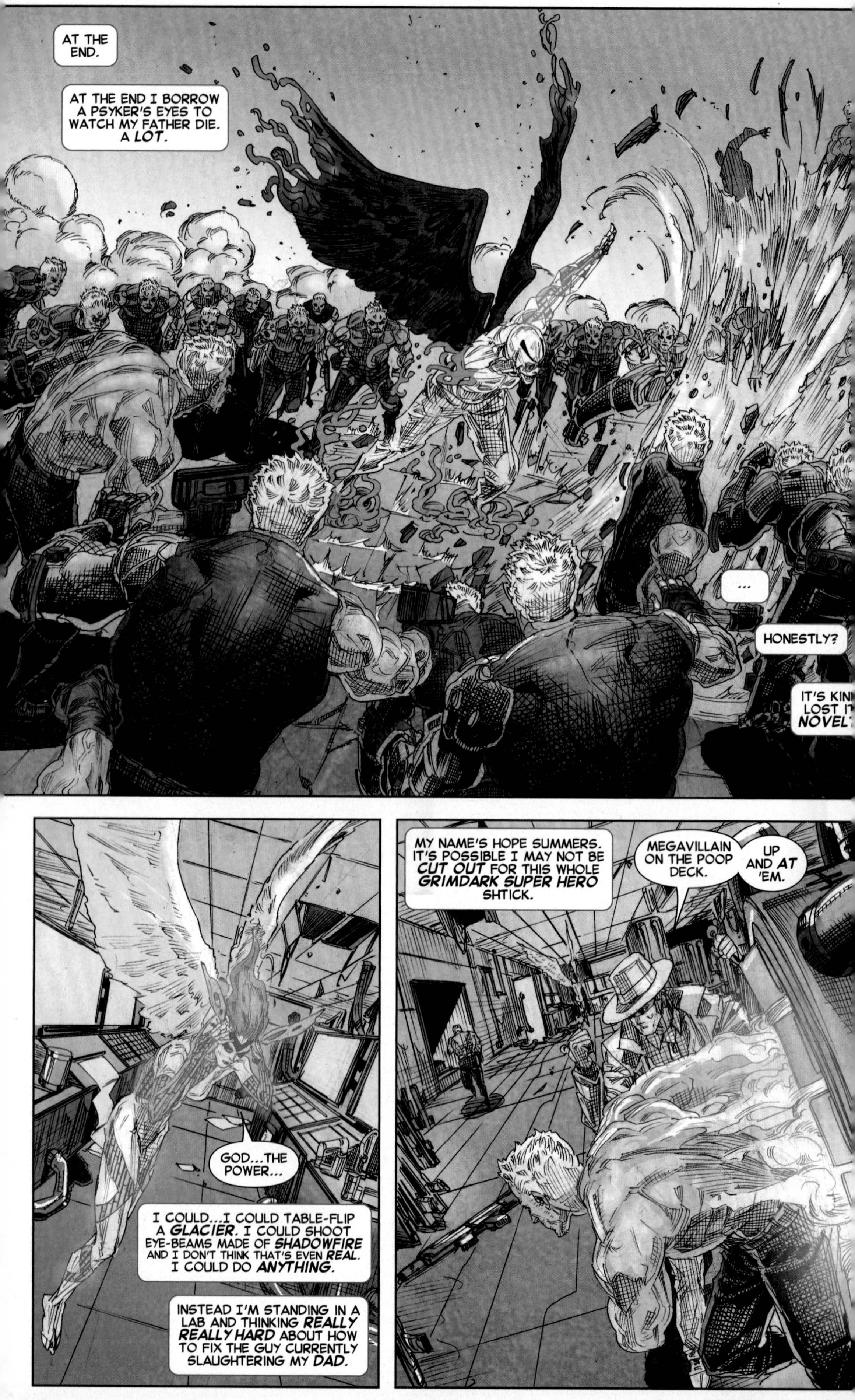
AT THE END.
AT THE END I BORROW A PSYKER'S EYES TO WATCH MY FATHER DIE. A *LOT*.
...
HONESTLY?
IT'S KIN LOST IT NOVEL
GOD... THE POWER...
I COULD... I COULD TABLE-FLIP A *GLACIER*. I COULD SHOOT EYE-BEAMS MADE OF *SHADOWFIRE* AND I DON'T THINK THAT'S EVEN *REAL*. I COULD DO *ANYTHING*.
INSTEAD I'M STANDING IN A LAB AND THINKING *REALLY REALLY HARD* ABOUT HOW TO FIX THE GUY CURRENTLY SLAUGHTERING MY *DAD*.
MY NAME'S HOPE SUMMERS. IT'S POSSIBLE I MAY NOT BE *CUT OUT* FOR THIS WHOLE *GRIMDARK SUPER HERO* SHTICK.
MEGAVILLAIN ON THE POOP DECK.
UP AND *AT* 'EM.

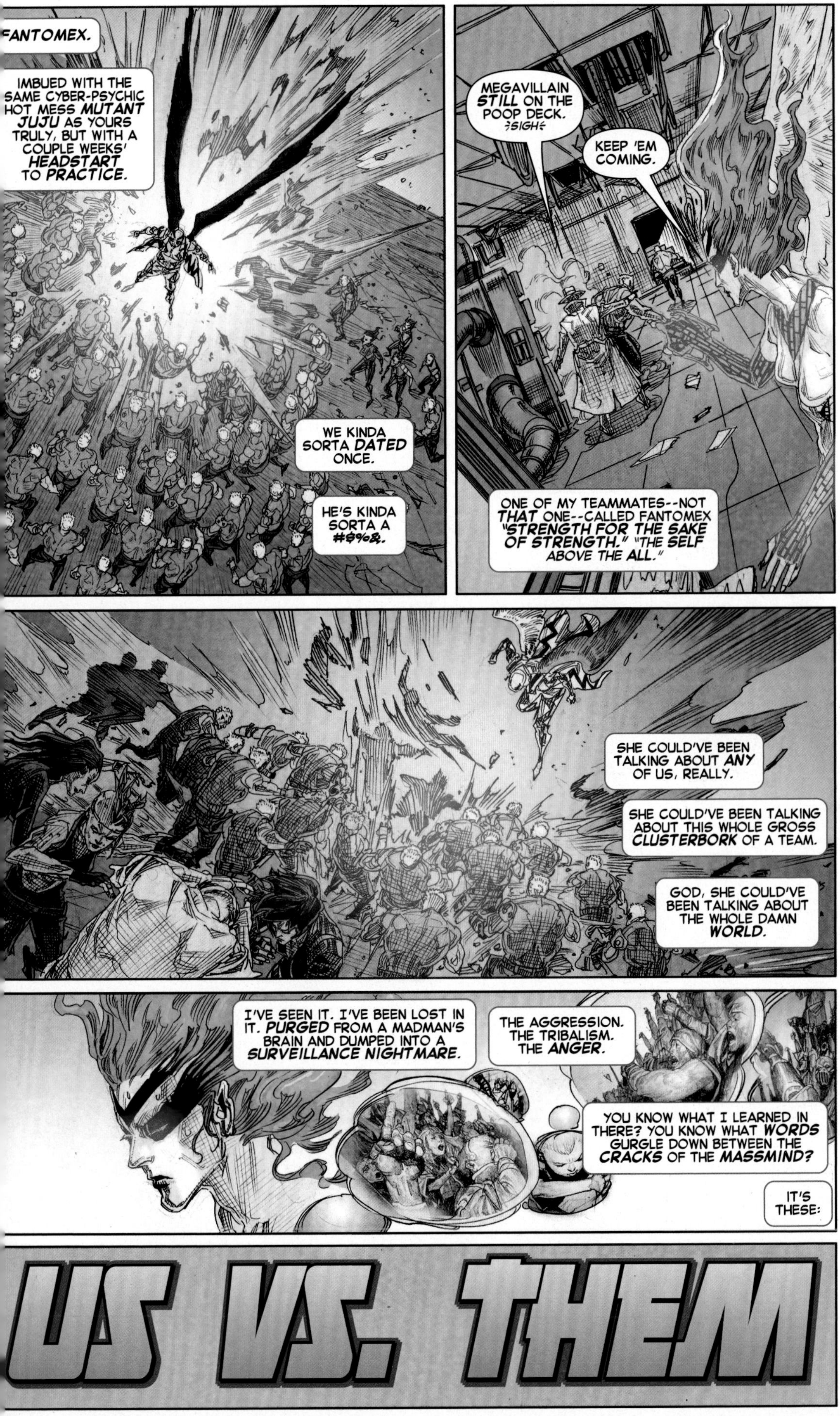
FANTOMEX.
IMBUED WITH THE SAME CYBER-PSYCHIC HOT MESS MUTANT JUJU AS YOURS TRULY, BUT WITH A COUPLE WEEKS' HEADSTART TO PRACTICE.
WE KINDA SORTA DATED ONCE.
HE'S KINDA SORTA A #$%&.
MEGAVILLAIN STILL ON THE POOP DECK. ƎSIGHƐ
KEEP 'EM COMING.
ONE OF MY TEAMMATES--NOT THAT ONE--CALLED FANTOMEX "STRENGTH FOR THE SAKE OF STRENGTH." "THE SELF ABOVE THE ALL."
SHE COULD'VE BEEN TALKING ABOUT ANY OF US, REALLY.
SHE COULD'VE BEEN TALKING ABOUT THIS WHOLE GROSS CLUSTERBORK OF A TEAM.
GOD, SHE COULD'VE BEEN TALKING ABOUT THE WHOLE DAMN WORLD.
I'VE SEEN IT. I'VE BEEN LOST IN IT. PURGED FROM A MADMAN'S BRAIN AND DUMPED INTO A SURVEILLANCE NIGHTMARE.
THE AGGRESSION. THE TRIBALISM. THE ANGER.
YOU KNOW WHAT I LEARNED IN THERE? YOU KNOW WHAT WORDS GURGLE DOWN BETWEEN THE CRACKS OF THE MASSMIND?
IT'S THESE:
US VS. THEM

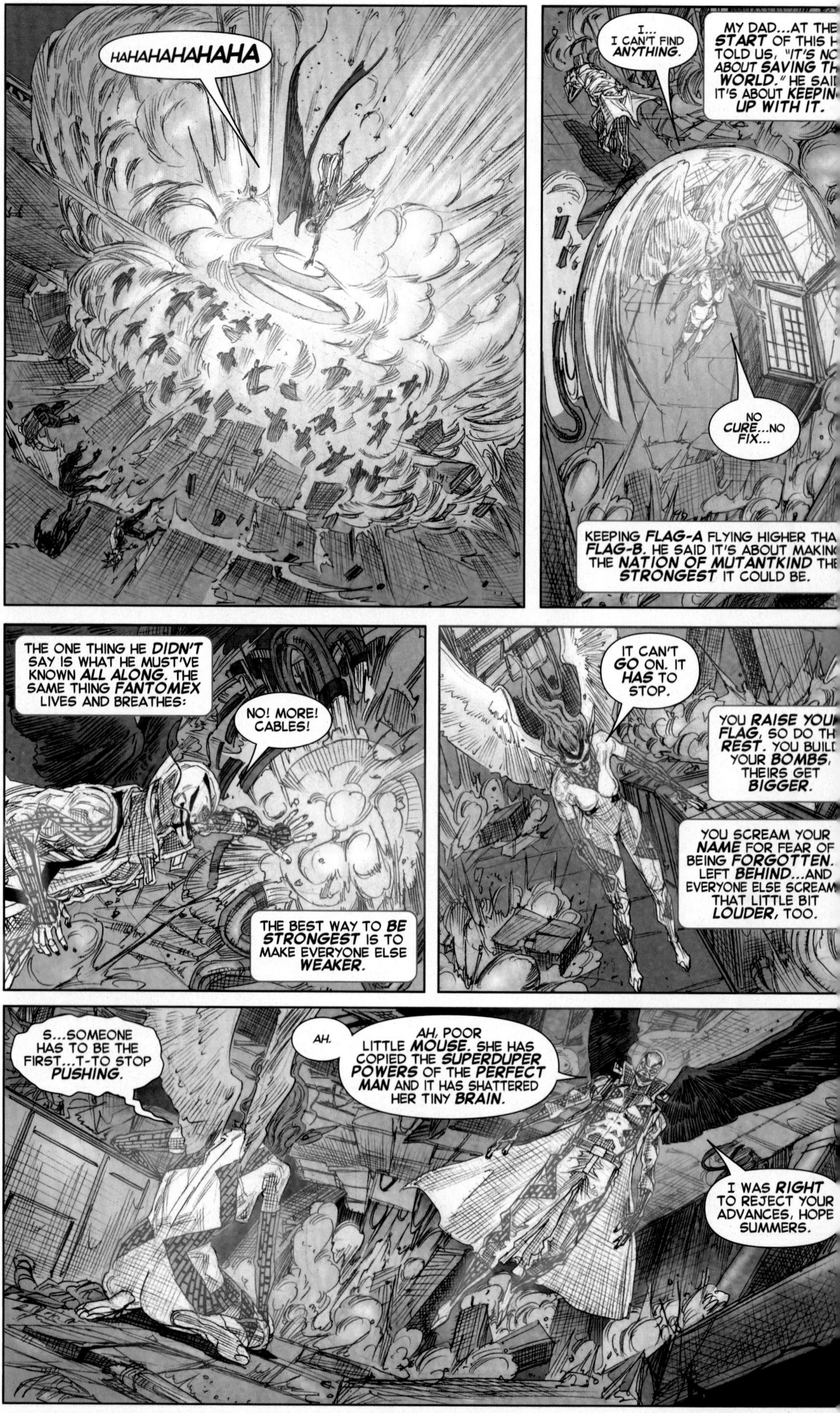

HAHAHAHAHAHA
I... I CAN'T FIND ANYTHING.
MY DAD...AT THE START OF THIS H TOLD US, "IT'S NO ABOUT SAVING TH WORLD." HE SAID IT'S ABOUT KEEPIN UP WITH IT.
NO CURE...NO FIX...
KEEPING FLAG-A FLYING HIGHER THA FLAG-B. HE SAID IT'S ABOUT MAKIN THE NATION OF MUTANTKIND TH STRONGEST IT COULD BE.
THE ONE THING HE DIDN'T SAY IS WHAT HE MUST'VE KNOWN ALL ALONG. THE SAME THING FANTOMEX LIVES AND BREATHES:
NO! MORE! CABLES!
THE BEST WAY TO BE STRONGEST IS TO MAKE EVERYONE ELSE WEAKER.
IT CAN'T GO ON. IT HAS TO STOP.
YOU RAISE YOU FLAG, SO DO TH REST. YOU BUIL YOUR BOMBS, THEIRS GET BIGGER.
YOU SCREAM YOUR NAME FOR FEAR OF BEING FORGOTTEN. LEFT BEHIND...AND EVERYONE ELSE SCREAM THAT LITTLE BIT LOUDER, TOO.
S...SOMEONE HAS TO BE THE FIRST...T-TO STOP PUSHING.
AH.
AH, POOR LITTLE MOUSE. SHE HAS COPIED THE SUPERDUPER POWERS OF THE PERFECT MAN AND IT HAS SHATTERED HER TINY BRAIN.
I WAS RIGHT TO REJECT YOUR ADVANCES, HOPE SUMMERS.

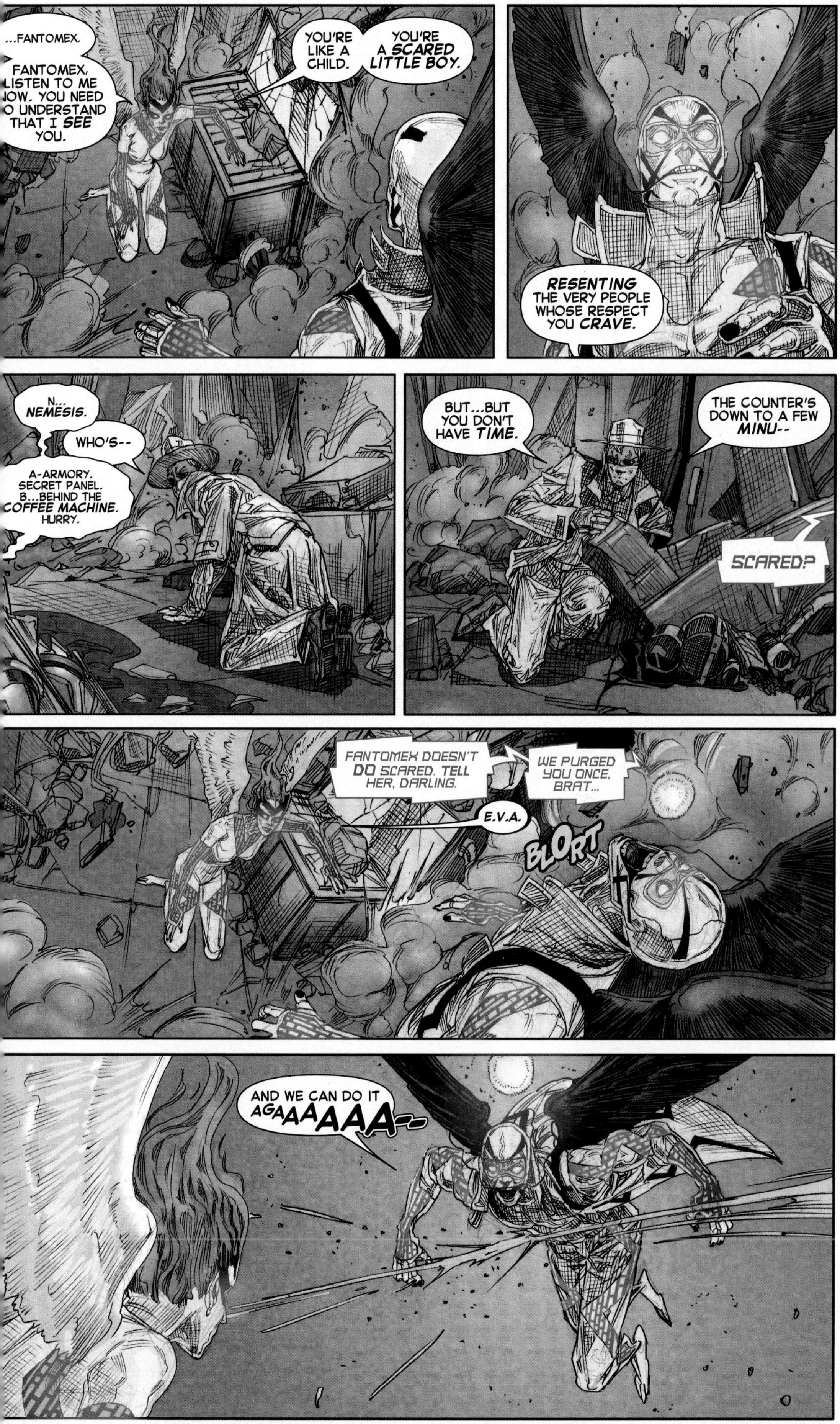
...FANTOMEX.
FANTOMEX, LISTEN TO ME NOW. YOU NEED TO UNDERSTAND THAT I SEE YOU.
YOU'RE LIKE A CHILD.
YOU'RE A SCARED LITTLE BOY.
RESENTING THE VERY PEOPLE WHOSE RESPECT YOU CRAVE.
N... NEMESIS.
WHO'S--
A-ARMORY. SECRET PANEL. B...BEHIND THE COFFEE MACHINE. HURRY.
BUT...BUT YOU DON'T HAVE TIME.
THE COUNTER'S DOWN TO A FEW MINU--
SCARED?
FANTOMEX DOESN'T DO SCARED. TELL HER, DARLING.
WE PURGED YOU ONCE, BRAT...
E.V.A.
BLORT
AND WE CAN DO IT AGAAAAAA--

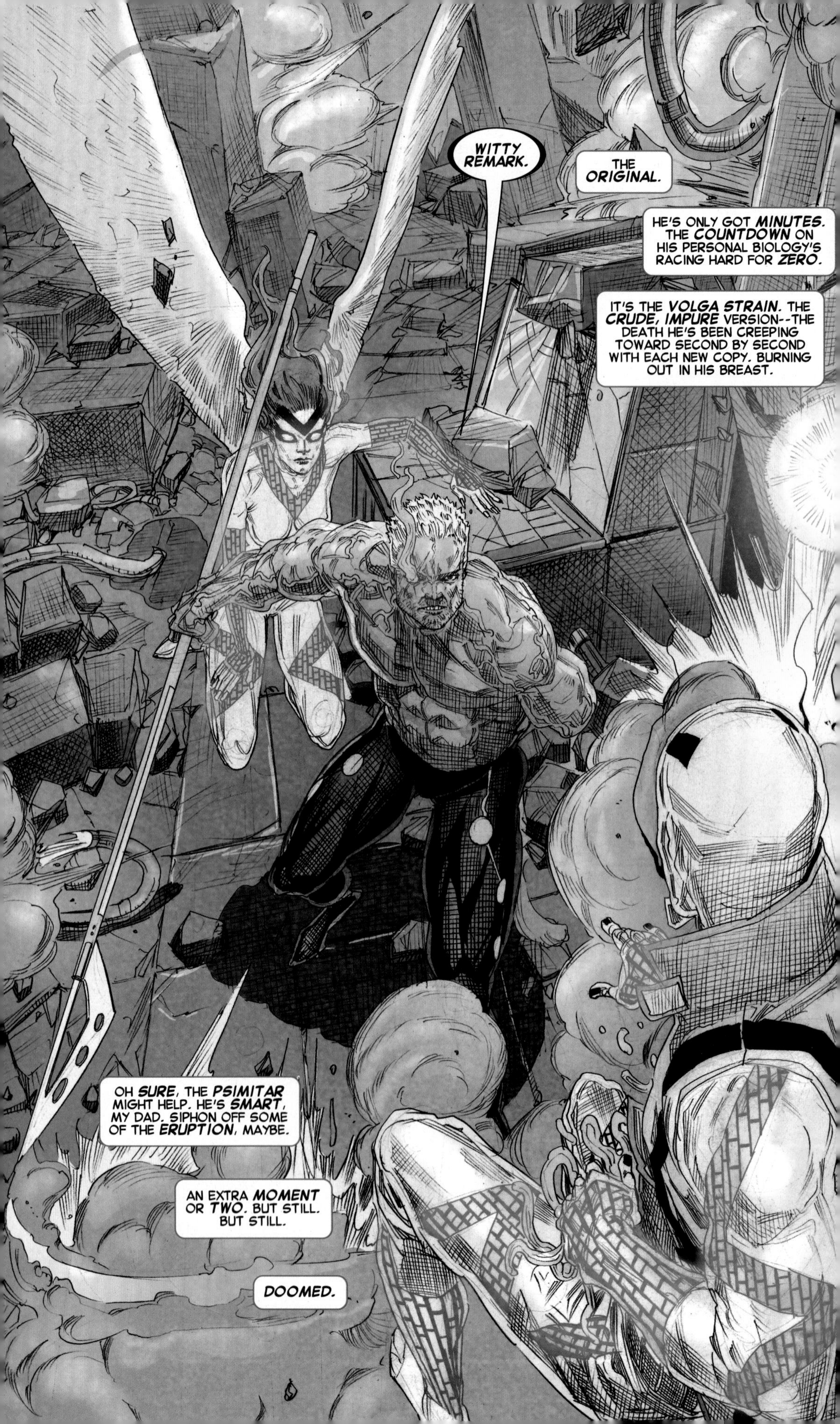
WITTY REMARK.
THE ORIGINAL.
HE'S ONLY GOT MINUTES. THE COUNTDOWN ON HIS PERSONAL BIOLOGY'S RACING HARD FOR ZERO.
IT'S THE VOLGA STRAIN. THE CRUDE, IMPURE VERSION--THE DEATH HE'S BEEN CREEPING TOWARD SECOND BY SECOND WITH EACH NEW COPY. BURNING OUT IN HIS BREAST.
OH SURE, THE PSIMITAR MIGHT HELP. HE'S SMART, MY DAD. SIPHON OFF SOME OF THE ERUPTION, MAYBE.
AN EXTRA MOMENT OR TWO. BUT STILL. BUT STILL.
DOOMED.

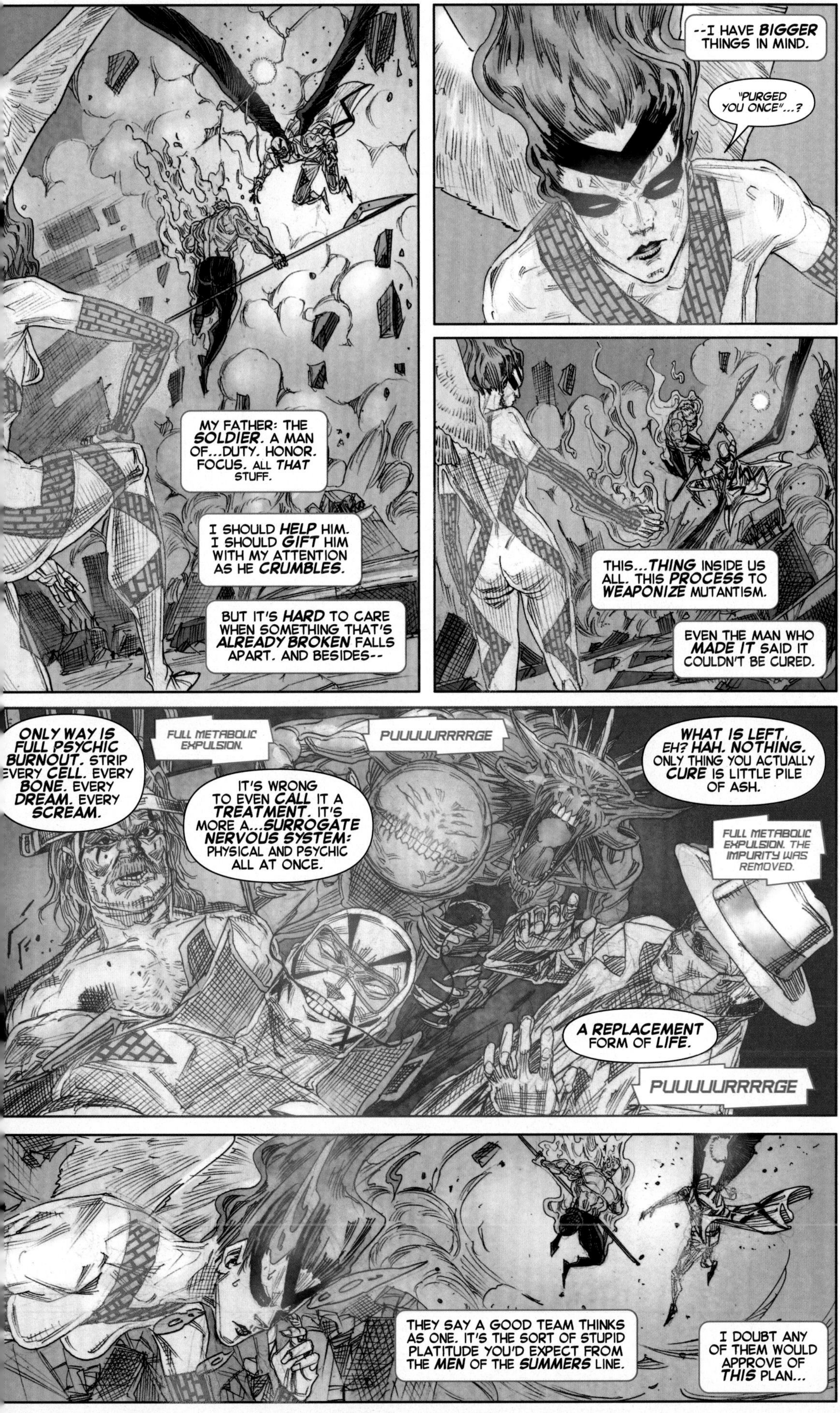
MY FATHER: THE SOLDIER. A MAN OF...DUTY. HONOR. FOCUS. ALL THAT STUFF.
I SHOULD HELP HIM. I SHOULD GIFT HIM WITH MY ATTENTION AS HE CRUMBLES.
BUT IT'S HARD TO CARE WHEN SOMETHING THAT'S ALREADY BROKEN FALLS APART. AND BESIDES--
--I HAVE BIGGER THINGS IN MIND.
"PURGED YOU ONCE"...?
THIS...THING INSIDE US ALL. THIS PROCESS TO WEAPONIZE MUTANTISM.
EVEN THE MAN WHO MADE IT SAID IT COULDN'T BE CURED.
ONLY WAY IS FULL PSYCHIC BURNOUT. STRIP EVERY CELL. EVERY BONE. EVERY DREAM. EVERY SCREAM.
FULL METABOLIC EXPULSION.
PUUUUURRRRGE
IT'S WRONG TO EVEN CALL IT A TREATMENT. IT'S MORE A...SURROGATE NERVOUS SYSTEM: PHYSICAL AND PSYCHIC ALL AT ONCE.
WHAT IS LEFT, EH? HAH. NOTHING. ONLY THING YOU ACTUALLY CURE IS LITTLE PILE OF ASH.
FULL METABOLIC EXPULSION. THE IMPURITY WAS REMOVED.
A REPLACEMENT FORM OF LIFE.
PUUUUURRRRGE
THEY SAY A GOOD TEAM THINKS AS ONE. IT'S THE SORT OF STUPID PLATITUDE YOU'D EXPECT FROM THE MEN OF THE SUMMERS LINE.
I DOUBT ANY OF THEM WOULD APPROVE OF THIS PLAN...

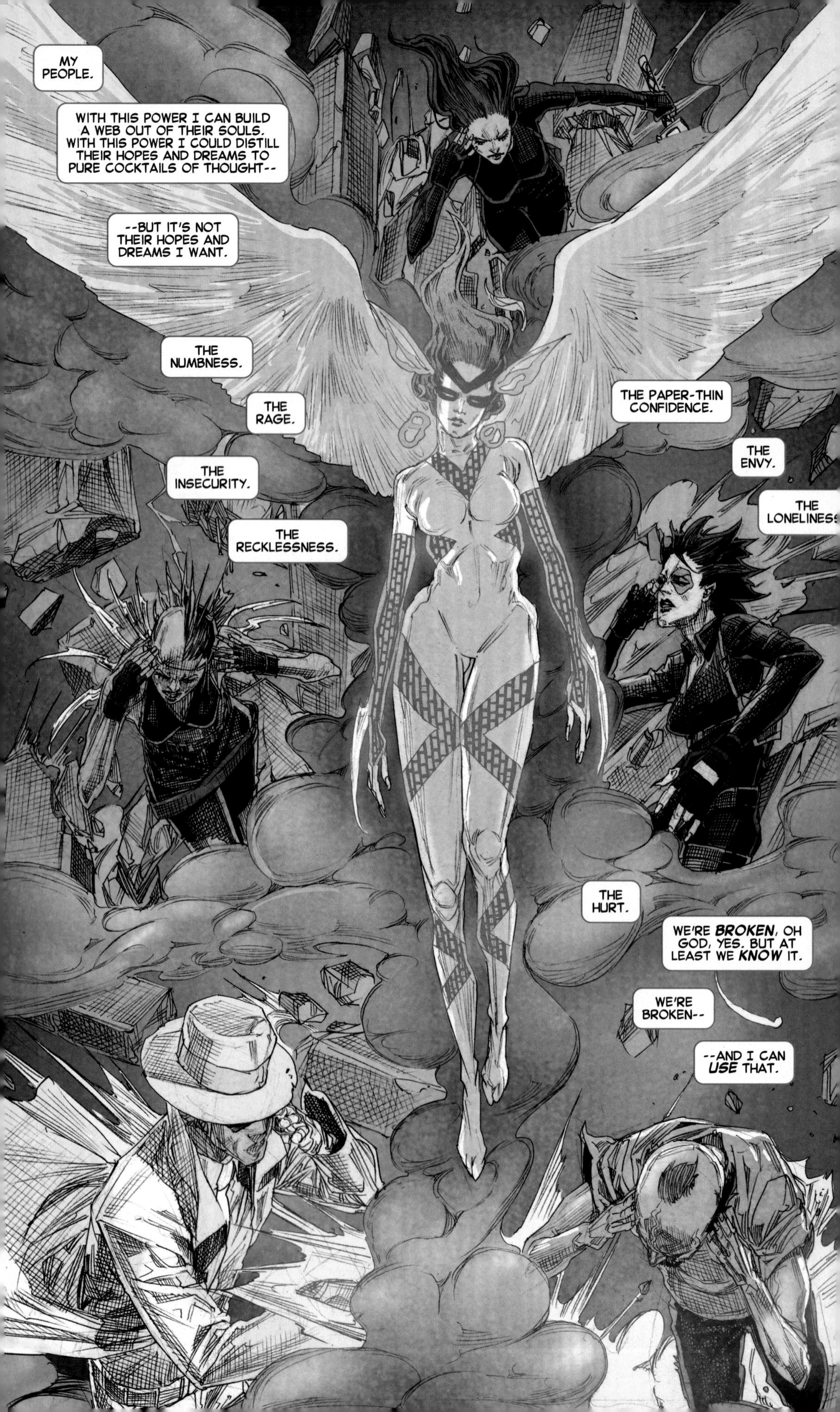
MY PEOPLE.
WITH THIS POWER I CAN BUILD A WEB OUT OF THEIR SOULS. WITH THIS POWER I COULD DISTILL THEIR HOPES AND DREAMS TO PURE COCKTAILS OF THOUGHT--
--BUT IT'S NOT THEIR HOPES AND DREAMS I WANT.
THE NUMBNESS.
THE RAGE.
THE INSECURITY.
THE RECKLESSNESS.
THE PAPER-THIN CONFIDENCE.
THE ENVY.
THE LONELINESS
THE HURT.
WE'RE **BROKEN**, OH GOD, YES. BUT AT LEAST WE **KNOW** IT.
WE'RE BROKEN--
--AND I CAN **USE** THAT.

RRRRRRRRRR.

A-ANTICLIMACTIC MESSIAH-GIRL! YOUR *COPYCATTERY* WON'T LAST FOREVER. WHATEVER OBSCENE *UNSCIENCE* YOU'RE DOING I SUGG--

STAY.

AWAY.

F-FROM *ME.*

STAND *TOGETHER*--! STAND *TOGE*--

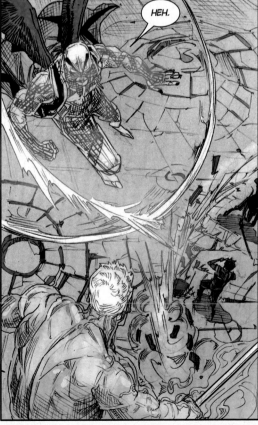

HEH.

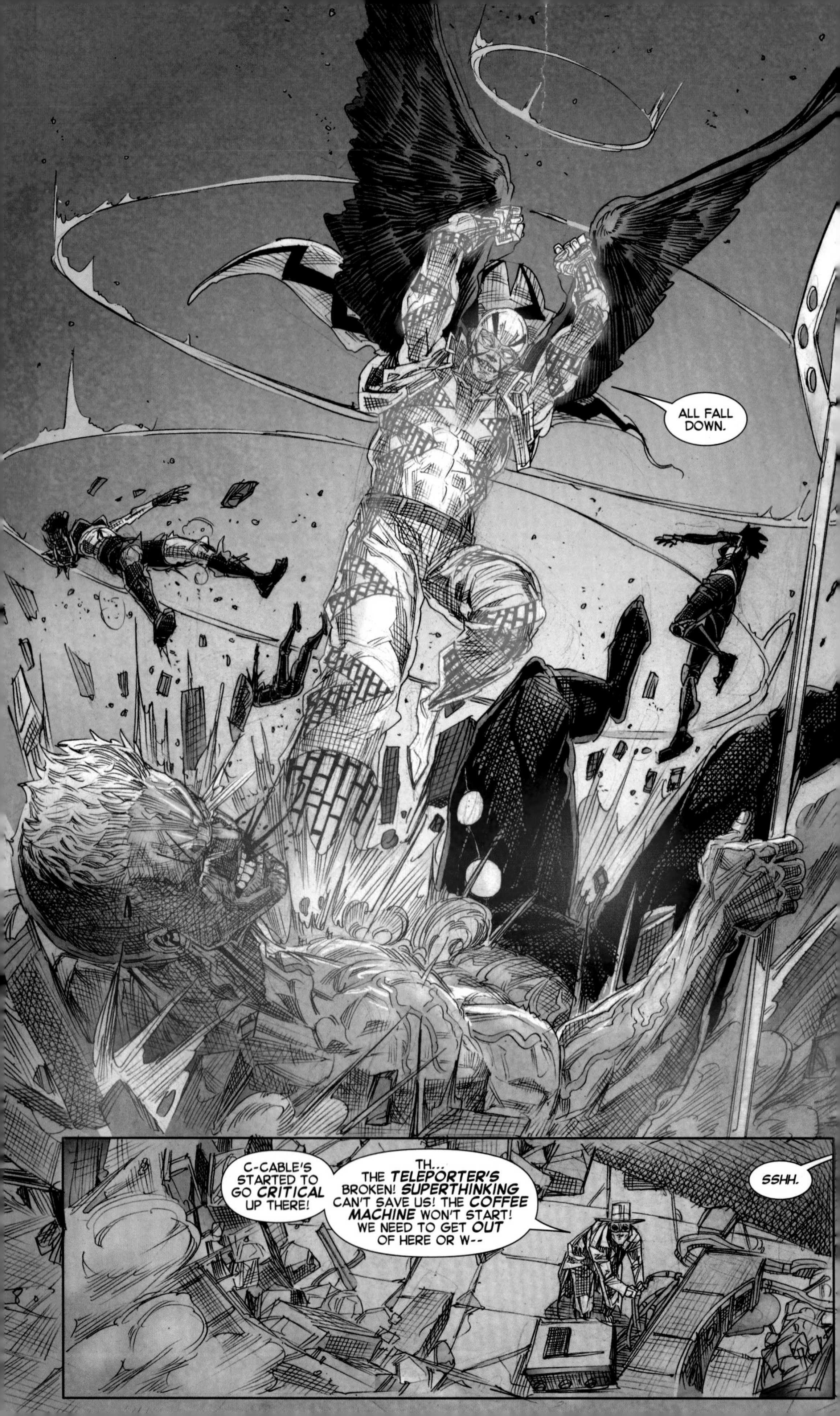
ALL FALL DOWN.
C-CABLE'S STARTED TO GO CRITICAL UP THERE!
TH... THE TELEPORTER'S BROKEN! SUPERTHINKING CAN'T SAVE US! THE COFFEE MACHINE WON'T START! WE NEED TO GET OUT OF HERE OR W--
SSHH.

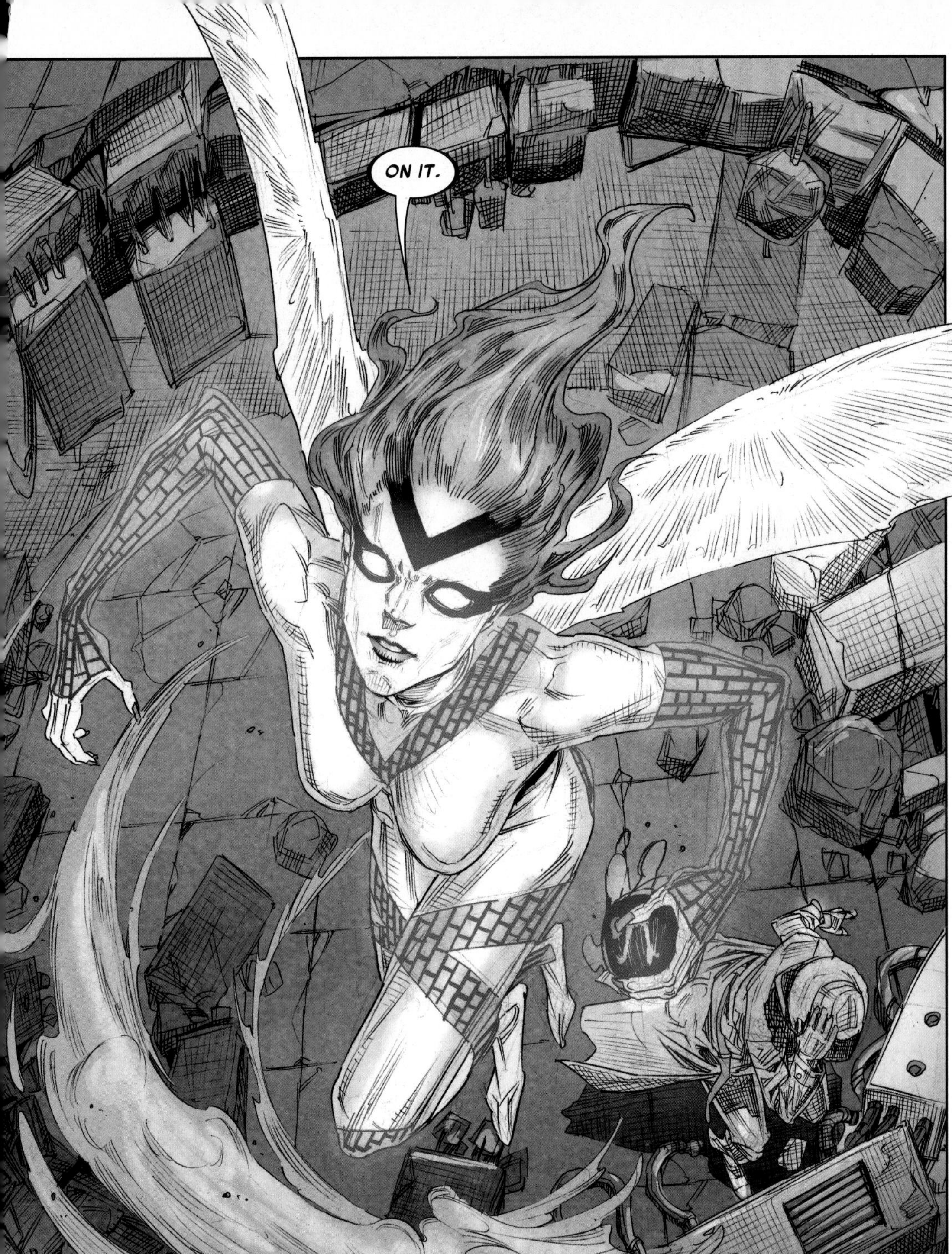
ON IT.

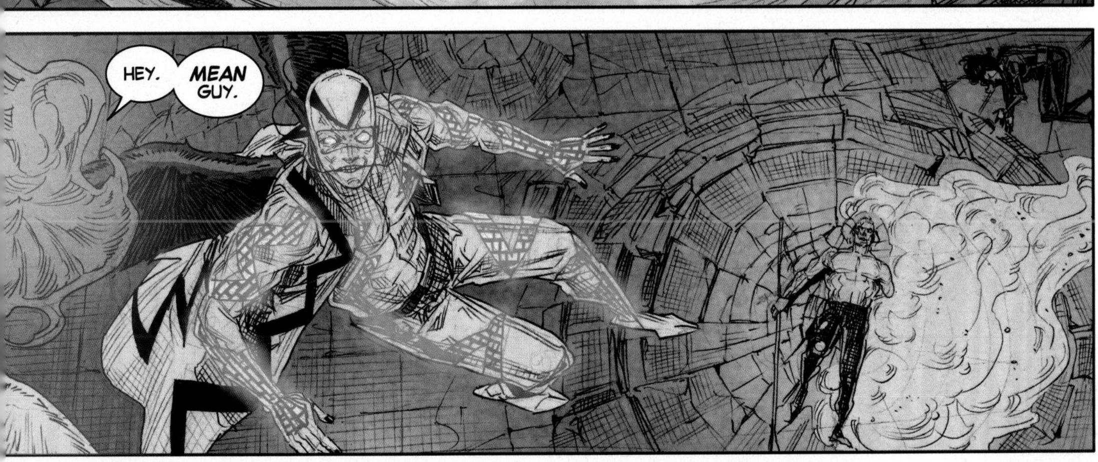
HEY.
MEAN GUY.

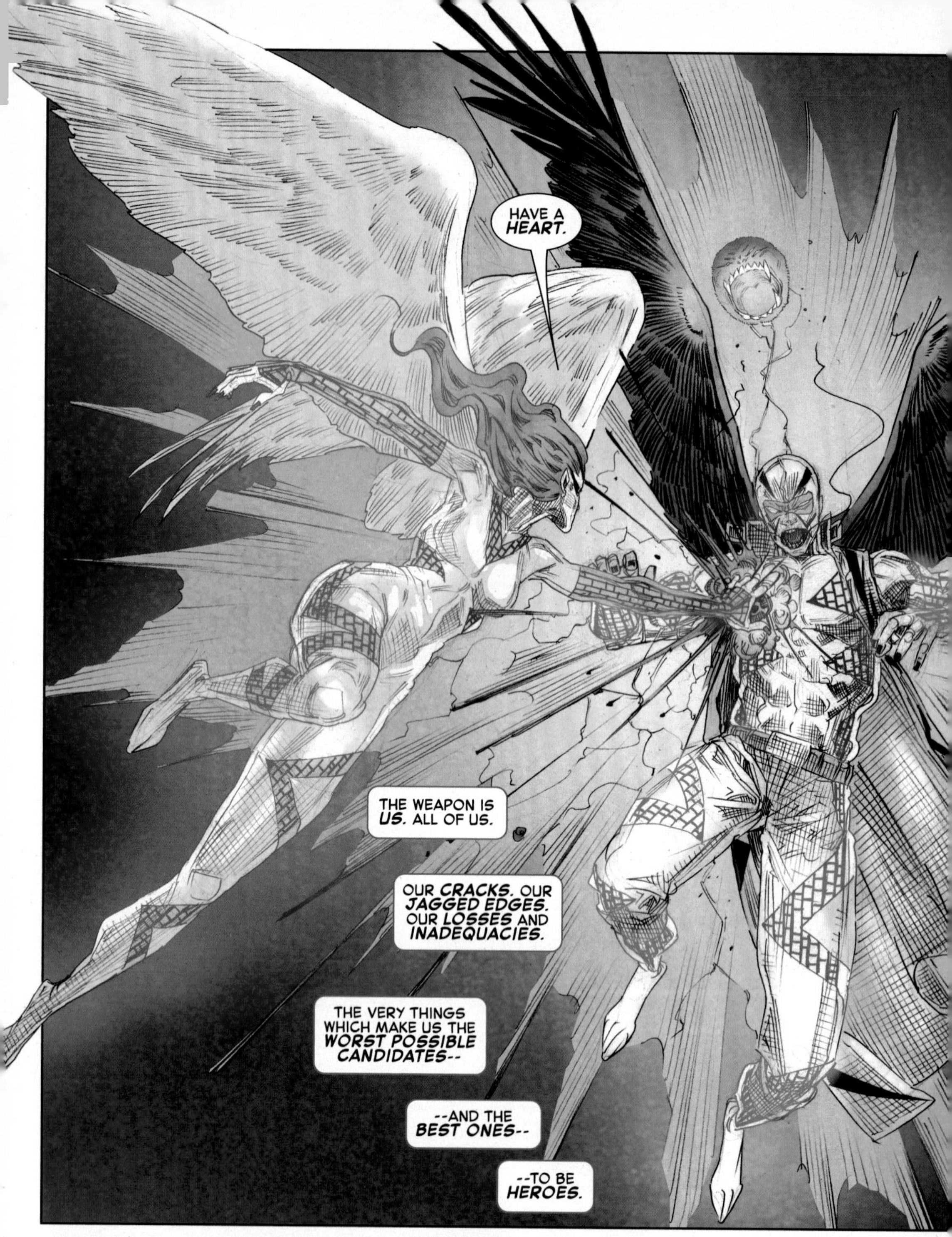
HAVE A HEART.
THE WEAPON IS US. ALL OF US.
OUR CRACKS. OUR JAGGED EDGES. OUR LOSSES AND INADEQUACIES.
THE VERY THINGS WHICH MAKE US THE WORST POSSIBLE CANDIDATES--
--AND THE BEST ONES--
--TO BE HEROES.

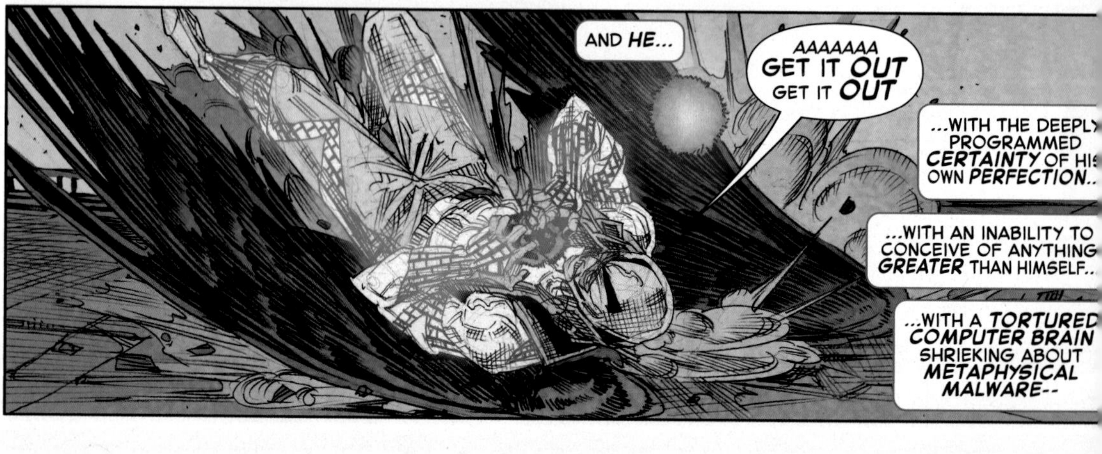
AND HE...
AAAAAAA GET IT OUT GET IT OUT
...WITH THE DEEPLY PROGRAMMED CERTAINTY OF HIS OWN PERFECTION...
...WITH AN INABILITY TO CONCEIVE OF ANYTHING GREATER THAN HIMSELF...
...WITH A TORTURED COMPUTER BRAIN SHRIEKING ABOUT METAPHYSICAL MALWARE--

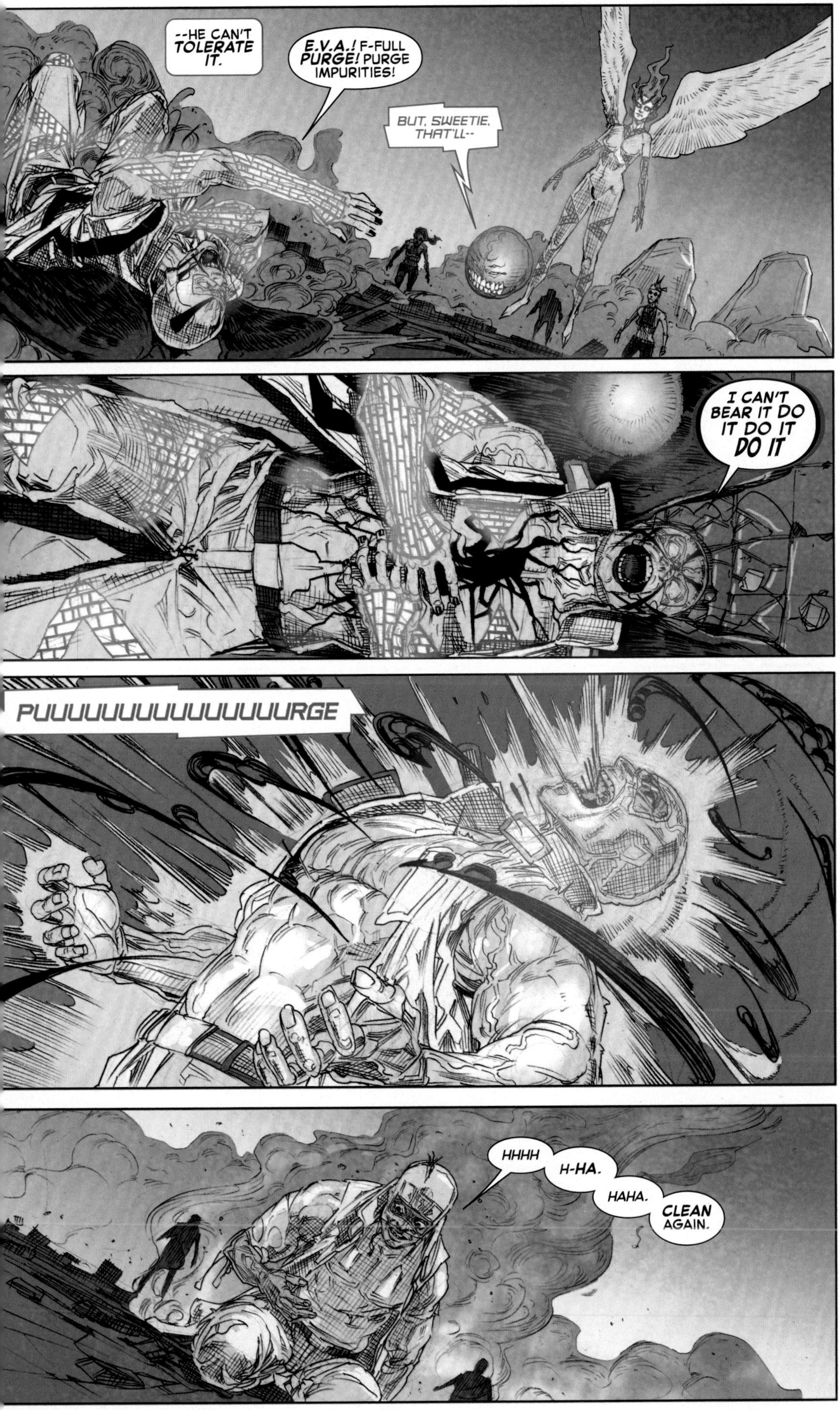
--HE CAN'T TOLERATE IT.
E.V.A.! F-FULL PURGE! PURGE IMPURITIES!
BUT, SWEETIE, THAT'LL--
I CAN'T BEAR IT DO IT DO IT DO IT
PUUUUUUUUUUUUUUURGE
HHHH
H-HA.
HAHA.
CLEAN AGAIN.

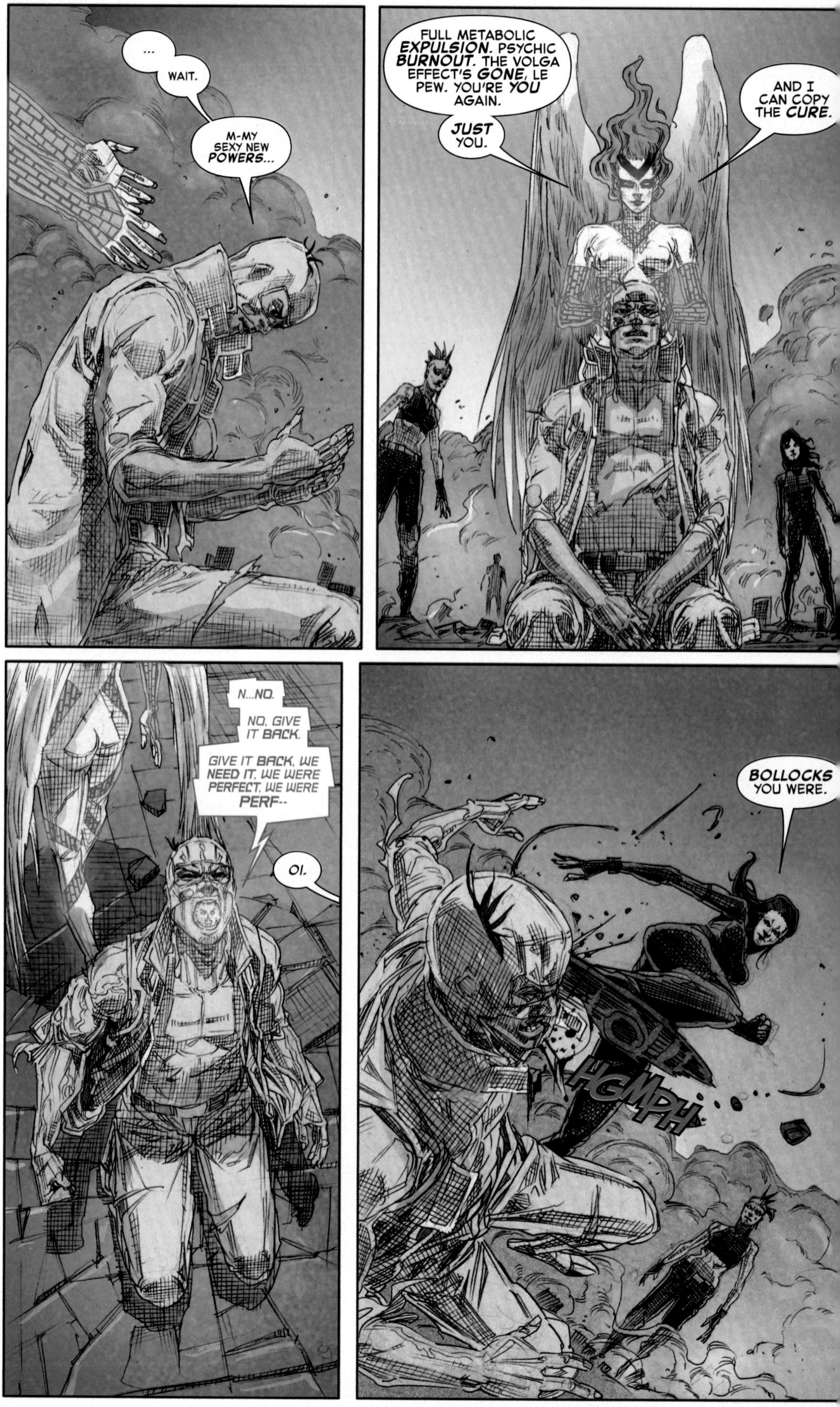
...
WAIT.
M-MY SEXY NEW POWERS...
FULL METABOLIC EXPULSION. PSYCHIC BURNOUT. THE VOLGA EFFECT'S GONE, LE PEW. YOU'RE YOU AGAIN.
JUST YOU.
AND I CAN COPY THE CURE.
N...NO.
NO, GIVE IT BACK.
GIVE IT BACK, WE NEED IT, WE WERE PERFECT, WE WERE PERF--
OI.
BOLLOCKS YOU WERE.
HGMPH

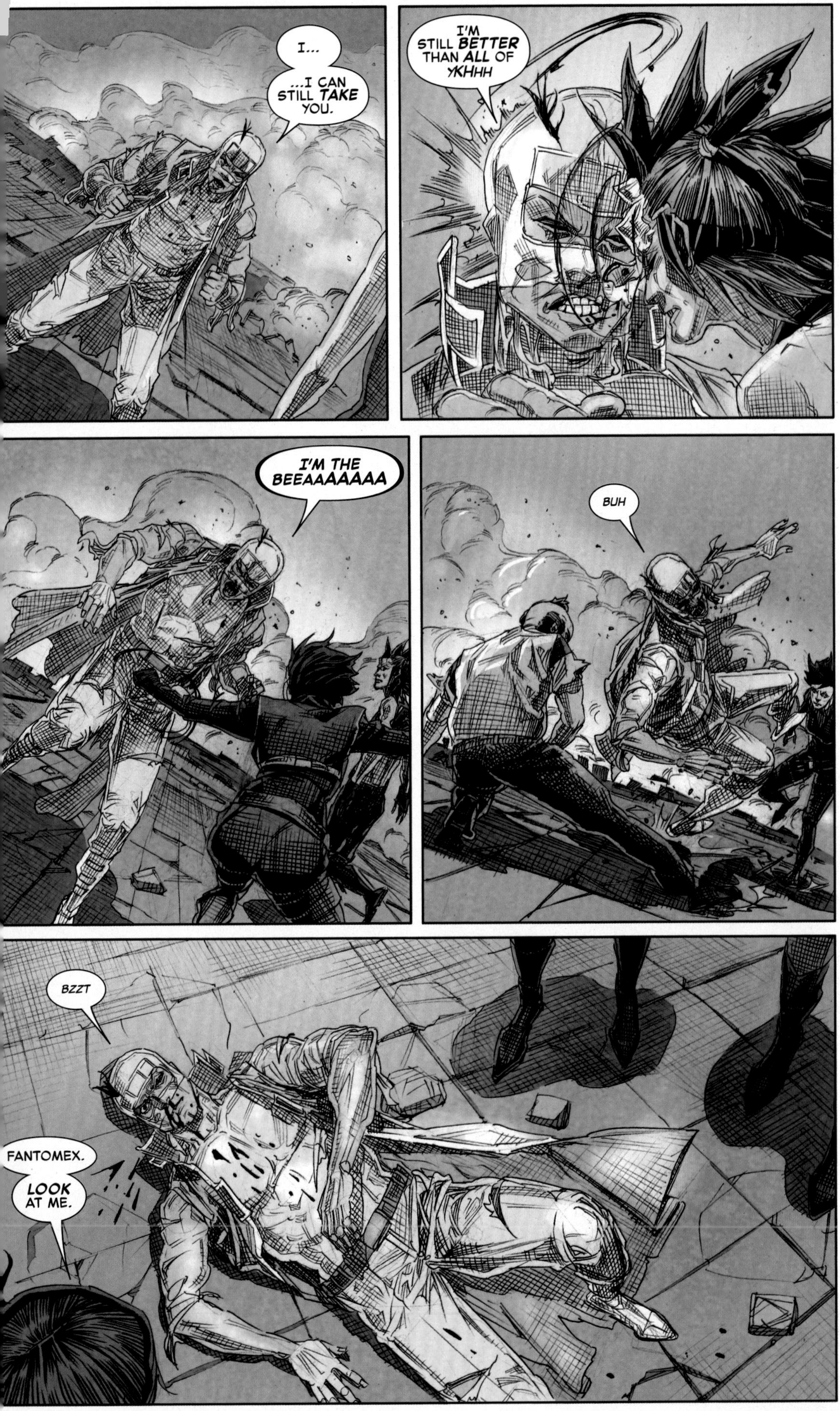
I...
...I CAN STILL TAKE YOU.
I'M STILL BETTER THAN ALL OF YKHHH
I'M THE BEEAAAAAAAA
BUH
BZZT
FANTOMEX.
LOOK AT ME.

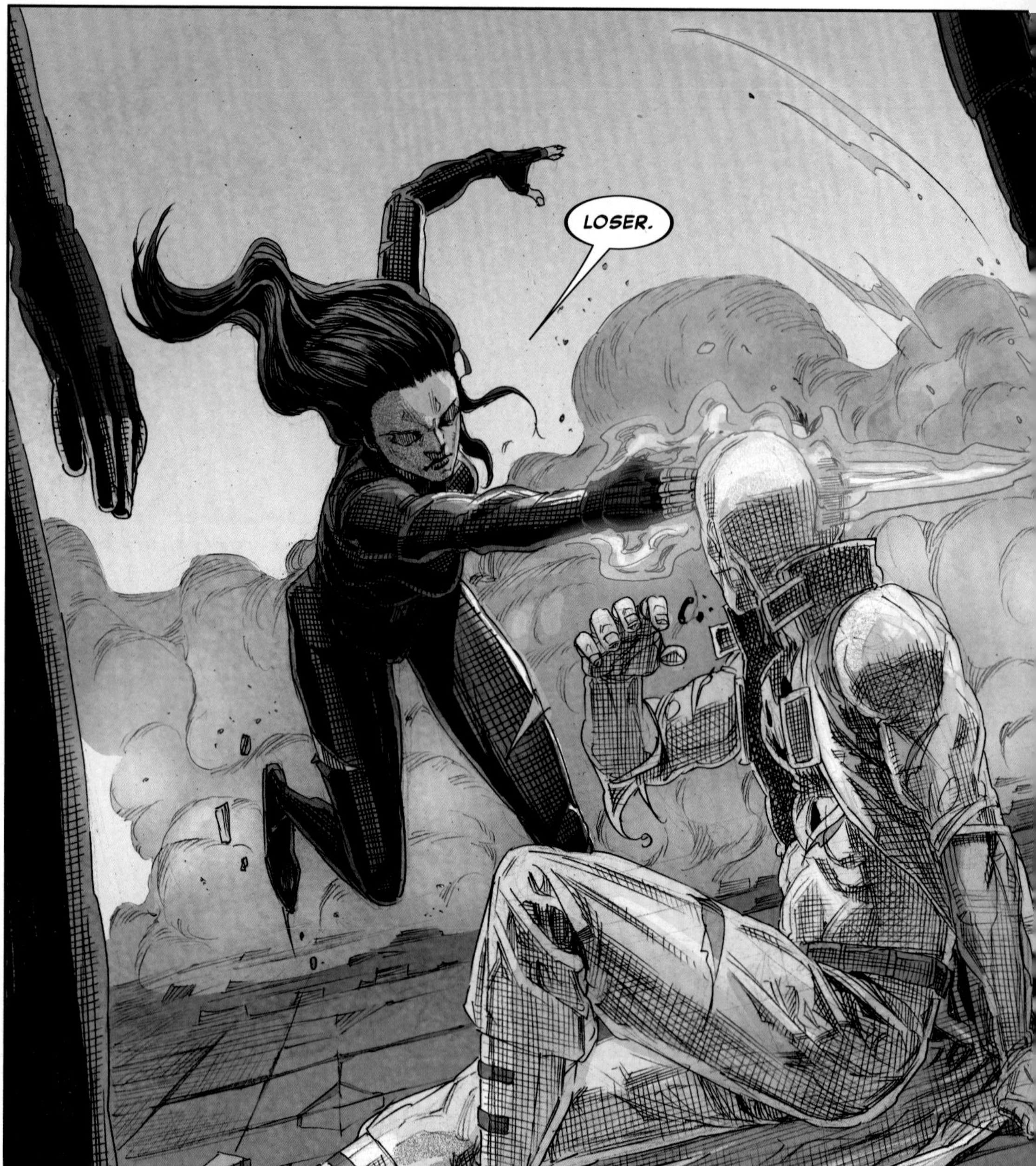
LOSER.
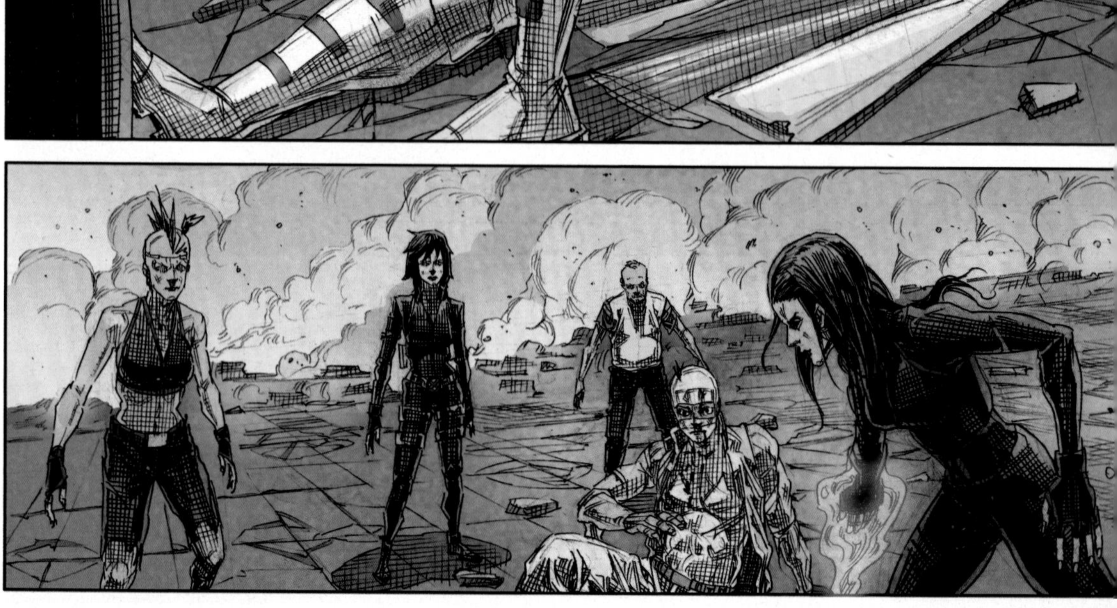

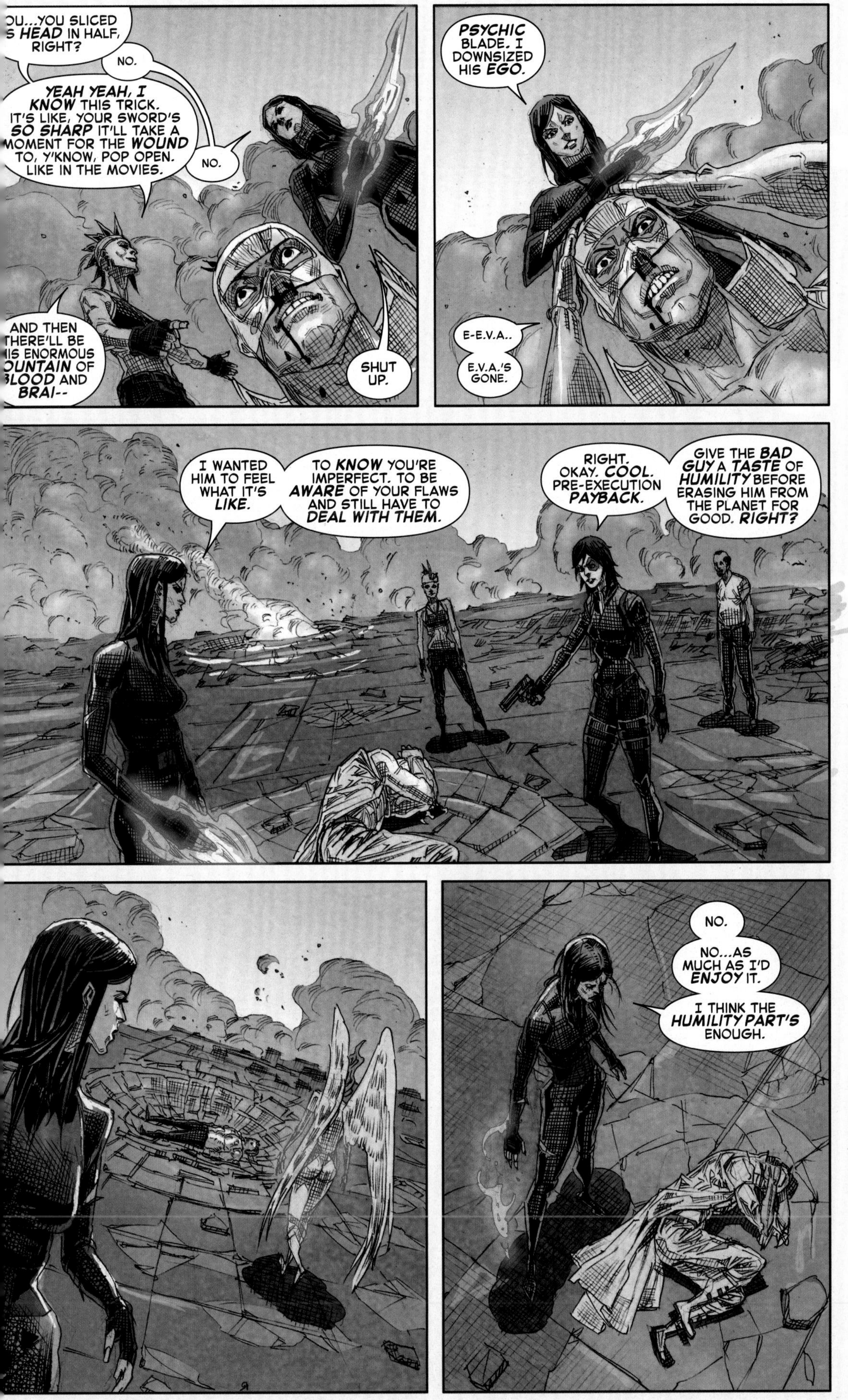
OU...YOU SLICED
S HEAD IN HALF,
RIGHT?
NO.
YEAH YEAH, I KNOW THIS TRICK. IT'S LIKE, YOUR SWORD'S SO SHARP IT'LL TAKE A MOMENT FOR THE WOUND TO, Y'KNOW, POP OPEN. LIKE IN THE MOVIES.
NO.
AND THEN THERE'LL BE IS ENORMOUS OUNTAIN OF BLOOD AND BRAI--
SHUT UP.
PSYCHIC BLADE. I DOWNSIZED HIS EGO.
E-E.V.A..
E.V.A.'S GONE.
I WANTED HIM TO FEEL WHAT IT'S LIKE.
TO KNOW YOU'RE IMPERFECT. TO BE AWARE OF YOUR FLAWS AND STILL HAVE TO DEAL WITH THEM.
RIGHT. OKAY. COOL. PRE-EXECUTION PAYBACK.
GIVE THE BAD GUY A TASTE OF HUMILITY BEFORE ERASING HIM FROM THE PLANET FOR GOOD. RIGHT?
NO.
NO...AS MUCH AS I'D ENJOY IT.
I THINK THE HUMILITY PART'S ENOUGH.

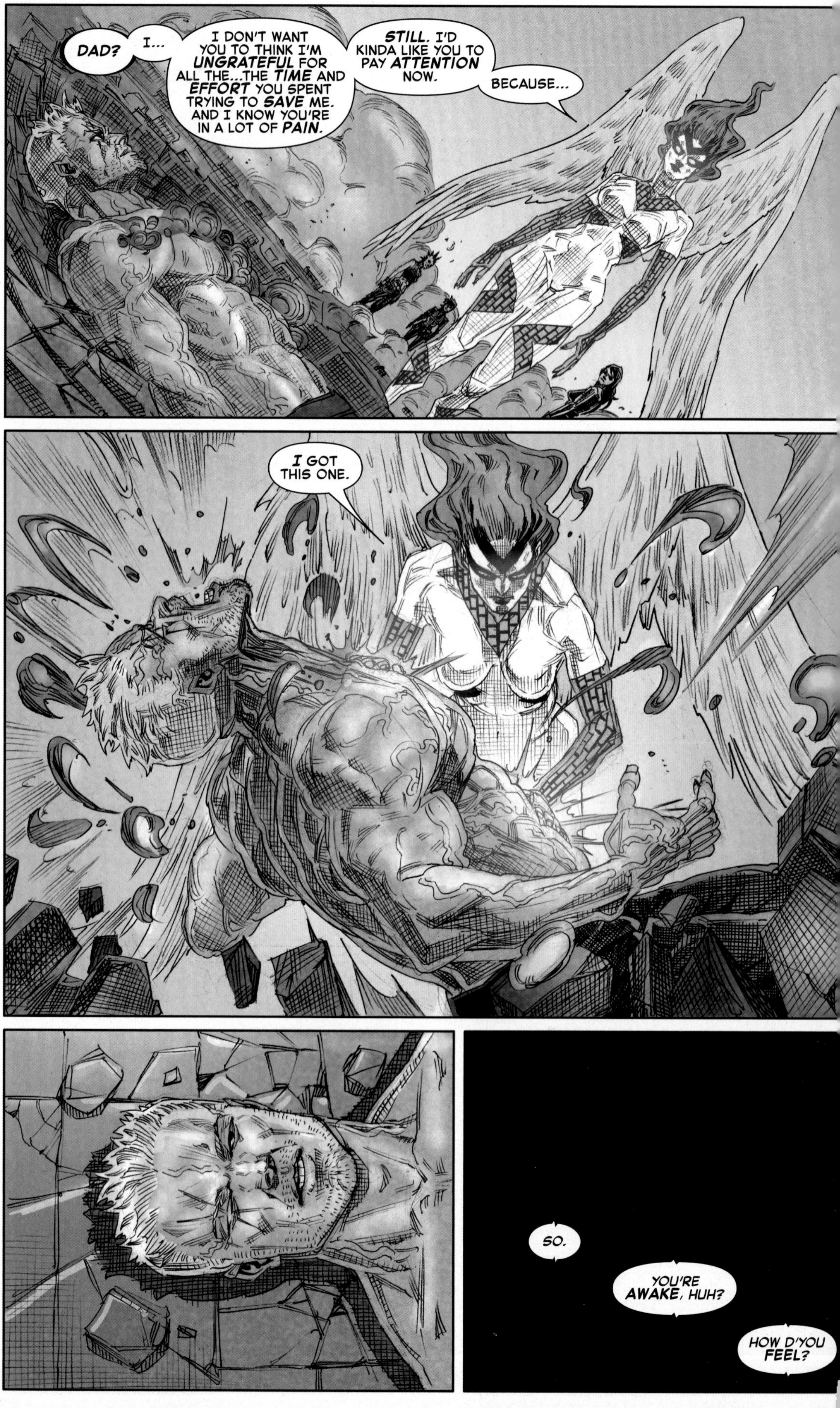
DAD?
I...
I DON'T WANT YOU TO THINK I'M UNGRATEFUL FOR ALL THE...THE TIME AND EFFORT YOU SPENT TRYING TO SAVE ME. AND I KNOW YOU'RE IN A LOT OF PAIN.
STILL. I'D KINDA LIKE YOU TO PAY ATTENTION NOW.
BECAUSE...
I GOT THIS ONE.
SO.
YOU'RE AWAKE, HUH?
HOW D'YOU FEEL?

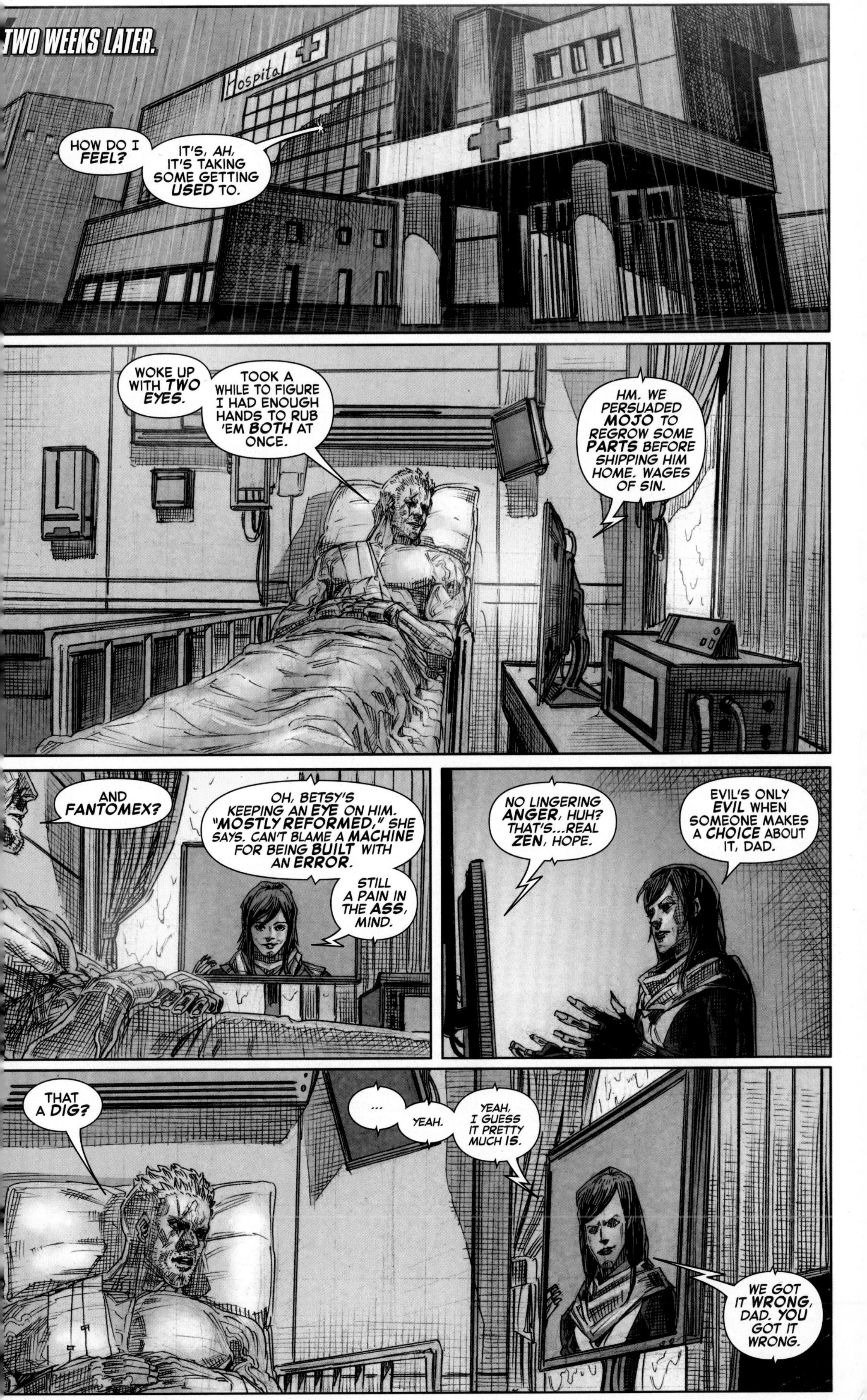
TWO WEEKS LATER.
Hospital
HOW DO I FEEL?
IT'S, AH, IT'S TAKING SOME GETTING USED TO.
WOKE UP WITH TWO EYES.
TOOK A WHILE TO FIGURE I HAD ENOUGH HANDS TO RUB 'EM BOTH AT ONCE.
HM. WE PERSUADED MOJO TO REGROW SOME PARTS BEFORE SHIPPING HIM HOME. WAGES OF SIN.
AND FANTOMEX?
OH, BETSY'S KEEPING AN EYE ON HIM. "MOSTLY REFORMED," SHE SAYS. CAN'T BLAME A MACHINE FOR BEING BUILT WITH AN ERROR.
STILL A PAIN IN THE ASS, MIND.
NO LINGERING ANGER, HUH? THAT'S...REAL ZEN, HOPE.
EVIL'S ONLY EVIL WHEN SOMEONE MAKES A CHOICE ABOUT IT, DAD.
THAT A DIG?
...
YEAH.
YEAH, I GUESS IT PRETTY MUCH IS.
WE GOT IT WRONG, DAD. YOU GOT IT WRONG.

YOU THINK IT'S ABOUT...BEING **STRONG**. STANDING UP TO BE **COUNTED**. A-AND THAT SOUNDS GOOD IN **PRINCIPLE**, SURE, BUT...

YOU TAKE THAT PATH AND YOU CAN'T **STOP**. TOUGHER, STRICTER, EXPLODIER. ENDLESS #$%&#$% **ESCALATION**.

MIND YOUR LANGUAGE, YOUNG LA--

IT'S NOT **ABOUT** "US VS. THEM," DAD. NOT REALLY. NEVER WAS.

IT'S ABOUT THE FOLKS WHO WANT TO **PARTICIPATE** VERSUS THE FOLKS WHO WANT TO **DOMINATE**.

... WHERE **ARE** YOU, HOPE?

DOESN'T **MATTER**. JUST... JUST **LISTEN**.

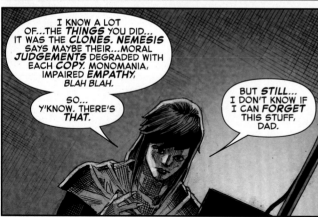

I KNOW A LOT OF...THE **THINGS** YOU DID... IT WAS THE **CLONES**. **NEMESIS** SAYS MAYBE THEIR...MORAL **JUDGEMENTS** DEGRADED WITH EACH **COPY**. MONOMANIA, IMPAIRED **EMPATHY**, BLAH BLAH.

SO... Y'KNOW. THERE'S **THAT**.

BUT **STILL**... I DON'T KNOW IF I CAN **FORGET** THIS STUFF, DAD.

I DON'T KNOW IF...IF I CAN BE **AROUND** YOU. **WORKING**, I MEAN. NOT FOR A LITTLE WHILE.

I THINK I NEED TO BE **BETTER** THAN THAT.

... ... I UNDERSTAND.

I...I DON'T **RESENT** YOU WANTING TO **LEAVE**. X-FORCE WILL BE HERE FOR YOU WHEN YOU'RE READY TO REJO--

NO.

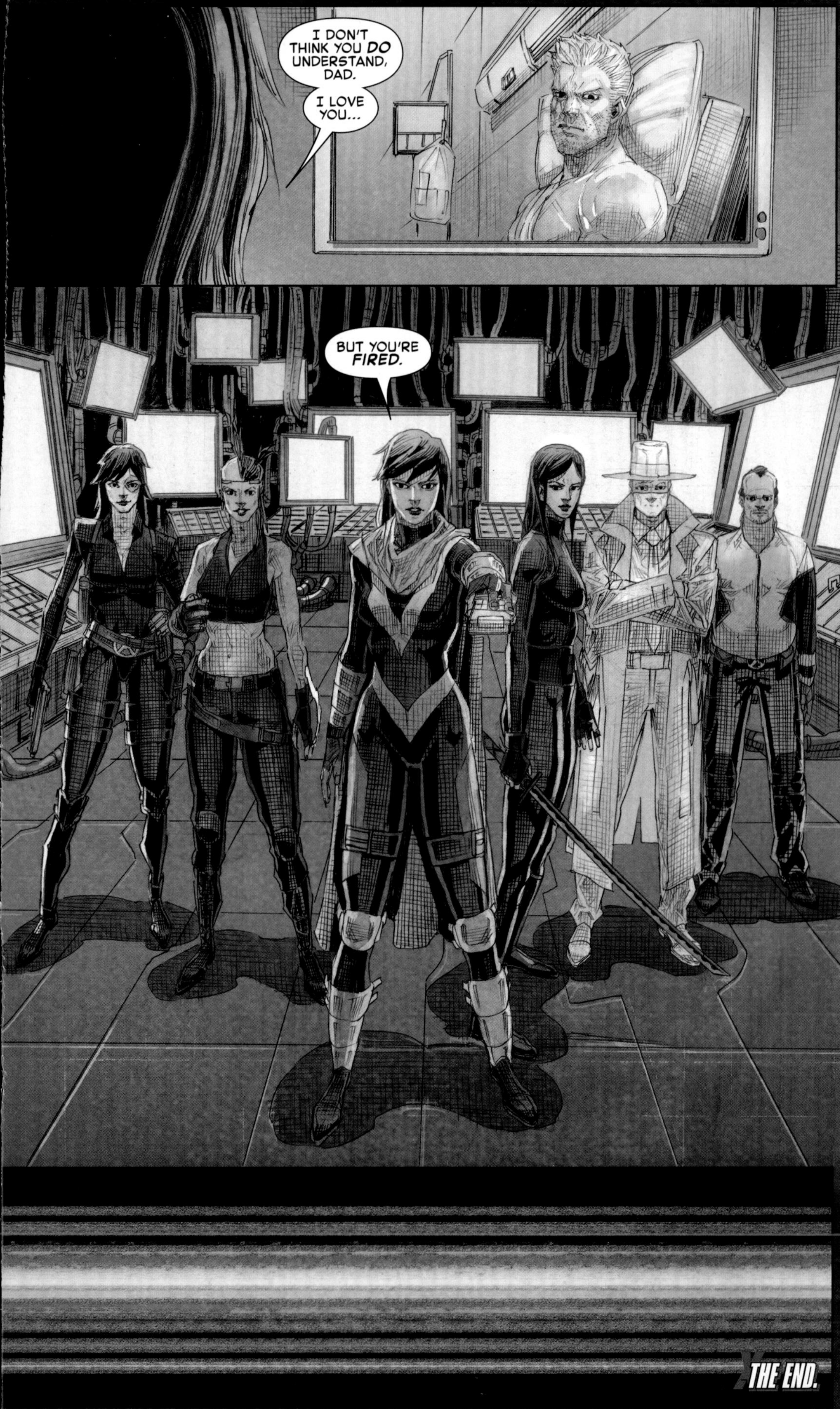
I DON'T THINK YOU *DO* UNDERSTAND, DAD.
I LOVE YOU...
BUT YOU'RE *FIRED.*
THE END.

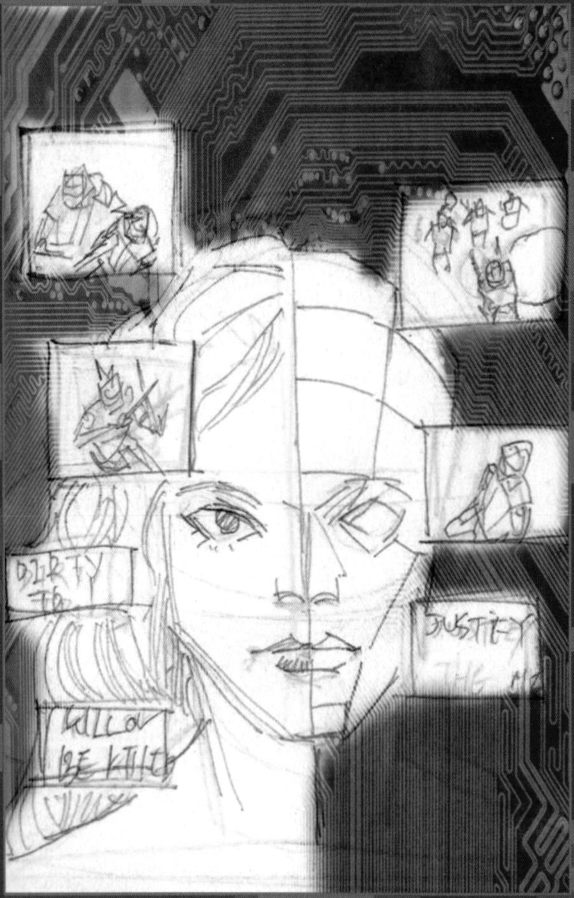

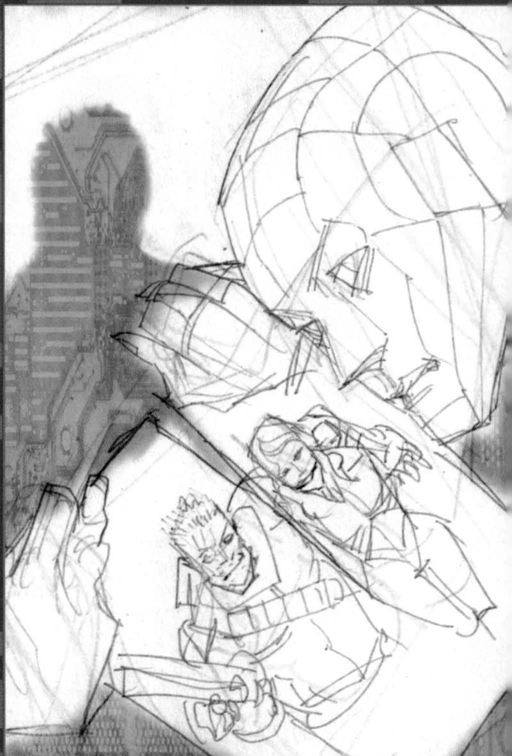

›› #13 COVER CONCEPTS BY ROCK-HE KIM ‹‹

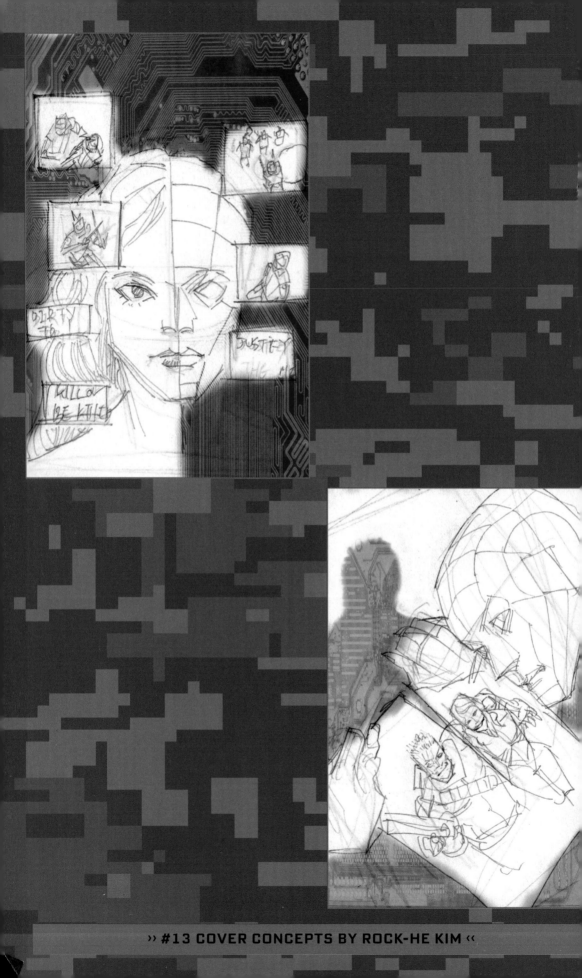

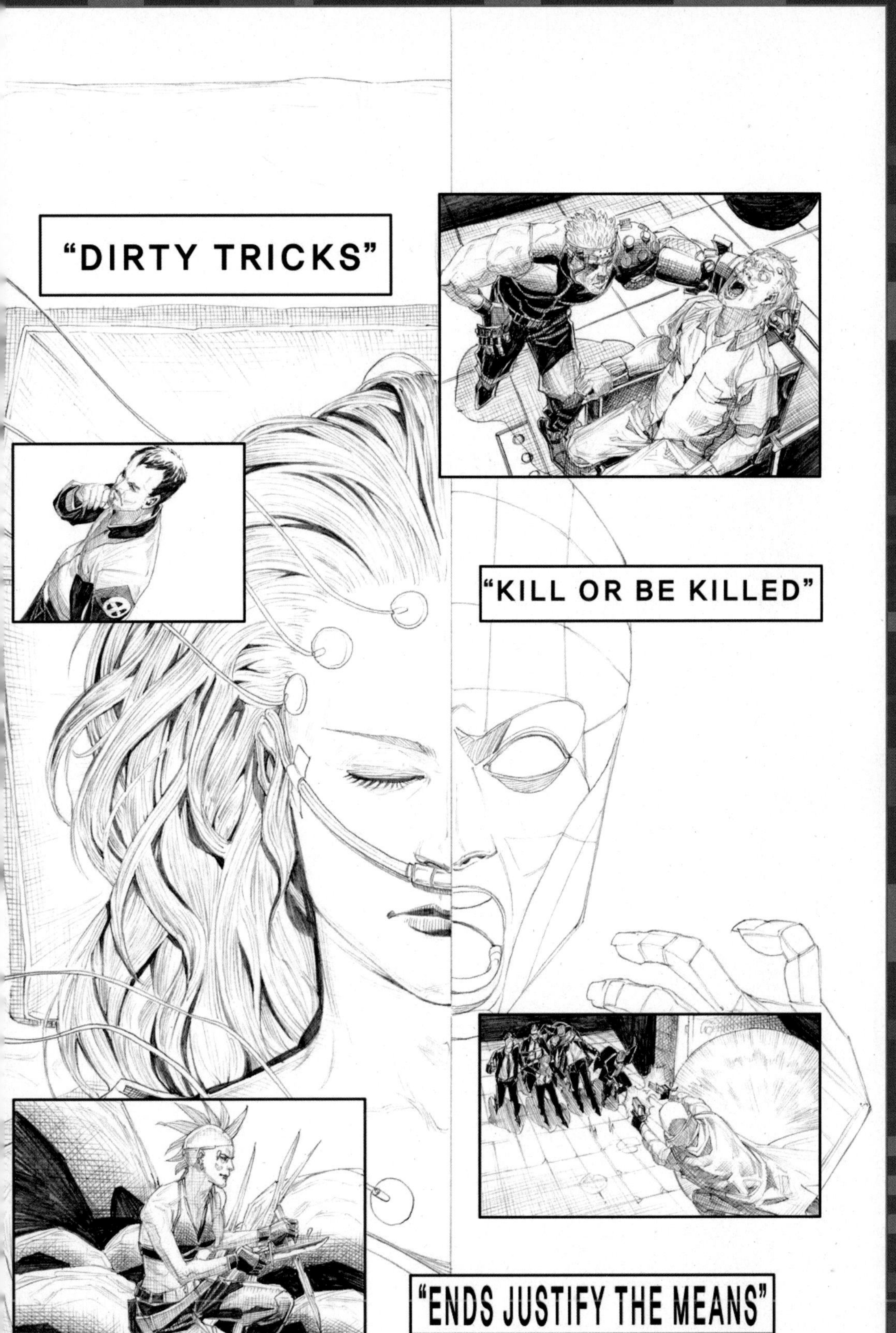
"DIRTY TRICKS"
"KILL OR BE KILLED"
"ENDS JUSTIFY THE MEANS"

›› #13 COVER ART WITH INITIAL LAYOUT BY ROCK-HE KIM ‹‹

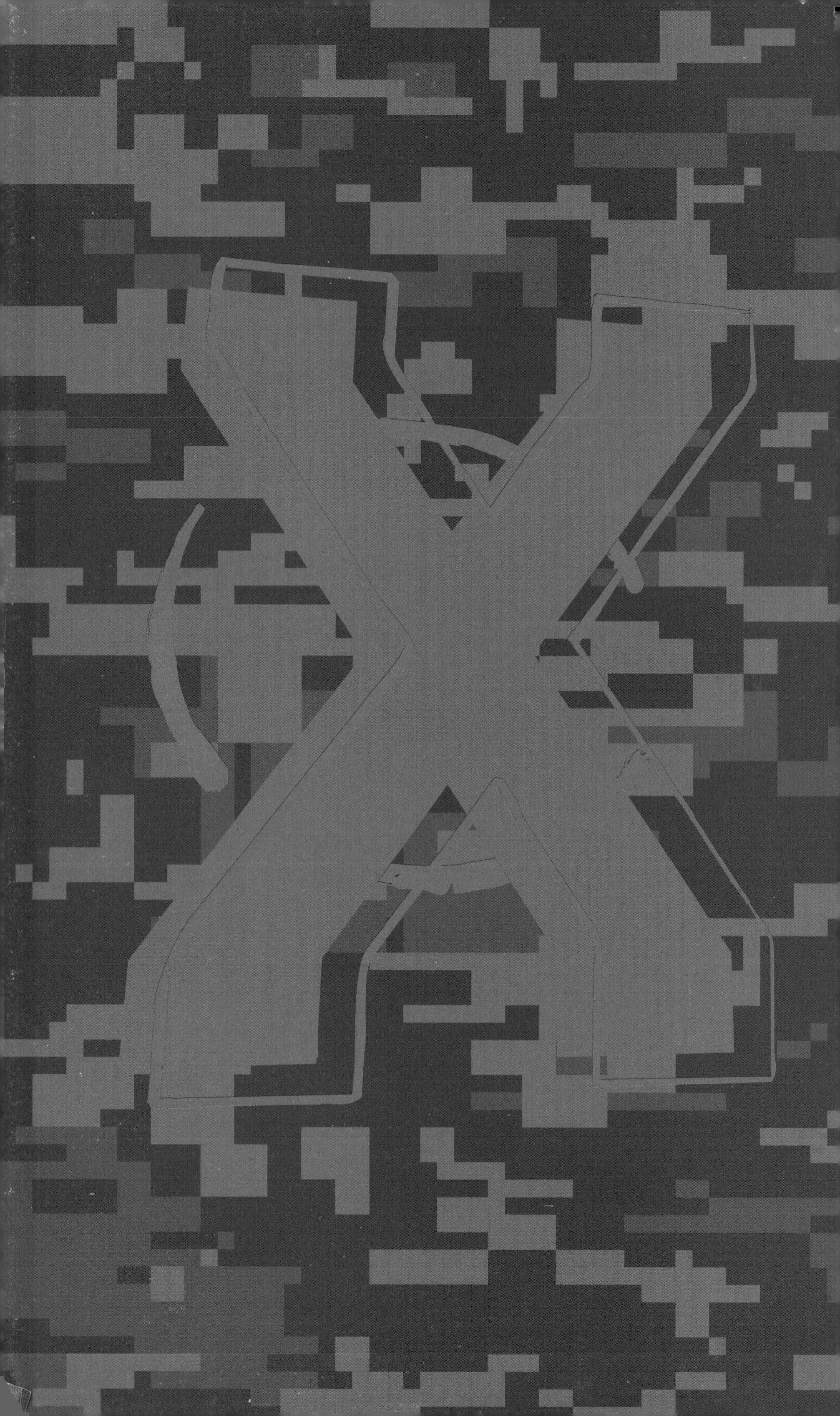